Guides to the Eucharist in Medieval Egypt

CHRISTIAN ARABIC TEXTS IN TRANSLATION

SERIES EDITOR
Stephen J. Davis, Yale University

ADVISORY BOARD
Jimmy Daccache, Yale University
Mark Swanson, Lutheran School of Theology
Alexander Treiger, Dalhousie University

Christian Arabic Texts in Translation (CATT) is a series dedicated to making Christian Arabic works available in English translation. Publications include works of biblical interpretation and commentary, treatises engaging with theological and ethical issues vital to Christian-Muslim encounters, as well as saints' lives, sermons, histories, and philosophical and scientific literature produced by Arabic-speaking Christians living in the medieval Islamicate world. Each accurate and accessible translation is presented with a concise, lucid, and engaging introduction to the historical context, authorship, and literary content of the work and selected critical notes providing resources for further study (biblical citations, bibliographical references, linguistic clarifications, etc.). These translations make it possible for Christian Arabic texts to be introduced to college, seminary, and graduate school curricula.

GUIDES TO THE EUCHARIST IN MEDIEVAL EGYPT

Three Arabic Commentaries on the Coptic Liturgy

YŪḤANNĀ IBN SABBĀʿ, ABŪ AL-BARAKĀT IBN KABAR, AND POPE GABRIEL V

TRANSLATED AND EDITED BY
ARSENIUS MIKHAIL

FORDHAM UNIVERSITY PRESS
New York • 2022

Fordham University Press also publishes its books in a variety of electronic formats. Some content that appears in print may not be available in electronic books.

Visit us online at www.fordhampress.com.

Library of Congress Cataloging-in-Publication Data available online at https://catalog.loc.gov.

Printed in the United States of America

24 23 22 5 4 3 2 1

First edition

To Marianne, whose love and patience itself is liturgy
and to Anastasia, who is growing to share our love for the liturgy

CONTENTS

Preface *ix*

Editorial Notes *xi*

List of Abbreviations *xiii*

Manuscripts *xv*

Map of Egypt *xviii*

Introduction 1

1 Abū al-Barakāt ibn Kabar, *The Lamp of Darkness* 31

2 Yūḥannā ibn Sabbāʿ, *The Precious Jewel* 60

3 Gabriel V, *The Ritual Order* 108

Appendix: Coptic Liturgical Chants *143*

Glossary *149*

Works Cited *159*

Biblical Index *175*

Manuscripts Index *177*

General Index *179*

PREFACE

The purpose of this volume is to provide the reader with an accessible English translation of three key works from the Copto-Arabic tradition describing the eucharistic liturgy of the Coptic Church. For a number of years, I have had the privilege to teach introductory courses on the Coptic liturgical heritage in at least five institutions. A standard component of these courses is a treatment of liturgy in medieval Egypt, which usually relies on descriptions of liturgical practices found in three key texts: *The Precious Jewel* by Yūḥannā ibn Sabbāʿ, *The Lamp of Darkness* by Abū al-Barakāt ibn Kabar, and *The Ritual Order* attributed to Pope Gabriel V. A common problem encountered when engaging with these texts has always been the lack of reliable English translations. Curiously, these texts have always been accessible only to readers of Arabic or those able to read the European languages in which these works have appeared so far: Latin, French, and Italian respectively. Simply put, most students in North America were prevented from engaging directly with these important works without significant language expertise. I am thus fortunate to present this volume as an attempt to remedy this situation.

In planning the translation and the accompanying notes, I had in mind two types of readers. On the one hand, those with professional training in the Christian Arabic heritage and/or Eastern liturgical history will find that the explanatory notes engage with literature from their respective scholarly fields, always seeking to read these primary texts within the broader context of Copto-Arabic culture and Eastern liturgical practice. For the wider readership interested in the liturgy of the Coptic Church, this volume presumes no prior knowledge of Arabic, Coptic, or Greek, nor does it demand a professional background in liturgiology. To this end also, a glossary at the end of the book provides helpful definitions for liturgical and ecclesiastical terms appearing both in the original texts as well as in my own notes commenting on them. They are designed to aid readers who have little previous exposure to the wide array of Greek, Coptic, and Arabic terms they will encounter in this book. It is my sincere hope that this work will place these key texts of Coptic liturgical history directly within the reach of scholars and students of Coptic studies, Christian Arabic studies, and liturgical history, as well as a wider readership in the Coptic community.

My sincere thanks for this wonderful opportunity are due first and foremost to Stephen J. Davis for his enthusiastic welcome of this work in the Christian Arabic Texts in Translation series (CATT), of which he is the series editor. I am grateful to the Monastery of Saint Antony (Red Sea, Egypt), in particular His Grace Bishop Yusṭus, Fr. Dūmādyūs al-Anṭūnī, and Fr. Deuscoros al-Anṭūnī, for facilitating my access to an important manuscript in the monastery's library concerning the date of departure of Abū al-Barakāt ibn Kabar. Stephen Davis read the first draft of this work and provided me with exceptional feedback and suggestions for improving the readability of the translation. Stephen also provided precious feedback as an expert in Egyptian Christianity and the Copto-Arabic literary heritage. In analogous fashion, Daniel Galadza kindly read a second draft of this work and suggested numerous improvements to its liturgiological content and intelligibility to scholarly readers of eastern liturgy. I am grateful also for Will Cerbone, editor at Fordham University Press, for his assistance throughout this project, Fr. Arsany Paul for his assistance with the indices, and my dear wife, Marianne Mikhail, for her careful reading of the manuscript and for enhancing the readability of the text.

Editorial Notes

A number of editorial choices were taken in the preparation of this volume that are explained here. A key concern was to ensure accuracy and clarity, while maintaining an appropriate level of accessibility to readers unfamiliar with the languages and/or the worship practices of Coptic Christians. Texts in the original scripts in Greek or Coptic are kept to a minimum, unless deemed necessary for explanatory notes. This is particularly the case with Greek diaconal responses, always rendered in Coptic manuscripts in nonstandard orthography. Transliteration is always provided for key terms and phrases. For Greek and Coptic, I follow the standards of the Society of Biblical Literature as found in *The SBL Handbook of Style for Ancient Near Eastern, Biblical, and Early Christian Studies*, edited by P. H. Alexander et al. (Peabody, MA: Hendrickson, 1999), and Richard Smith, *A Concise Coptic-English Lexicon* (Atlanta: Society of Biblical Literature, 1999), respectively. However, since all Coptic texts in this volume are in the Bohairic dialect, some key modifications to these systems are implemented for accessibility. Namely, the Bohairic ϧ (*khai*) is rendered as *kh*, Ϭ (*chima*) is rendered as *ch*, and the letter ϣ (*shai*) as *sh*. Arabic is always given in transliteration, following the standards of the ALA–Library of Congress (http://www.loc.gov/catdir/cpso/romanization/arabic.pdf). The only exception to this is in rendering ى (*alif maqṣūrah*) as *ā* and not the *á* demanded by the ALA rules.

While the RSV English translation of the Bible was consulted, the Arabic scriptural verses provided by the authors frequently diverged enough that it was deemed preferable to provide a literal translation for accuracy. All references to the book of Psalms are based on the Septuagint (LXX) numbering, with the Hebrew (Masoretic) numbering provided in parentheses.

Providing the readers with an accurate but readable translation of medieval Arabic texts is always a challenge. This is especially the case with the texts in this volume, which heavily employ technical/ritual language often comprehensible only to members of the Coptic community well versed in the details of their own liturgical practices. For the sake of clarity, the present translation often departs from the exact syntax of the original text while preserving the meaning. Other strategies were also employed, though sparingly, to aid in comprehension. For example, square brackets [. . .] are utilized for insertions intended to clarify the meaning and are not explicitly present in the original text. This applies also to headings provided for the selections from *The Lamp of Darkness* and from *The Ritual Order*, where no such titles exist in the manuscripts. Such headings—introduced by the translator—are meant to provide a convenient roadmap to the reader following standard divisions of the eucharistic service common in liturgical scholarship. Parentheses (. . .) are used to give a transliteration of the Arabic word used in the original. The notes should also be mentioned in this regard, whose main function is to explain difficult passages or at least indicate when the exact meaning of a passage has eluded even the translator.

At times, liturgical terms are provided in their exact form as they appear in the source, supplemented by an explanation in the notes. At other times, a commonly accepted liturgical term was found to be sufficient to convey the meaning without burdening the reader with a large amount of technical Copto-Arabic terms in the body of the text. Thus, where the text may use *qurbān* (oblation) or *quddās* (from *qaddasa*, to consecrate or sanctify), I usually employ the widely understood term *liturgy*. Often the exact term in the original is provided in the notes.

For the reader's convenience, a glossary of liturgical terms is provided in the end, which includes terms of Greek, Coptic, and Arabic origin as well as technical terms common in liturgical scholarship and used in this volume. Throughout the texts, especially chapter 1 from Ibn Kabar's *Lamp of Darkness*, liturgical hymns are referenced only by their Coptic incipit, familiar to chanters. In order to make this hymnography accessible to the reader while not overburdening the notes with lengthy texts, an appendix to this volume gives the full text of all such chants arranged in alphabetical order by their English titles. In the notes themselves, the reader is directed to that appendix whenever such hymns occur.

Abbreviations

BSAC	*Bulletin de la Société d'Archéologie Copte*
CE	*The Coptic Encyclopedia*, ed. Aziz S. Atiya. 8 volumes. New York: Macmillan, 1991.
CMR	*Christian-Muslim Relations: A Bibliographical History*, ed. David Thomas et al. 8 volumes. Leiden: Brill, 2009–16.
CSCO	Corpus Scriptorum Christianorum Orientalium
EI²	*Encyclopaedia of Islam*, 2nd edition, ed. P. Bearman et al. 12 volumes. Leiden: Brill, 1986–2004.
GCAL	*Geschichte der christlichen arabischen Literatur*, ed. Georg Graf. 5 volumes. Studi e Testi 118, 133, 146, 147, 172. Vatican City: Biblioteca Apostolica Vaticana, 1944–52.
OCA	Orientalia Christiana Analecta
OCP	*Orientalia Christiana Periodica*
ODB	*The Oxford Dictionary of Byzantium*, ed. Alexander P. Kazhdan et al. 3 volumes. New York: Oxford University Press, 1991.
PO	Patrologia Orientalis
SC	Sources Chrétiennes
SOC	*Studia Orientalia Christiana*

Manuscripts

The following is a list of manuscripts of each of the three works presented in this volume. In listing them, I include only those manuscripts that were utilized in preparing the translation. Readers interested in a complete list of manuscripts for *The Precious Jewel* of Ibn Sabbāʿ and *The Lamp of Darkness* of Ibn Kabar are referred to the respective entries in *Christian-Muslim Relations: A Bibliographical History*, vol. 4. The notes in this section refer to catalogue entries or other scholarly works describing the manuscripts in question. The symbols below are utilized in the notes throughout this book rather than the full shelf mark for each manuscript.

The Lamp of Darkness and the Elucidation of the Service

P203 *Paris, BnF Ar. 203* (AD 1363–1369)[1]
U12 *Uppsala O. Vet. 12* (AD 1547) (= Tornberg 486)[2]

The Precious Jewel on the Ecclesiastical Sciences

P207 *Paris, BnF Ar. 207* (14th c.)[3]

1. Gérard Troupeau, *Catalogue des Manuscrits arabes*, 171–172; Villecourt, "Les observances (Ch. XVI–XIX de la Lampe des ténèbres)," 249–250.
2. Tornberg, *Codices Arabici, Persici et Turcici*, 306–309; Villecourt, "Les observances," 250.
3. Troupeau, *Catalogue des Manuscrits arabes*, 178; Mistrīḥ, *Pretiosa margarita*, xx.

CM15 *Cairo, Coptic Museum Lit. 15* (AD 1634) (= Graf 32; Simaika 180)[4]
P208 *Paris, BnF Ar. 208* (AD 1638)[5]
DK221 *Cairo Dār al-Kutub Theol. 221* (AD 1750)[6]

The Ritual Order

P98 *Paris, BnF Ar. 98* (17th c.)[7]

4. Marcus Simaika and Yassa ʿabd al-Masiḥ, *Catalogue*, 1:89; Georg Graf, *Catalogue de Manuscrits arabes chrétiens*, 14–15; William F. Macomber, *Final Inventory, Rolls A1–20*, 215–216; Mistrīḥ, *Pretiosa margarita*, xx–xxi.

5. Troupeau, *Catalogue des Manuscrits arabes*, 178–179; Mistrīḥ, *Pretiosa margarita*, xxi.

6. Mistrīḥ, *Pretiosa margarita*, xix–xx.

7. Troupeau, *Catalogue des Manuscrits arabes*, 75–76; ʿAbdallah, *L'ordinamento*, 44–52.

Guides to the Eucharist in Medieval Egypt

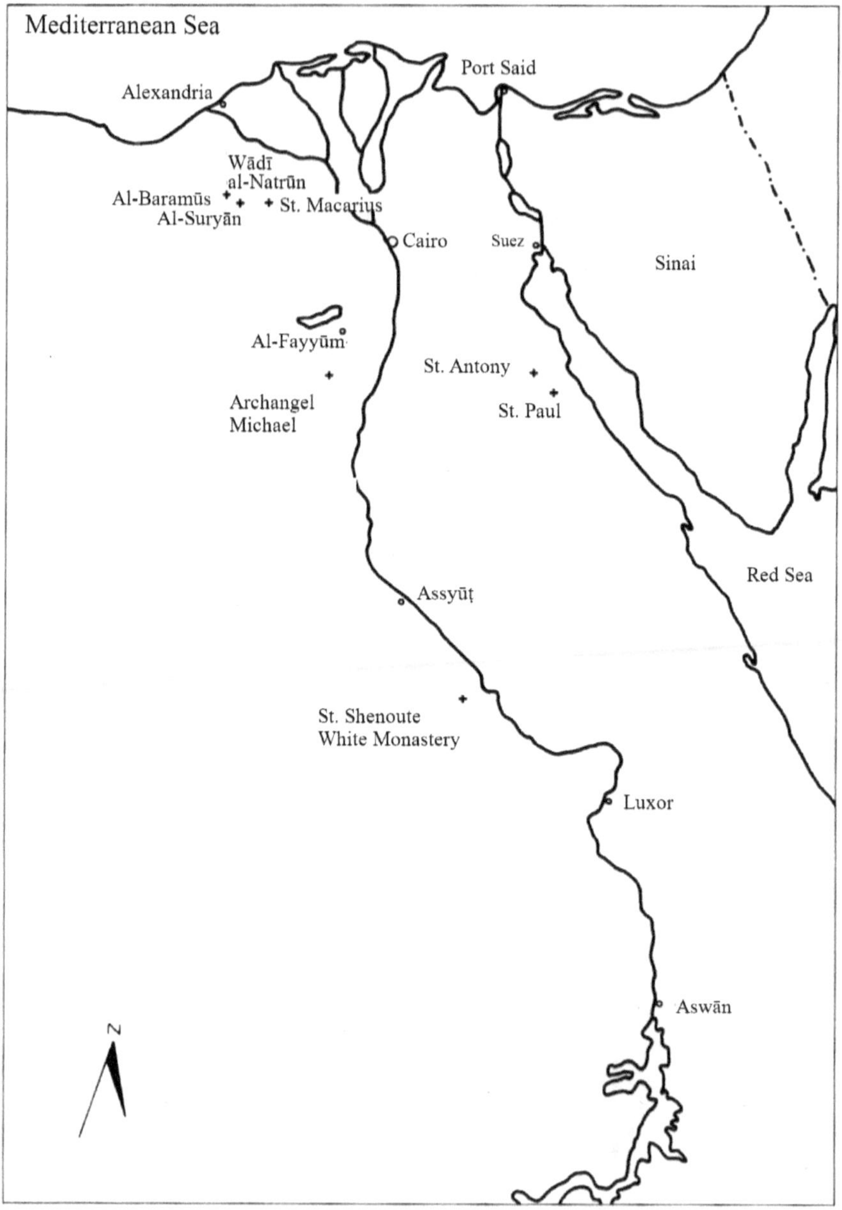
Mediterranean Sea
Alexandria
Port Said
Wādī
al-Natrūn
Al-Baramūs
Al-Suryān
St. Macarius
Cairo
Suez
Sinai
Al-Fayyūm
St. Antony
St. Paul
Archangel
Michael
Red Sea
Assyūṭ
St. Shenoute
White Monastery
Luxor
Aswān
N

Introduction

It can be safely assumed that worship occupied a central place in the life of Egypt's Coptic Christian community throughout late antiquity and the Middle Ages. This is unequivocally attested by the vast number of liturgical manuscripts that survived these periods, as well as the witness of ancient churches, artifacts, and countless references to liturgical practices in patristic sources, as well as medieval historical and canonical literature. Yet, for the entire first millennium, no author has left us a commentary or a detailed description of the Coptic eucharistic liturgy, the central event of the Church's worship life. We do not possess for example any catechetical homilies on the sacraments such as those attributed to Cyril of Jerusalem, Theodore of Mopsuestia, or Ambrose of Milan.[1] Nor is there a theological commentary on the Alexandrian liturgy, such as was developed in Byzantium by Maximus Confessor, Germanus of Constantinople, or

1. There is the exception of a relatively obscure catechetical homily preserved in the fifteenth-century Ethiopic manuscript *Paris, BnF Eth. MS D'Abbadie 66–66bis* and given the title *The Order of the Mystery* in modern scholarship. Although the single manuscript of this work is from the fifteenth century, Heinzgerd Brakmann has argued on more than one occasion that the liturgy it describes can be traced ultimately to fifth-century Alexandria. For Brakmann's remarks, see Brakmann, "Le déroulement de la Messe copte," 107–132, at 109; Brakmann, "Neue Funde und Forschungen zur Liturgie der Kopten (1988–1992)," 9–32, at 11–12. For an English edition, translation, and commentary of this obscure text, see Emmanuel Fritsch, "The Order of the Mystery," 195–263. Although Brakmann's arguments carry significant weight, the exact origin of this homily—if not simply Ethiopia—remains unknown and its attribution to fifth-century Alexandria tentative.

Nicholas Cabasilas,[2] or in the Syriac East by George of the Arab tribes or Moses bar Kepha.[3]

However, by the fourteenth and fifteenth centuries, writings began appearing that dealt systematically with the liturgical practices of the Coptic Church. This phenomenon coincided with a broader rise in Coptic religious literature in Arabic that came to be known as the "Golden Age" of Copto-Arabic literature.[4] This volume presents selections from three of these works in English translation with ample explanatory notes. Although the three works represented in this volume are all united around the topic of the eucharistic liturgy, it will become clear to the reader that the three authors differ in their purpose and approach in treating the ritual unfolding of the Coptic liturgy of the Middle Ages.

The Lamp of Darkness by Ibn Kabar

The first text presented here is quite well known among scholars of Copto-Arabic literature and liturgical studies. Usually referred to as Abū al-Barakāt ibn Kabar, his full name is Shams al-Ri'āsah Abū al-Barakāt ibn al-Akmal al-As'ad ibn Kabar.[5] Born to a wealthy Cairo family, Ibn Kabar began his career as a secretary or *kātib* to Mamluk prince Baybars al-Dawādār, a prestigious government position that must have required a great deal of expertise in Arabic, accounting, and knowledge of Islamic culture. However, he eventually had to abandon his post due to governmental oppression, namely, the decree in 1293 by the Sultan Al-Malik al-Ashraf (AD 1290–1293) banning Christians from all positions in the government.

2. The best study of the genre of Byzantine liturgical commentaries remains René Bornert, *Les commentaires byzantins de la Divine Liturgie du VIIe au XVe siècle*. See also Paul Meyendorff, *St Germanus of Constantinople on the Divine Liturgy*, and the commentary by Nicholas Cabasilas in J. M. Hussey and P. A. McNulty, *A Commentary on the Divine Liturgy*. See also the classic study of Robert F. Taft aiming to situate the genre of Byzantine liturgical commentaries in their historical context. Taft, "The Liturgy of the Great Church," 45–75. See also another classic work on the subject, Hans-Joachim Schulz's *The Byzantine Liturgy*, 184.

3. R. H. Connolly and H. W. Codrington, *Two Commentaries on the Jacobite Liturgy*.

4. Adel Y. Sidarus, "The Copto-Arabic Renaissance in the Middle Ages," 141–160; Sidarus, "La Renaissance copte arabe du Moyen Âge," 311–340.

5. See, among others, Khalil Samir, "L'encyclopédie liturgique d'Ibn Kabar († 1324) et son apologie d'usages coptes," 619–655; Wadī' Awaḍ, "Al-Shams ibn Kabar," *CMR* 4:762–766; Georg Graf, *GCAL* 2:438–445.

Ibn Kabar left his position to be eventually ordained a priest in 1300 for the famous Al-Muʿallaqah (Hanging) Church in Old Cairo, likely taking the name Barṣawmā. However, when widespread riots against the Copts and destruction of churches broke out in 1321,[6] Ibn Kabar was nowhere to be found. It is likely that he was protected by his former employer, Prince Baybars, and he was able to go into hiding undetected.[7] Ibn Kabar died between 1323 and 1325.[8] According to one source, this took place exactly on May 10, 1324, though this particular date could not be verified.[9]

6. On these riots, reported by the Mamluk historians Al-Maqrīzī and Al-ʿAynī, see Donald P. Little, "Coptic Conversion to Islam under the Baḥrī Mamlūks," 552–569, esp. 562–565.

7. Samir, "L'encyclopédie liturgique d'Ibn Kabar," 626.

8. The information can be deduced from a colophon in a manuscript preserved in the *Berlin Staatsbibliothek* numbered *Berlin, Staatsbibliothek 10173 (Diez A fol. 41)*, a book of the biographies of sixteen Old Testament prophets, whose copying was completed on May 8, 1325. This manuscript itself is a copy of an older manuscript that used to be the property of Ibn Kabar. In the colophon of *Diez A fol. 41*, the scribe copied the following note from the original exemplar: "This blessed book became the property of the wretched sinner, who is unworthy of being called a human being let alone a priest, Barṣawmā, servant of the Hanging Church in Qaṣr al-Jamʿ in Cairo, in the early months of the Coptic year 1040" (fol. 257v). This Coptic year corresponds to AD 1323, showing that Ibn Kabar was at least alive at that point. The scribe of *Diez A fol. 41* continues, "That book, I mean the original from which this copy was made, is now the property of his daughter, I mean of the priest Al-Shams ibn Kabar, may God repose his soul with his saints and righteous ones, amen." Thus, at the time of making this copy in 1325, Ibn Kabar had already reposed. This allows us to place his death at some time between 1323 and 1325. For information on this manuscript and the text of the colophon, see Samir, "L'encyclopédie liturgique d'Ibn Kabar," 623–626.

9. According to an account by Jirjis Filūthāʾus ʿAwaḍ, a manuscript in the Monastery of Saint Antony near the Red Sea, *Liturgy 446*, contains—among a collection of forty-two orations attributed to Ibn Kabar—a funeral oration Ibn Kabar is supposed to have written for himself. ʿAwaḍ reports the title of the oration as "a funeral oration by its composer the master, the presbyter, Al-Shams ibn Kabar, when great weakness had befallen him and he reposed on the 15th of Bashans of the year 1040." This date translates to May 10, 1324. For this information, ʿAwaḍ relies on a transcribed list of titles of these forty-two orations in the handwriting of Hegumen ʿAbd al-Masīḥ Ṣalīb al-Masʿūdī al-Baramūsī, which he penned in an edition of a shorter list of twenty-three orations published by Ḥabīb Jirjis. See ʿAwaḍ, *Ibn Kabar*, 115–123, esp. 120. For the collection of orations published by Ḥabīb Jirjis, where Hegumen ʿAbd al-Masīḥ penned his notes, see Jirjis, *Al-jawharah al-nafīsah fī khuṭab al-kanīsah*. For the reference to this manuscript and the alleged date of Ibn Kabar's death, see also Graf, *GCAL* 2:443. Based on personal inspection of this manuscript, the title is in fact "A funeral oration arranged by the mentioned father the priest

Besides his famous crowning achievement, *The Lamp of Darkness* (*Miṣbāḥ al-ẓulmah*), Ibn Kabar also left behind a dictionary of the Bohairic dialect of the Coptic language known as *The Great Ladder* or the *Scala magna* in Western scholarship.[10] He also wrote a number of homilies for various feasts. Ibn Kabar's identity as a priest in Cairo's famous Hanging Church, as well as the relatively secure dates of his activity, allow us to contextualize his *Lamp of Darkness* and the liturgical information contained in it.

The title of the work in full is *The Lamp of Darkness and the Elucidation of the Service* (*Miṣbāḥ al-ẓulmah wa-īḍāḥ al-khidmah*). Consisting of twenty-four chapters, this work also covers a range of topics, including dogma, Scripture, church canons, and liturgical observances. The preface to *The Lamp* gives no indication that the work was intended as an official guide for the purpose of reform. Instead, the author begins by thanking God for granting him such knowledge of the Church and for the gift of the priesthood. The author then writes a prayer that he be found faithful in discharging his duties. He indicates his interest in providing a manual for the clergy—especially the deacons—that would provide a helpful compendium of the Church's rituals and services, saving the clergy the effort of locating this information in a large number of external sources.[11] Although Ibn Kabar hints at the confusion and discord that results from ignorance and disagreements over rituals, he seems to be providing this work out of a personal sense of duty rather than any official mandate to adjudicate on matters of ritual. It is not clear when Ibn Kabar wrote *The Lamp of Darkness*, a work that must have occupied a large amount of time and research. It is clear at least that he did so after his ordination to the priesthood in 1300; that much is discernible from his introduction. One reasonable suggestion would be that he wrote it during his years of

Shams al-Ri'āsah in his weakness and was read at the time of his departure during his funeral at the Mu'allaqah [Hanging Church]. It was read by the priest Al-Akram." (fol. 12r). I am grateful to the Monastery of Saint Antony (Red Sea, Egypt) and Father Dūmādiyus al-Anṭūnī for allowing me the opportunity to inspect this manuscript. In recent times, Ibn Kabar's commemoration on Bashans 15 has been incorporated in some versions of the Copto-Arabic Synaxarion, the official liturgical book containing the lives of the saints throughout the year and read during the eucharistic liturgy. See, for example, the recent edition published by the Monastery of the Virgin Mary Al-Suryān: The Synodal Committee for Rituals, *Kitāb al-Sinaksār*, 231.

10. Athanasius Kircher, *Lingua aegyptiaca restituta*, 39–272.

11. *Paris, BnF Ar. 203* (AD 1363–1369), fol. 2v–4r.

service as a priest in Cairo between 1300 and 1321. Ibn Kabar's position as the priest of one of the most important churches in Cairo, near the patriarchate and with access to written resources and perhaps even official support, would have made such a scholarly endeavor more feasible. His practical experience presiding over services at the Hanging Church and his likely exposure to frequent disagreements over ritual would have made his work that much more necessary.

Following two introductory chapters on the Christian faith and dogmatic positions (chs. 1–2), Ibn Kabar provides a summary of the incarnation and the apostolic preaching (chs. 3–4). This is followed by a chapter on the received canonical tradition as well as a relatively unique bibliography of Copto-Arabic works known to him (chs. 5–6).[12] Liturgical chapters commence in earnest with chapter 8, on the consecration of churches and vessels, and chapter 9, on the consecration of the chrism used in anointing newly baptized faithful. A sequence of chapters on ordination rites from patriarchs down to monastics follows (chs. 10–14). The remaining chapters focus on baptism and chrismation (ch. 15), daily prayer (ch. 16), the eucharistic liturgy (ch. 17), Lent and holy week (ch. 18), various feasts of the liturgical year (ch. 19),[13] betrothal and marriage (ch. 20), and funerals and anointing of the sick (ch. 21). The last three chapters cover the lectionary cycle, the epact calculation of Easter,[14] and a chronological chapter on world history (chs. 22–24).

Chapter 17 of *The Lamp of Darkness*, on the eucharistic liturgy, is similar in scope to the other two texts in this volume. Ibn Kabar appears less

12. As ʿAwaḍ points out, the only other comparable bibliography appears in chapter 1 of Al-Muʾtaman ibn Al-ʿAssāl's *Majmūʿ uṣūl al-dīn*. For Ibn Kabar's bibliography in chapter 7 of *The Lamp*, see Wilhelm Riedel, "Der Katalog der christlichen Schriften in arabischer Sprache von Abū 'l-Barakāt," 635–706.

13. The chapter begins with a brief description of the rituals on the feasts of the Resurrection, Ascension of Christ, and Pentecost. A listing of all major feasts related to Christ's life include the Nativity, Baptism (Theophany), the Transfiguration, Palm Sunday, Resurrection, Ascension, and Pentecost. This is followed by a second list of other feasts, "that follow them and are equal to them," including the Annunciation of Christ's birth, Circumcision, the entry of Christ to the temple, his entry to Egypt, Great Thursday, Great Friday, the first Sunday after the Resurrection, and the Feast of the Cross on Baramhāt 10.

14. The Epact calculation is a work of chronology that explains how to calculate the date of Easter for any given year. The complicated calculations of the annual Easter are traditionally attributed to Patriarch Demetrius I of Alexandria (AD 189–231). For more on the Epact calculation in general, see Khalil Samir, "Book of Epact," *CE* 2:409a–411b.

concerned overall with an abstract liturgical theology, unlike his near-contemporary Ibn Sabbāʿ, the author of the second selection in this volume. Rather, he delves into the intricate details of the liturgy with firsthand expertise, which has made his work a favorite of liturgical scholars seeking a window into the unfolding of the Coptic liturgy in fourteenth-century Cairo. Ibn Kabar's description at times is quite detailed, providing the first few words of all prayers and chants in Coptic as well as stage directions for what each liturgical "actor"—priest, deacon, chanters—ought to do. His description becomes the most complex when he attempts to provide variations in the ritual according to different seasons. Perhaps of particular interest to scholars of liturgy is Ibn Kabar's clear awareness of regional diversity in Coptic liturgical practice.[15] Throughout late antiquity and for much of the medieval period, the liturgical practices of local Christian communities throughout Egypt often differed on a number of points, ranging from the language(s) used and locally venerated saints to the texts used for the eucharistic prayer itself. By the fourteenth century, this regional diversity was rapidly declining due to the centuries-long influence of the patriarchate and the monasteries of Scetis, yet Ibn Kabar still has much information to share about this aspect of Coptic liturgical practice. Examples of this awareness are when he speaks of the unique vesting habits of the monks of Saint Macarius and when he explains how the psalm and gospel are to be chanted in the Liturgy of the Word, a role assigned to different ranks of chanters and/or clergy throughout Egypt. The meticulous attention to liturgical practice and analysis in the work has rightfully earned Ibn Kabar's *The Lamp of Darkness* its place as an essential text for studying the medieval Coptic liturgy, especially given the scarcity of such works delving into the minutiae of liturgical practices.

The text is given here from the oldest known manuscript of *The Lamp*, preserved in the National Library of France (*Paris, BnF Ar. 203*; AD 1363–1369). Variant readings—when deemed substantive—are provided in the notes from the second-oldest manuscript to contain chapter 17, preserved in Uppsala University Library in Uppsala, Sweden (*Uppsala O. Vet. 12*; AD

15. The regional nature of medieval Coptic liturgy is discussed in more detail in what follows. Similarly, Byzantine liturgical sources are beginning to be read through this regional lens, paying close attention to issues of provenance and the local context of various manuscripts and texts. On the regional history of the Byzantine liturgy, see Stefano Parenti, "Towards a Regional History," 109–121.

1547), itself copied from an older manuscript dated AD 1357.[16] While no critical edition of the entire *Lamp of Darkness* has appeared to date, a French translation of chapter 17 utilizing both of these manuscripts was published by Louis Villecourt.[17] An edition also appeared in Egypt by Father Samuel al-Suryānī, although he does not explicitly identify the manuscript source.[18] More recently, an edition of the earliest surviving manuscript from Paris was published in the Arabic journal *Madrasat al-Iskandariyyah* following a more scholarly editorial method, though without a translation to any Western language.[19]

The Precious Jewel by Ibn Sabbāʿ

The second text in this volume is the work of an obscure author, about whom very little is known with certainty.[20] His full name as given in some manuscripts is Yūḥannā ibn Abī Zakariyyā known as Ibn Sabbāʿ (vocalized by some as Ibn Sibāʿ). Ibn Sabbāʿ was not a prolific author or a well-known ecclesiastical figure. The present work, *The Precious Jewel*, is the only text attributed to him that has come down to us. A remark in chapter 26 of the work mentions that more than 1,300 years have passed since the time of the disciples, which, if true, would place Ibn Sabbāʿ's work around the middle of the fourteenth century, ca. AD 1350, perhaps about two or three decades after the death of Ibn Kabar.[21]

16. See the colophon of the manuscript on fol. 258r. Cf. Carl Johan Tornberg, *Codices Arabici, Persici et Turcici*, 306–309; Louis Villecourt, "Les observances liturgiques (Ch. XVI–XIX de la Lampe des ténèbres)," 249–292, at 250.

17. Villecourt, "Les observances liturgiques," 201–280.

18. Samuel al-Suryānī, *Miṣbāḥ al-ẓulmah fī īḍāḥ al-khidmah.*

19. Fādī Ra'fat Ramzī, "Tartīb al-quddās wa-al-qurbān (1)," 193–214.

20. Much of the biographical information in this section is based on the brief notes in the following works: Graf, *GCAL* 2:448–449; Mark N. Swanson, "Ibn Sabbāʿ," *CMR* 4:918–923.

21. The internal reference in question reads, "Those who believe it [the Gospel] have been for years, whose number now has reached more than (*yanīf*) one thousand three hundred years." See Vincentio Mistrīḥ, *Pretiosa margarita*, 63 (Arabic), 424 (Latin). Taking the age of the Gospel to refer to the period after the life of Christ (i.e., more than AD 30) implies that Ibn Sabbāʿ must have written his work later than AD 1330 and likely even later. Curiously, a number of modern authors place Ibn Sabbāʿ's work in the middle or late thirteenth century instead. See, e.g., Samir, "L'encyclopédie liturgique d'Ibn Kabar,"

In his study of the dogmatic theology of Ibn Sabbāʿ, Milad S. Zakhary attempted to mine the *Precious Jewel* for clues about the author's identity. He observed Ibn Sabbāʿ's intimate knowledge of ritual details, even ones that would require unhindered access to the sanctuary, where most of the intricate ritual actions take place. He also noted the author's familiarity with patriarchal administrative affairs, and his particular manner of speaking of and to other members of the clergy throughout the work. In conclusion, Zakhary proposed the high likelihood that Ibn Sabbāʿ must have been a person entrusted with managing the ritual and administrative affairs of the patriarch, a role logically fulfilled by an archdeacon.[22] On the other hand, the ritual details described by Ibn Sabbāʿ in his work often differ radically from those described by Ibn Kabar in the *Lamp of Darkness.* Such stark contrast on some key ritual details between these two nearly contemporaneous works may in fact suggest that Ibn Sabbāʿ was more familiar with a rite geographically far removed from Cairo, such as that practiced in southern Egypt. At any rate, nothing more is known about the enigmatic Ibn Sabbāʿ and his background.

The full title of Ibn Sabbāʿ's work is *The Precious Jewel on the Ecclesiastical Sciences* (*al-Jawharah al-nafīsah fī ʿulūm al-kanīsah*). Though the work has gained in popularity in recent times among Egyptian scholars studying liturgical history, *The Precious Jewel* is much more than a book of ritual. Consisting of 113 chapters—though some chapters are no more than one page in the critical edition—the work covers a range of subjects: dogmatic, biblical, spiritual, and liturgical. After the initial two chapters discussing the unity of God's essence and the Trinity, the author turns to a lengthy exposition of Scripture and salvation history from Creation to the preaching of the apostles, consisting of chapters 3–26. Hereafter, Ibn Sabbāʿ turns to discuss ecclesiastical and liturgical matters, though not without some digressions. He begins by explaining the church building, the ranks of the clergy and how each is reflected in Christ's ministry, and baptism. Then he turns to a number of key Christian practices, such as fasting, prayer, faith, and almsgiving. Mark Swanson has noted that this order of topics may be reminiscent of the similar five "pillars" of Sunni Islamic prac-

620, and the study of Milad Zakhary cited in the following note as evidenced in its very title, which identifies Ibn Sabbāʿ as a thirteenth-century author.

22. Milad Zakhary, *De la Trinité à la Trinité*, 98–130.

tice known as *arkān al-islām*, which are faith, prayer, almsgiving, fasting, and pilgrimage.[23] Naturally, Ibn Sabbāʿ presents these topics in their Christian expression, taking the opportunity of this broad similarity in practices to introduce Christian fasts, a commentary on the Our Father prayer, and an analysis of the Nicene Creed. In chapters 37–42, the author discusses a number of communal virtues and practices: love of neighbor, humility, avoidance of anger, purity, marriage, avoiding adultery, and second marriage.

Particularly ecclesiastical and liturgical subjects resume with chapter 44 on the clerical ranks (chs. 44–52), incense (ch. 53), the consecration of churches and icons (chs. 54–56), proper liturgical conduct (ch. 57), the eucharistic liturgy, including the ordination rites for clerical ranks up to patriarch (chs. 58–84), various patriarchal administrative affairs (chs. 85–98), the rites of major feasts (ch. 99), Holy Week (chs. 100–105), the Pentecost period (chs. 106–107), the Feast of the Cross (ch. 108), anointing of the sick and funerals (chs. 109–110), further remarks on patriarchal pastoral activity (chs. 111–112), and the use of cymbals in church (ch. 113).

As can be seen from this synopsis, *The Precious Jewel* covers an eclectic collection of topics of importance to the community's beliefs, traditions, and proper conduct, often earning it the title of an encyclopedia of religious sciences.[24] For the purpose of this volume, only those chapters covering the eucharistic liturgy are presented, 58–73 and 83–84.[25]

Part of chapter 84 includes a homily by the presiding priest about the Eucharist, placed immediately before communion in the unfolding of the liturgy. The homily is an exhortation for more frequent communion, albeit after the requisite spiritual preparation and repentance from major sins,

23. Swanson, "Ibn Sabbāʿ," 919. For more information on the five pillars of Islam, see S. Nomanul Haq, "Rukn," *EI²* 8:596b–597b, as well as individual entries for each practice under its Arabic term: faith (*shahāda*), prayer (*ṣalāt*), fasting (*ṣawm*), almsgiving (*zakāt*), and pilgrimage to Mecca (*ḥajj*). It is unclear if the order of the analogous topics in *The Precious Jewel* is significant.

24. See, for example, Swanson, "Ibn Sabbāʿ," 918. Zakhary frequently refers to *The Precious Jewel* as an encyclopedia, for example in the title of chapter 3, "L'encyclopédie et ses source": Zakhary, *De la Trinité à la Trinité*, 131.

25. The intervening chapters on clerical ordinations (chs. 74–82) are excluded. This was decided both for considerations of space and also since ordinations represent an extraordinary feature outside the regularly celebrated eucharistic service. Chapter 83 itself continues with rites related to the consecration of the patriarch of Alexandria. Halfway through that chapter, the author returns to the explanation of the regular eucharistic service after the patriarch has been consecrated.

as well as scriptural witnesses for the mystery of the Eucharist. Overall, the homily lacks any of the distinctive theological features apparent in the rest of Ibn Sabbāʿ's discourse on the liturgy. In fact, one suspects that it may not originally belong to the work, but rather could be an anonymous homily of the kind common in homiletic collections of Christian Arabic literature.[26]

Throughout these chapters, the readers will notice Ibn Sabbāʿ's particular method of interpretation. Not contenting himself with merely describing the ritual activities as they unfold, the author often inserts spiritual and theological explanations that at times seem somewhat far-fetched, at least to modern ears, such as the remark that the wine is mixed with water in the eucharistic rites in imitation of the Virgin's habit of drinking wine with water during her pregnancy. In reality, however, Ibn Sabbāʿ shows a remarkable knowledge of both early patristic literature and the later Copto-Arabic tradition of his period. Milad Zakhary has analyzed the patristic sources of Ibn Sabbāʿ's writing, which he suggested could have included Origen, Clement, and Cyril of Alexandria.[27] More notably, and especially for the chapters included here, the influence of the writings of Pseudo-Dionysius are quite clear.[28] On more than one occasion, Ibn Sabbāʿ is specifically concerned with demonstrating that the worship of the church on earth is a reflection of the heavenly eternal worship of the angels before God's throne. Thus, we find Ibn Sabbāʿ asserting that "the earthly Church resembles the heavenly Jerusalem in that the minds of the luminous angels praise and hallow the Holy Trinity, the Father and the Son and the

26. See, for example, Graf, *GCAL* 2:467–468.

27. Zakhary, *De la Trinité à la Trinité*, 174–176, 324–325. However, Zakhary's treatment of these influences is minimal. See the critique in Stephen J. Davis, "Review of *De la Trinité à la Trinité*," 733–737. It is worth noting that the transmission of the writings of Origen and Clement of Alexandria is very sparse in the Arabic tradition generally, which renders the idea—if true—that Ibn Sabbāʿ shows influence from these sources remarkable. I am grateful to Stephen J. Davis for this information on the writings of Origen and Clement in Arabic.

28. Dionysius the Areopagite is the alleged author of the theological works known as *The Celestial Hierarchy*, *Ecclesiastical Hierarchy*, *Mystical Theology* and *Divine Names*. This anonymous author presents himself as the disciple of Paul the Apostle (Acts 17:34), but is likely from the early sixth century, though his exact identity is unknown. Pseudo-Dionysius is notable for treating such topics as the Godhead, the Trinity, Creation, and eschatology relying heavily on Neoplatonic language. For a brief introduction, see Robert Browning, "Dionysius the Areopagite, Pseudo-," *ODB* 1:629–630.

Holy Spirit" (ch. 64), which is reminiscent of Pseudo-Dionysius's entire approach in the *Celestial Hierarchy* as providing a model of the Church's worship.[29] This cosmological approach lies behind many of Ibn Sabbāʿ's explanations for particular points of Coptic ritual, such as his assertion that the leader of the earthly rank—the bishop—has the privilege of pronouncing the conclusion of each prayer recited by other clergy, or that the word *Holy* in the course of the Trisagion chant is repeated a total of nine times in the likeness of the nine ranks of heavenly beings. This approach also seems to lie behind Ibn Sabbāʿ's constant attention to proper hierarchical order: the deacon, who stands "higher" than the priest further east behind the altar, should restore the proper order at a later point by performing a prostration to the priest. The clergy, who enter the sanctuary prior to the bishop for the preparation of the bread and wine, must also at a later point bow before the bishop, who reads a prayer of absolution over them (ch. 64).

The Precious Jewel owes much also to the Copto-Arabic literature current at the time. In particular, it is clear that Ibn Sabbāʿ was intimately familiar with writings that passed under the name of the tenth-century bishop and apologist Sāwīrus ibn al-Muqaffaʿ.[30] Thus, certain curious explanations in *The Precious Jewel* seem to have originated in *The Book of Elucidation* (*Kitāb al-īḍāḥ*), attributed—most likely falsely—to Sāwīrus, such as the notion that the wine is mixed with water for the Eucharist because this is how the Virgin Mary used to drink wine during her pregnancy (ch. 64)![31]

Altogether, *The Precious Jewel*'s explanation of the eucharistic liturgy is a fascinating text with many layers and nuances. For scholars of liturgical development, it provides a valuable counterweight to the other famous

29. See, for example, the *Celestial Hierarchy* 1.3, where one reads, "The sacred institution and source of perfection established our most pious hierarchy. He modeled it on the hierarchies of heaven." See Colm Luibheid, *Pseudo-Dionysius*, 146. For a summary of Ibn Sabbāʿ's cosmological vision, see Zakhary, *De la Trinité à la Trinité*, 495–500.

30. Zakhary, *De la Trinité à la Trinité*, 177; Swanson, "Ibn Sabbāʿ," 920.

31. On the authorship and dating of the *Book of Elucidation*, see Graf, *GCAL* 2:309–311; Mark N. Swanson, "*Kitāb al-īḍāḥ*," *CMR* 3:265–269. By comparison with Sāwīrus's other writings, Swanson doubts that the *Book of Elucidation* is an authentic work of Sāwīrus, given its popular style and diction. Stephen J. Davis has pointed out that the *Book of Elucidation* shows an elaborate understanding of the nature of angels, inconsistent with the other genuine writings of Sāwīrus. The common attribution of this work to Sāwīrus is no longer commonly accepted. See, for example, the remark in Mark N. Swanson, "A Copto-Arabic Catechism of the Later Fatimid Period," 483n38; Davis, *A Disputation over a Fragment of the Cross*, 20n28; Davis, *Coptic Christology in Practice*, 230–231.

fourteenth-century work *The Lamp of Darkness* by Ibn Kabar, showing a diversity of practices in that period when attention is paid to their intricate ritual details. At the same time, the interesting mix of the patristic heritage and the medieval Christian Arabic literature reveals an astute author interested in presenting a Coptic Christian orthodoxy and orthopraxy that is both appealing to his coreligionists and understandable to a wider Islamic readership.[32]

The Precious Jewel was published by the Franciscan Vincentio Manṣūr Mistrīḥ from a manuscript from the *Dār al-Kutub* in Cairo (*Cairo, Dār al-Kutub Theol. 221*), with a Latin translation and introduction.[33] Mistrīḥ took the date of this manuscript to be 1164 according to the Era of the Martyrs (= AD 1448). However, Samir Khalil has suggested that the date on fol. 115r should be rather understood as 1164 according to the Islamic calendar (= AD 1750).[34] At any rate, the oldest manuscript of the *Precious Jewel* is the fourteenth-century manuscript *Paris, BnF Ar. 207.* The text presented here is from this latter manuscript. Occasionally, variant readings of interesting content are provided in the notes from two later manuscripts from the Coptic Museum in Cairo and from the National Library of France: *Coptic Museum Lit. 15* (AD 1634) and *BnF Ar. 208* (AD 1638), respectively.

The Ritual Order by Pope Gabriel V

To the reader of the biography of Pope Gabriel V (AD 1409–1427) found in the *History of the Patriarchs*, it would appear that Gabriel's was an unremarkable tenure on the patriarchal throne, besides the brief remark that his famous predecessor Matthew I, known as Mattā al-Miskīn (Matthew the Poor), had miraculously prophesied Gabriel's elevation to the patriarchate.[35] Belonging to a slightly later period, after the "Golden Age" of Copto-Arabic

32. As Mark Swanson points out, chapter 1 of the *Precious Jewel,* on the unity (*tawḥīd*) of God, would have been immediately accessible to a Muslim reader. The description of the Trinity as God the *nāṭiq* (speaking, i.e., the rational Word), and *ḥayy* (living, i.e., the Holy Spirit) was a common strategy employed in the context of Christian-Muslim disputes to convey the Trinity using traditional Muslim attributes of God. See Swanson, "Ibn Sabbā‘," 920.

33. Mistrīḥ, *Pretiosa margarita,* b.

34. Kussaim Samir, "Contribution à l'étude du Moyen Arabe des Coptes," 153–209, at 161–164. Cf. Zakhary's list in Zakhary, *De la Trinité à la Trinité*, 511–512; and Swanson, "Ibn Sabbā‘," 921.

35. Antoine Khater and O. H. E. Burmester, *History of the Patriarchs of the Egyptian Church*, 3.3:158 (Arabic), 272 (English).

literature, Gabriel began his career as a government official in charge of tax collection. Later in his life, he entered monasticism by the name of Gabriel at the Monastery of Saint Samuel of Qalamūn near Fayyūm. Although the entry on his tenure in the *History of the Patriarchs* implies an uneventful period in the history of the Coptic Church, the Muslim historian al-Maqrīzī described this period as "the worst days through which Christians had ever passed." This was in reference to pressures on the community from many fronts. During his papacy, the government decreed that one to four dinars be collected from each Christian annually as a poll tax (*jizyah*) rather than demand the lump sum from the community as a whole. This meant that rather than the community in general being responsible for providing a fixed amount in taxes, each and every person, rich or poor, had to pay this poll tax individually, which probably disadvantaged the community's poorest members. A resurgent attempt to enforce the special dress code (*ghiyār*) for Christians likely exacerbated their second-class status. Customary aid from the Ethiopian Church was withheld, indicating strained relations between the two Churches. Finally, it was also during his time that Venetian merchants stole the revered head of Mark the Evangelist.[36]

Notwithstanding these difficult circumstances, Gabriel V seem to have taken a keen interest in matters of ritual and the orderly celebration of the liturgy. As we learn from the short preface to his *Ritual Order*, the only surviving work attributed to him, the patriarch oversaw the collection of a number of ritual manuscripts (*'iddat tarātīb*) testifying to the diversity of practices current at the time for the purpose of collating them into a single authoritative book of ritual.[37] On May 3, 1411, if the text's own statement is to be believed, the pope gathered a group of priests, notables, deacons, and laity, who agreed to authorize the new composite ritual reform to become thereafter the only sanctioned order for celebrating the various sacraments of the Coptic Church. This claim for success appears to be supported by the vast number of Euchologion manuscripts copied after 1411. Euchologion manuscripts are books containing the prayers needed by the priest to pray any of the three eucharistic prayers current in the Coptic Church. Such manuscripts and their present-day printed versions contain two types of texts, prayers to be recited by the priest and ritual

36. Al-Maqrizi's remark and the situation at the time are described in Mark N. Swanson, *The Coptic Papacy in Islamic Egypt*, 120–123. See also the biography in the *Coptic Encyclopedia*, Khalil Samir, "Gabriel V," *CE* 4:1130a–1133a.

37. Alfonso 'Abdallah, *L'ordinamento liturgico*, 113 (Arabic), 319 (Italian).

instructions for how the priest is to perform the rites (e.g., when to offer incense, how to distribute communion, etc.). While such rubrics were minimal or entirely absent in manuscripts prior to the fifteenth century, one finds the text of the *Ritual Order* inserted verbatim as ritual instructions in the appropriate places in Euchologia produced after that date.[38]

The work itself is titled in the manuscript *Kitāb tartīb* (*A Book of Order*),[39] though it has been customarily referenced in scholarly literature as *The Ritual Order* by way of specificity, especially since the edition by Alfonso ʿAbdallah gave it the Italian title *L'ordinamento liturgico*. As implied by the title, and as distinct from the previous two works, Gabriel's *Book of Order* is only concerned with ritual matters, as can be seen from the following outline of its contents:

1. Baptism and the postbaptismal absolution
2. Betrothal and marriage
3. Anointing of the sick
4. The ritual of Abū Tarbū[40]
5. Evening and morning prayer
6. The Liturgy of Saint Basil
7. Clerical ordinations
8. Monastic consecrations
9. Funeral rites
10. The rite of the filling of the chalice[41]
11. Consecration of the altar vessels and icons[42]

In keeping with this volume's theme of presenting selections on the eucharistic liturgy, only chapter 6 of *The Ritual Order*, on the liturgy of

38. For the liturgical legacy of Gabriel V, see ibid., 67–73.

39. *Paris, BnF Ar. 98* (17th c.), fol. 1r. See ʿAbdallah, *L'ordinamento*, 113 (Arabic), 319 (Italian).

40. On this curious medieval Coptic ritual meant to cure someone who has contracted rabies through a dog bite, see Ramez Mikhail, "A Magical Cure for Rabies," 267–289.

41. This is a service usually prescribed for emergencies if the original chalice at a liturgy is spilled, or its contents found to be corrupted, and appears to be based on an ancient rite of Alexandrian presanctified liturgy, i.e., a liturgical service in which communion is administered from a new chalice and particles of the body that have been kept from a liturgy on a previous day. On this rite, see Īrīs Ḥabīb al-Maṣrī, "The Rite of the Filling of the Chalice," 77–90; Ramez Mikhail, "The Coptic Church and the Presanctified Liturgy," 2–30, at 16–21.

42. See also the detailed outline with page numbers corresponding to ʿAbdallah's edition in Samir, "Gabriel V," 1132a–b.

Saint Basil, is given here. Some remarks about this text are in order. First, Gabriel's attention to ritual details and gestures—going as far as instructing the priests to enter the sanctuary with their right foot and exit with their left—is quite noticeable though expected given the purpose of the work to regulate liturgical practices. In fact, the author's explicit agenda aimed at providing a single authoritative set of rituals explains why he makes no mention of any such variant practices throughout Egypt. Clearly the purpose was to establish authoritative norms and not to inform the readers about practices followed elsewhere and deemed irregular.

However, *The Ritual Order* is no mere innovation or an attempt to impose new or foreign practices from above. As noted previously, a remark in the preface indicates that Gabriel gathered a number of orders—that is, ritual manuscripts—in preparation for this authoritative edition, and indeed the work shows familiarity with an earlier example from this genre of ritual orders titled *The Guide to the Beginners and the Disciplining of the Laity*, attributed—perhaps falsely—to Patriarch Cyril III ibn Laqlaq (AD 1235–1243).[43] After beginning his explanation of the liturgy, Gabriel's *Ritual Order* makes a digression to explain the reasons that gave rise to this reform. He paints a picture of ritual confusion throughout the Church, with fights often breaking out between deacons and priests over the exact manner of performing the rites. This entire segment in *The Ritual Order* is a quotation and an expansion of a similar section in *The Guide to the Beginners*.[44] Clearly, Gabriel considered the complaints in *The Guide to the Beginners* still relevant and appropriate for the present situation, necessitating a more detailed and exact ritual manual than Cyril III's *Guide to the Beginners*, with which Gabriel was clearly familiar.

43. *The Guide to the Beginners and the Disciplining for the Laity* (*Dallāl al-mubtadi'īn wa-tahdhīb al-ʿalmāniyyīn*), is a short treatise of twenty chapters on matters of ritual and discipline during the services. The oldest known manuscript of this work is from the fourteenth century and is found in the Vatican Apostolic Library under the shelf mark *BAV Vatican Ar. 117* (AD 1323). The treatise on folios 197r–205v of this manuscript was copied from an older manuscript from AD 1286. See the German edition: Georg Graf, "Liturgische Anweisungen," 119–134.

44. This section on the urgent need for a liturgical guide appears nearly one hundred years prior to Gabriel's *Ritual Order* in one of the manuscripts of Cyril's *Guide to the Beginners, Baramūs Canons 9* (AD 1353), fol. 3r–39r. For this version of the text, see Mīṣā'īl al-Baramūsī, "Dallāl al-mubtadi'īn wa-tahdhīb al-ʿalmāniyyīn," 117–169.

Although the stated purpose of the work is to reform and standardize liturgical practices, *The Ritual Order* frequently comments on the spiritual meaning of the rituals as well, even more so than Ibn Kabar does in *The Lamp*. After explaining the Liturgy of the Word, Gabriel provides a symbolic allegorical commentary on the rites just explained. Ritual actions are compared to Old Testament events with a view toward their spiritual efficacy in the present. Thus, the priest's sevenfold circling with the censer around the altar and church is a reminder of Israel's sevenfold procession around Jericho under Joshua's leadership and so is meant to result in an analogous tearing down of the power of sin. Likewise, the act of breaking the body of Christ before communion is connected in its details to various aspects of salvation: the descent of Christ to Hades is represented by moving a particle of the body from top to bottom in the paten; the transfer of mankind from left to right, that is, their salvation, is represented by moving a particle from left to right in the paten. For priests and deacons, the ones who perform and/or observe such intimate liturgical acts taking place on the altar, such explanations may have functioned for their spiritual edification as well as material to be used in catechism and preaching. For everyone else in the laity, who would not have had the opportunity to observe these actions up close, such description and symbolic interpretation may have been one way to provide a rare peek into the intricate mechanics of ritual celebration.[45]

As remarked earlier, the ritual instructions of *The Ritual Order* were included in subsequent centuries as rubrics in most manuscripts of the Euchologion. However, as a cohesive text, *The Ritual Order* is preserved in only two manuscripts. The main manuscript, and the one this volume relies on, is from the seventeenth century and is found in the National Library of France (*Paris, BnF Ar. 98*), the only source containing the chapter on the eucharistic liturgy. A later manuscript from the same century preserved in the Vatican Apostolic Library (*BAV Vatican Copt. 46*; AD 1719) contains a chapter from the same work on the consecration of altars and is thus not utilized in this volume.[46] The only edition of the entire work—utilizing both manuscripts—is by Alfonso ʿAbdallah, together with an Italian translation.

45. For a discussion of the genre of liturgical commentaries in the patristic and the Byzantine traditions, see Paul Meyendorff, *On the Divine Liturgy*, 23–54.

46. *BAV Vatican Copt. 46* (AD 1719), fol. 136r–143r.

One Liturgy, Different Approaches

Despite sharing a common subject matter—the liturgical ceremonies of the Coptic Church—each of the three works presented in this volume employs a different approach to this subject, likely for different objectives. This is an important point to emphasize, so as not to fall into the trap of divorcing a text from its author and the background of its composition. Often, these texts have been consulted by students and scholars of liturgy as ideal and disembodied representations of liturgical practice in their given time, assuming that the liturgical details of these texts truly reflect actual practice on the ground as these authors knew it and lived it. However, such an approach to these works does not give sufficient regard to their authors, the authors' backgrounds, and, most important, to their differing motivations for writing these works. I attempt here to offer some suggestions for reading *The Lamp*, *The Precious Jewel*, and *The Ritual Order* in context as three very different works about the same subject.[47]

Ibn Kabar's treatment of rituals in *The Lamp of Darkness* reads like a technical manual of liturgical performance for specialists. Ibn Kabar was known as a multilingual scholar and a polymath whose very prominence in government circles likely protected him in the latter part of his life. His frequent references to regional practices among the Copts and the customs of neighboring Christian communities highlight his scholarly background and scientific approach to his subject matter. Of the three texts presented here, *The Lamp* is perhaps the most comprehensive in its scope and reads most as a true reference manual for the benefit of priests and deacons aimed at informing and not reforming in the strict sense.

By contrast, *The Precious Jewel* displays a more deliberate goal of influencing the interpretation of the rites, not merely giving instructions on how they are to be performed. As discussed before, Ibn Sabbāʿ employs the traditional language of Pseudo-Dionysius to highlight the hierarchical nature of the Church and its modeling of the hierarchical division of the heavenly beings into ranks successively leading up to the throne of God. The author employs this language to great effect in order to emphasize the expected and proper behavior among the various ranks of the clergy within

47. I am grateful to the insight of Stephen J. Davis for the following comparison of the three texts and their respective approaches, which has helped clarify my thoughts on this topic.

the church. This is seen, for example, in his remarks on how deacons are to embody their respect toward higher clergy in specific ritual gestures and how particular liturgical phrases are to be reserved for bishops alone as the highest-ranking officiants. Unfortunately, very little is known about the identity of Ibn Sabbāʿ. But if Zakhary's conclusion is true, namely that the author of *The Precious Jewel* was an archdeacon in the papal entourage, one may wonder if this specific hermeneutical approach was motivated by an underlying desire to reinforce the papacy's prestige, and by extension that of the ecclesiastical hierarchy in general, by means of a consistent and articulated vision of ritual. In other words, for Ibn Sabbāʿ, liturgy could have been—among other things—the very context in which a proper disposition toward the Church's hierarchy can be theologically defended and bodily enacted.

Appearing approximately a century after the first two works, Gabriel's *Ritual Order* represents a culmination of this genre of Coptic liturgical guides. Alongside its interest in the rites and their meaning, it also presents itself as an official ecclesiastical reform, prompted by the perceived chaos in liturgical practice. Given such chaos, *The Ritual Order* makes clear its aim to minimize disagreement among liturgical performers by providing a clear and authoritative guide for the main liturgical functions and ceremonies of the Coptic Church. Yet, as remarked earlier, Gabriel's work does not content itself with the technicalities of ritual performance, though technical it certainly is. Nor does it appear to employ a particular hermeneutic key aimed at advocating for a particular disposition toward the hierarchy. Instead, the author alternates between providing exact stage directions for liturgical actors and supplying short excurses on the meaning of these rituals, usually by explaining the rites in light of parallel episodes from the Old Testament.

It is highly plausible that Gabriel and his assistants were intimately familiar with the previous works of Ibn Kabar and Ibn Sabbāʿ. All three works were produced by prominent ecclesiastics in Cairo near the center of authority in the Coptic Church within a century of one another and were specifically and uniquely engaged with liturgical practices and customs. Yet despite this likely familiarity with previous works, *The Ritual Order* clearly sets itself apart from its predecessors. Gabriel and the bishops who assented to this liturgical reform seem uninterested in the regional variety of liturgical practice evident in *The Lamp*. In fact, the text departs in minor ritual details from Ibn Kabar's description, written only a century earlier, and it also shows no apparent influence from or even knowledge of

Ibn Sabbāʿ's *Precious Jewel.* If the reformers of the early fifteenth century under Gabriel V's leadership were familiar with the previous works of Ibn Kabar and Ibn Sabbāʿ, they clearly had a different approach in mind and chose to put together a different sort of text that would serve as a lasting and authoritative guide for liturgical practice. The success of this endeavor can be seen clearly in the ubiquity of manuscripts of the Euchologion copied in subsequent centuries that include the exact text of *The Ritual Order* as a basis for ritual actions throughout the liturgical service. This success would be also apparent for any modern reader intimately familiar with the ritual details of the Coptic liturgy, who would recognize in *The Ritual Order* a liturgy identical to current practice in most—if not all—details, compared to the other two works in this volume.

Yet to focus solely on the ultimate normativity of *The Ritual Order* would risk missing the unique and significant contribution of the other two works for our knowledge of the medieval Coptic liturgy. In a sense, the field of Coptic liturgical history is enriched by having access to such unique descriptions of liturgical practice written in relatively close succession, which precisely because of their differing approaches and content provide us a more well-rounded knowledge of Coptic ritual in the medieval period.

Liturgy in Medieval Egypt

The eucharistic liturgy described in the texts that follow represents the result of centuries of historical development in worship patterns. In fact, one can speak of the rites described by these medieval authors as a later phase in the evolution of the Coptic liturgy. These are descriptions of liturgical customs virtually identical to the eucharistic liturgy as practiced and experienced by Copts today, minor variants in ritual notwithstanding, which are explained in the notes accompanying each text. It may be helpful therefore to provide a brief synopsis of this evolution and to place this late medieval phase in the broader context of Egyptian and Eastern Christian worship traditions. Unfortunately, a systematic analysis of the history of the Coptic liturgy has yet to be attempted, although the scholarly field is continuously enriched by contributions to various aspects of this history cited throughout this work.[48]

48. By comparison, the history of the Byzantine liturgy was analyzed first by Juan Mateos and subsequently by Robert F. Taft in a series on the history of the liturgy of

The history of the Eucharist before the fourth century is on the whole rather murky and presents a number of unanswered questions for scholars of early liturgical history.[49] Beginning in the fourth century, Christian communities began to consolidate around the regional system of dioceses and—eventually—patriarchates. This in turn provided a natural impetus toward the consolidation of the disparate local eucharistic practices of earlier centuries into so-called ritual families, largely coterminous with each patriarchate, though of course a considerable degree of local variety continued to exist within each family. Thus, one can begin to speak of broad regional rites in East and West, such as the Antiochian, Jerusalem, Byzantine, and Roman traditions.[50]

Within this context, liturgical sources by the fourth or fifth century show the emergence of a number of liturgical prayers and practices distinctive of Egyptian Christianity and centered on the "capital" of the Egyptian Church in the city of Alexandria. To mention just one example, a distinctive structure characteristic of Alexandrian prayers for the consecration of the Eucharist (known as anaphoral prayers) can be seen already in sources of this period. Examples include the *Strasbourg Papyrus* containing fragments of the Anaphora of Saint Mark, the anaphoral prayer in the prayer book attributed to Sarapion of Thmuis, and the so-called *Barcelona Papyrus*, all sources from the fourth or fifth century

---

Saint John Chrysostom published in *Orientalia Christiana Analecta*, of which five (out of six) volumes have appeared so far: Juan Mateos, *La célébration de la Parole*; Taft, *The Great Entrance*; Taft, *The Diptychs*; Taft, *The Precommunion Rites*; Taft, *The Communion, Thanksgiving, and Concluding Rites*. For the Roman Mass, see the still-influential work by Josef A. Jungmann, *Missarum Sollemnia*, 2 vols. A more inclusive history of Western liturgy has appeared recently: Jürgen Bärsch and Benedict Kranemann, *Geschichte der Liturgie in den Kirchen des Westens*. Recently, Athanasius al-Maqārī published a two-volume work on the history of the Coptic liturgy. Despite succeeding in introducing the topic to Arabic readers and providing frequent helpful insights, the work as a whole suffers from an inconsistent quality of scholarship and remains somewhat inaccessible outside Egypt. Al-Maqārī, *Al-quddās al-ilāhī*.

49. See, for example, Paul F. Bradshaw, *Eucharistic Origins*; Bradshaw, *The Search for the Origins of Christian Worship*; Andrew B. McGowan, *Ancient Christian Worship*, to name only a few notable and recent contributions. For a comprehensive analysis of the Eucharist in relation to Judaism, Greco-Roman society, patristic tradition, and iconography, see David Hellholm and Dieter Sänger, *The Eucharist: Its Origins and Contexts*.

50. For a more detailed description of these liturgical families, see Ephrem Carr, "Liturgical Families in the East," 11–24; Gabriel Ramis, "Liturgical Families in the West," 25–32.

with eucharistic prayers belonging to the Alexandrian tradition.[51] Space does not allow here for a detailed discussion of these sources, which are often difficult to contextualize and to interpret definitively.[52] Information on early Alexandrian liturgical practices continues to fascinate scholars, in part due to the distinct nature of these practices compared to other neighboring Eastern traditions and in part due to the scarcity of detailed sources, which range from fragmentary texts to elusive references in the writings of Alexandrian authors.[53]

In the centuries following the council of Chalcedon (AD 451), Egyptian Christianity itself was divided into several factions adhering to various beliefs concerning Christ's incarnation and the exact relationship between his humanity and divinity.[54] The immediate effect this had on liturgical practices was likely limited. One example where these theological disagreements manifested themselves on the ground was in regard to church buildings. Conflicts over ownership of churches, their painting programs, and their rites of consecration represented a metaphorical battleground in which various communities sought to assert their legitimacy

51. For the *Strasbourg Papyrus*, whose exact library shelf mark is *P. Strasbourg Gr. Inv. 254*, see the English text in R. C. D. Jasper and G. J. Cuming, *Prayers of the Eucharist*, 53–54. See also the analysis of this important source in Cuming, *The Liturgy of St Mark*, xxiii–xxvii; H. A. J. Wegman, "Une anaphore incomplète?" 432–450; Jürgen Hammerstaedt, *Griechische Anaphorenfragmente*, 22–41. The most updated edition and commentary on the prayers attributed to Sarapion of Thmuis is Maxwell E. Johnson, *The Prayers of Sarapion*. Finally, for an edition and analysis of the anaphoral prayer in the *Barcelona Papyrus*, or *P. Monts.Roca inv. 128–178*, see Michael Zheltov, "The Anaphora and the Thanksgiving Prayer from the Barcelona Papyrus," 467–504.

52. For a helpful and most-recent overview of research on Alexandrian/Egyptian liturgy, see Brakmann, "New Discoveries and Studies in the Liturgy of the Copts (2004–2012)," 457–481.

53. For a brief overview of the state of the question, see Maxwell E. Johnson, *Liturgy in Early Christian Egypt*. See also the still-influential work, Theodor Schermann's *Ägyptische Abendmahlsliturgien des ersten Jahrtausends*.

54. For a helpful narrative of the events surrounding the council of Chalcedon, the reader is referred to Price, "The Council of Chalcedon (451): A Narrative," 70–91. On the roots of the Christological controversies in the writings of Cyril of Alexandria and the council of Ephesus in AD 431, see John McGuckin, *St. Cyril of Alexandria: The Christological Controversy*, 126–226. For a more detailed analysis of the Christological debate following the council of Chalcedon, see Alois Grillmeier and Theresia Hainthaler, *Christ in Christian Tradition*, vol. 2, pt. 2.

as the only lawful Church of Alexandria, a dynamic that continued even after the Arab conquest in AD 642.[55]

Gradually, the worship practices of Egypt's Christian communities evolved into two distinct sets of practices or rites: the Alexandrian Melkite tradition observed by the Chalcedonian Church of Alexandria and the liturgy of the non-Chalcedonian Coptic Church. The origins of this bifurcation are not exactly clear. We simply do not know when, where, or how the first instance occurred that the liturgical practices of one community would have been recognizably different to members of the other group. We do know that surviving manuscripts of the Liturgy of Saint Mark, for example, can be clearly categorized into a Greek Melkite version and a Coptic version, the latter transmitted under the name of Cyril of Alexandria.[56] Other examples of these two divergent sets of practices include rites for ordination to the clergy, marriage, and for blessing the water of the Nile River.[57] In terms of location, the Melkite Alexandrian tradition was observed mainly in Alexandria and a few towns in the Nile Delta with concentrations of Chalcedonian Christians before eventually becoming extinct by the late thirteenth century due to the increasing influence of the Byzantine liturgical tradition of the city of Constantinople.[58] In the meantime, the Coptic liturgy had as its strongest center the monas-

55. Leslie S. B. MacCoull, "A Dwelling Place of Christ, a Healing Place of Knowledge," 1–16. For the overall inter-confessional dynamics before and after the Arab conquest, especially in the area of liturgical and religious practices, see Maged S. A. Mikhail, *From Byzantine to Islamic Egypt*.

56. For the Greek medieval version of the Liturgy of Saint Mark, see Cuming, *The Liturgy of St Mark*, especially his overview of the manuscripts in xxix–xxxi. The Coptic version of this liturgy has yet to be analyzed independently. For an English translation of the thirteenth-century manuscript *Oxford, Bodleian Hunt. 360* with additions from later liturgical books, see F. E. Brightman, *Liturgies Eastern and Western*, 144–188.

57. See respectively, Heinzgerd Brakmann, "Die altkirchlichen Ordinationsgebete Jerusalems," 108–127; Gabriel Radle, "Uncovering the Alexandrian Greek Rite of Marriage," 49–73; Roshdi Wassef Behman Dous, "Ο Αγιασμός των υδάτων του Νείλου Ποταμού."

58. On the Melkite liturgy of the patriarchates of Alexandria, Jerusalem, and Antioch and their eventual demise under Constantinopolitan influence, see Joseph Nasrallah, "La liturgie des Patriarcats melchites de 969 à 1300," 156–181; Nasrallah, *Histoire*, III.1:359–384. While the question of the "Byzantinization" of the Patriarchate of Alexandria has not been adequately studied, the similar process was analyzed for the Patriarchate of Jerusalem in Daniel Galadza, *Liturgy and Byzantinization in Jerusalem*.

tic establishments in Scetis, also known as Wādī Habīb and Wādī al-Naṭrūn in the later Arabic tradition.

Meanwhile, the liturgy of the Coptic Church—celebrated in both Greek and Coptic—continued to develop in line with ecclesiastical and societal factors influencing the community. The Monastery of Saint Macarius in Wādī al-Naṭrūn (Scetis) played a central role in protecting the Coptic Alexandrian patriarchate and preserving its traditions in the postconquest period.[59] For this reason, the Coptic liturgy came to be decisively shaped by the local practices of Scetis, part of a broader regional tradition that can be termed the northern Egyptian liturgy. In addition, this northern tradition gained many influences from practices of West Syrian Christianity, such as the adoption of certain priestly prayers before and after the eucharistic prayer proper, termed the *Prayer of the Veil* and the *Prayer of the Fraction*, respectively. Indeed, the ultimate rise of the Egyptian Liturgy of Saint Basil—a prayer structured in a similar pattern to most Syriac eucharistic prayers—to become the most commonly celebrated liturgy of the Coptic Church can itself be seen as a sign of the same trend toward the "Syrianization" of the Coptic liturgy in the Middle Ages.[60] This was likely due to the close relationship between the Copts and their Syrian Orthodox coreligionists as well as a number of influential Coptic popes of Syrian background, notably Damian (AD 576–605), Simon I (AD 692–700), and Afrahām ibn Zur'ah (AD 975–978).[61]

Meanwhile, and until at least the fourteenth century, communities in southern Egypt continued to observe their own local practices, usually in Sahidic Coptic with some Greek. This is mainly attested in manuscripts of the famous White Monastery near Akhmīm—mostly fragmentary—and those of the ancient monastery of Archangel Michael in the Fayyūm region, now preserved in the Morgan Library and Museum in New York. Texts from these two monastic establishments are what are termed collectively

59. See, for example, Martin Krause, "The Importance of Wadi al-Natrun for Coptology," 1–11; Ugo Zanetti, "Liturgy at Wadi al-Natrun," 122–141.

60. On this trend as a formative influence of Coptic liturgical history, see Jean Maurice Fiey, "Coptes et syriaques: contacts et échanges," 295–365. This liturgical connection between the two non-Chalcedonian communions is also discussed in Brakmann, "New Discoveries and Studies in the Liturgy of the Copts (2004–2012)," 462–463.

61. Johannes den Heijer, "Les patriarches coptes d'origine syrienne," 45–63.

the southern Egyptian liturgy.[62] Ultimately however, as indeed happens in many contexts in which a distinction can be seen between an influential center—in this case places like Scetis and Cairo—and a relatively subordinate periphery such as southern Egypt, the liturgical practices of the latter became gradually extinct, no longer to appear in the sources after scattered references to them in Ibn Kabar's *Lamp of Darkness.*

As the Coptic Church entered the second millennium, the overall Arabization of the community and its written tradition also left its tangible mark on the liturgy, seen foremost in the spread of liturgical manuscripts with a parallel Arabic translation of the Coptic texts.[63] By the twelfth century, this set of liturgical practices originally of northern provenance and now practiced mainly in Arabic and the Bohairic dialect of Coptic had established itself as the official liturgy of the Coptic papacy, especially in Scetis and Cairo. This was such that Pope Gabriel II ibn Turaik (AD 1131–1145) could endorse a canonical pronouncement forbidding the celebration of any prayers of the Eucharist other than the three common to Scetis and the north generally, namely, those attributed to Saints Basil, Gregory, and Mark/Cyril.[64] In many ways, the liturgy of the medieval Coptic Church as seen in the texts presented here represents an advanced stage of a protracted process of evolution influenced by a variety of cultural, historical, and linguistic factors. By the time we arrive at the fifteenth century and *The Ritual Order* of Gabriel V, the Coptic eucharistic service had essentially reached the shape and content recognized today by millions of Copts worldwide, even to the level of seemingly minor liturgical details, such as the number of times a priest should place incense in the censer or the ratio of water to wine to be poured into the chalice for the Eucharist.

62. Much of the work on this rich heritage of liturgical practices, including anaphoras, lectionaries, and hymnography, remains to be done, conducted mainly by Diliana Atanassova. For a helpful summary of the state of research, see Atanassova, "The Primary Sources of Southern Egyptian Liturgy," 47–96.

63. The literature on the Arabization process in the Coptic Church is rich. For the classic treatment of the subject from the perspective of the written tradition, see Samuel Rubenson, "Translating the Tradition," 4–14. The oldest surviving Arabic translations of the Coptic liturgy have been studied by Fr. Wadīʿ al-Fransiskānī in "Aqdam al-tarjamāt al-ʿarabiyyah," 217–235.

64. Canon 26. See O. H. E. Burmester, "The Canons of Gabriel Ibn Turaik," 5–45, at 40–41.

The importance of the texts presented below becomes strikingly clear when viewed in the context of other sources of the Coptic liturgy. For the liturgical historian, the primary body of evidence is usually the liturgical manuscripts themselves, prayer books of various types written by hand in or very close to the time period under consideration. In the case of the Coptic eucharistic liturgy, there are three main types. The first is the Euchologion, traditionally providing only the prayers for the celebrant. The second is the Diaconicon, known in Arabic as *Khidmat al-shammās* (*The Service of the Deacon*), and providing both the responses/acclamations of the deacon and congregational chants. The third is the Lectionary, the book of scriptural readings arranged into sections for each liturgical celebration.[65] Unfortunately, the earliest attested manuscripts of Euchologia from the north date to the thirteenth century, which renders it difficult to make any assertions about practices prior to that period.[66] To make matters worse, the oldest Euchologion manuscripts prior to the fifteenth century usually provide only the prayers of the celebrant. In other words, they do not describe any ritual movements or gestures, nor do they provide any short, easily memorable formulas said by the celebrant, nor even the diaconal and congregational responses that are to accompany each prayer.[67] This renders descriptive texts such as the ones presented here of paramount importance

65. This is a very simplified summary of the topic of Bohairic liturgical manuscripts, many of which in reality defy a simple classification. For a closer analysis, see Ugo Zanetti, "Bohairic Liturgical Manuscripts," 65–94.

66. For example, a late-thirteenth-century Euchologion from the Monastery of Saint Antony near the Red Sea containing the three liturgies of Basil, Gregory, and Cyril, and the service of the "Filling of the Chalice." It is currently preserved in the Vatican Apostolic Library under the name *BAV Vatican Copt. 17*, copied in AD 1288. See the publication of the Arabic text of the liturgy of Saint Basil from this manuscript in Wadīʿ ʿAwaḍ, "Testo della traduzione araba della Messa Copta di San Basilio Secondo," 129–149. See also the French translation in Mamdouh Chéhab, "Traduction de la version arabe de la messe copte de s. Basile," 49–68. For a description of the manuscript, see Adolph Hebbelynck and Arnold van Lantschoot, *Codices Coptici Vaticani Barberiniani Borgiani Rossiani*, 1:58–63; Achim Budde, *Die ägyptische Basilios-Anaphora*, 111.

67. In addition to the Vatican manuscript in the previous note, examples from the thirteenth century alone include *London, British Library Or. 1239*, *Oxford, Bodleian Hunt. 360*, and *Manchester, Rylands Copt. 426*. Unfortunately, none of these manuscripts are published as such, with the exception of F. E. Brightman's edition of the Liturgy of Saint Cyril from the Bodleian manuscript, which he supplemented by rubrics and chants from printed editions. For descriptions of these manuscripts, see Budde, *Die ägyptische Basilios-Anaphora*, 108–112.

for a holistic view of the Coptic liturgy as ideally conceived by these particular authors, with all liturgical roles integrated into a cohesive description. Yet at the same time, one must always keep in mind the common problems of critical interpretation and possible agenda inherent to any text.

Finally, a brief synopsis of the Coptic liturgy itself would be helpful. Rather than provide a detailed account of all the ritual actions and words discussed in the following texts, I provide here only a brief outline intended to familiarize readers with the major stages of the Coptic eucharistic liturgy, while those interested in a detailed analysis of particular points are referred to the plentiful notes accompanying each text. In the following description, I adhere to a level of detail general enough so as to apply equally to all three texts presented in this volume. As a reading of the commentaries presented here reveals, minor points of ritual variance among the texts exist within the common scheme described below.[68]

Following the morning service, the clergy, chanters, and readers put on their liturgical vestments, after which the appropriate hours of prayer from the Book of Hours (*Ajbiyyah*) are prayed.[69] These introductory rites lead into the eucharistic service proper, which begins with the prothesis rite or the preparation of the offerings of bread and wine for the subsequent eucharistic meal. The purpose of this stage is to choose the eucharistic bread and to prepare the chalice of wine and water in view of the subsequent consecration of these gifts in the anaphora. As such, the prothesis rite has its roots in the ancient practices of receiving these gifts as donations by the people and their placement on the altar in a solemn procession, a ritual that became extinct by the fourteenth century but that can still be glimpsed in vestigial form in Ibn Sabbāʿ's commentary.[70] Though preparatory in nature, the prothesis rite is a visible and public part of the service and thus

68. A detailed description of the Coptic eucharistic liturgy can be found in the classic work by O. H. E. Burmester, *The Egyptian or Coptic Church*, 46–90. See also John Paul Abdelsayed, "Liturgy: Heaven on Earth," 143–159.

69. Since the Early Church, a daily system of prayer units—also called offices or hours—developed, which in later Coptic tradition became seven in number, corresponding to the following hours of the day: First, third, sixth, ninth, eleventh (or sunset), twelfth (or compline), and midnight. It eventually became customary to pray certain of these hours of prayer before commencing the eucharistic service. For the historical development of the so-called liturgy of the hours, see Robert F. Taft, *The Liturgy of the Hours*, esp. 249–259 on the Coptic tradition specifically.

70. I discuss this transformation and the subsequent history of the Coptic prothesis rite in Ramez Mikhail, *The Presentation of the Lamb*. For remarks on this transformation,

consists of prayers by the celebrant, diaconal responses, congregational chants, and a procession of the gifts around the altar. The details of the prothesis rite, with a few differences in details, are described in the texts presented in this volume.

After the prothesis rite and the priest's reading of a prayer for the forgiveness of the clergy and other liturgical assistants at the entrance of the sanctuary, all reenter the sanctuary for the rites of the Liturgy of the Word. This service of scriptural readings, chants, and prayers commences with the offering of incense in the sanctuary and throughout the church's interior, likely deriving from exorcising uses of incense in late antiquity, where the sight and smell of incense in the air highlights the presence of God in the liturgical assembly, though a parallel view of incense burning as a propitiatory offering is also attested.[71] The Coptic liturgy of northern Egypt assigns four scriptural readings for every liturgy from the Pauline epistles, the catholic or non-Pauline epistles, the Acts of the Apostles, and the Gospels.[72] In an era subsequent to that of the texts presented here, these sections of the service also came to include a reading from the *Synaxarion*, which provides a brief synopsis of the lives of the saints commemorated that day. The Liturgy of the Word is also the locus of variable chants appropriate for the day, especially on solemn feasts. Most notably, the Trisagion chant, "Holy God, Holy mighty, Holy immortal," is chanted every service and forms a high point in preparation for the Gospel reading, as evidenced by the solemnity accorded it in the commentary by Ibn Sabbāʿ. Traditionally, the climax of the Liturgy of the Word included the sermon or homily, a word of exhortation delivered by one of the clergy either extemporaneously or from a prepared text.[73] After the sermon, a series of prayers entreating for the sick, those who are traveling, and those preparing for baptism, among other segments of the community, concludes the Liturgy of the Word. Although in late antiquity at this point in the service it was common to dismiss the catechumens (those preparing for baptism and membership in the Church),

---

see Emmanuel Fritsch, "The Preparation of the Gifts and the Pre-Anaphora," 97–152; Al-Maqārī, *Al-quddās al-ilāhī*, 1:270–277.

71. Taft, *The Great Entrance*, 49–51.

72. The primary study of the northern Egyptian lectionary system remains Ugo Zanetti, *Les lectionnaires coptes annuels*.

73. For a detailed study of the homily in the early Church, see Alexandre Olivar, *La predicación cristiana antigua*. See also Mary B. Cunningham and Pauline Allen, *Preacher and Audience*.

by the medieval period this practice had become extinct, owing in large part to the demise of the adult catechumenate itself.[74]

A series of rites follows on the heels of the Liturgy of the Word and constitute the bridge between the service of Scripture and the Eucharist known as the pre-anaphoral rites. These start with the three great prayers for the universal Church, the hierarchs, and the security of the church gathering in this particular place. This is followed by the recitation of the confession of faith of Nicaea-Constantinople, a feature of the ritual in Eastern liturgies at this point. Meanwhile, the priests perform their own acts of preparation, namely, the washing of hands and the silent reading of the *Prayer of the Veil*, a prayer of Syrian influence requesting the grace to approach the altar and perform the mysteries. This prayer owes its name to its traditional place of recitation before the veil of the sanctuary. As a final act of preparation, the clergy and people exchange a kiss of peace following a prayer by the same name, once again a standard feature of Eastern pre-anaphoral rites.[75]

The anaphora of Saint Basil itself begins with the ancient greeting of the celebrant, "The Lord be with you," found also in the Roman Mass and other Eastern liturgies. What follows is the anaphoral or eucharistic prayer by the celebrant, a lengthy discursive prayer characteristic of fourth-century developments in eucharistic history, in which the celebrant gives thanks to God, recalls the major events of salvation history, and ultimately calls upon the Holy Spirit to consecrate the bread and the wine. Notable highlights along the way include the chanting of the angelic praise, "Holy, Holy, Holy Lord of hosts," based on the vision in Isaiah 6:3 and known in liturgical scholarship as the *Sanctus*, the retelling of the account of the establishment of the Eucharist at the Last Supper, the epiclesis prayer for the consecration of the bread and wine, and a lengthy commemoration of the names of well-known saints such as the Virgin Mary, John the Baptist, Stephen the Protomartyr, as well as particularly Egyptian saints, such as Athanasius, Cyril, Dioscorus, and Antony. A concluding doxology that the Father's name "be glorified, blessed, and exalted in everything that is honored and blessed with Jesus Christ, your beloved Son, and the Holy Spirit" concludes the prayer of the anaphora.

74. Michel Dujarier, *A History of the Catechumenate*; Marcel Metzger, Wolfram Drews, and Heinzgerd Brakmann, "Katechumenat," 498–574.

75. The pre-anaphoral rites of the Byzantine liturgy, containing many of the same elements, were analyzed in Robert Taft's groundbreaking study *The Great Entrance*.

After the anaphora, attention shifts toward the imminent communion in the body and blood of Christ. A *Prayer of the Fraction*, so called because it accompanies the physical breaking of the body by the celebrant, invokes the language of the people's sonship to God, which grants them the boldness to call him Father, thus forming a prelude to the reciting of the Lord's Prayer, "Our Father." This in turn leads to a prayer by the celebrant asking for the people to be absolved of their sins, while the people are prostrating, one of many such prayers pronounced throughout the service. This is transformed into the jubilant cry of the celebrant, "The holy things for the holy ones," an ancient call to communion that also asserts a requisite holiness on the part of the would-be communicants. By way of a final declaration of faith in the Eucharist, the priest proclaims a series of faith statements that this is indeed the body and blood of Christ, to which the people give their assent by saying amen.

Communion is given by the celebrant, assisted by other priests and/or deacons. Coptic tradition preserves the ancient manner of distributing the body and the blood separately. The body is placed directly in the mouth of the communicant, while the blood is administered by means of a communion spoon dipped in the chalice. During this procedure, chanters sing Psalm 150, the traditional and essential communion chant of the Coptic rite. Additional chants in either Coptic or another language may be added as needed. At the conclusion of communion, the celebrant returns to the altar, where he consumes the remainder of the Eucharist and washes the vessels. A dismissal prayer accompanied by the sprinkling of water upon the people concludes the service. Following the dismissal rites, the priest will usually distribute small pieces from oblation breads prepared for that day's service but not chosen for the Eucharist, commonly termed *ūlūjiyyah* (Gr. εὐλογία, blessing).

Reading through the three texts presented here from *The Lamp of Darkness*, *The Precious Jewel*, and *The Ritual Order*, the reader will readily notice the adherence of their respective authors to the general outline of the eucharistic service in the Coptic tradition I have just described. Yet it is the minor differences in details and interpretation in these texts that make them so fascinating to study in parallel. Their juxtaposition here together in a single volume is thus a rewarding experience in studying the liturgy of medieval Egypt as well as how ritual practices represented a central concern in the life of the Coptic Church during that period.

CHAPTER

1

The Lamp of Darkness and the Elucidation of the Service

(Miṣbāḥ al-Ẓulmah wa-Īḍāḥ al-Khidmah)

By Abū al-Barakāt ibn Kabar

Chapter 17

Concerning the Order of the Liturgy and the Oblation

That which the holy canons have prescribed for the liturgy is for the words of the holy books to be interpreted,[1] then that the presbyter is to carry the bread and the cup of thanksgiving, while the bishop carries the incense and circles with it around the altar three times.[2] The bishop is to hand the censer of incense to the presbyter, who is to go around with it to the entire congregation. Once they have finished chanting, the deacons are

1. The author begins here by providing a quick summary of the liturgy in its broad strokes. He includes the following main stages. First are the readings from Scripture or other holy books before the liturgy, perhaps in reference to the Gospel reading in the morning service. The term translated here as "interpreted" (*yufassar*) could also mean "to translate," in which case it may be referring to the practice of reading aloud the scriptural lessons in Coptic followed by an Arabic translation. This is followed by the prothesis rite, offering of incense, the Liturgy of the Word, the prayers or litanies before the anaphora, the kiss, the hand washing by the celebrant, the removal of the veil covering the gifts, the breaking of the body, and communion. The text here is based on the thirteenth-century Nomocanon of al-Ṣafī ibn al-ʿAssāl, where the author references the *Didascalia Arabica* 10, 23, and 38. See Jirjis Fīlūthāʾus ʿAwaḍ, *Al-majmūʿ al-ṣafawī*, 1:123.

2. Here and elsewhere, the word "presbyter" is meant to specify members of the second rank of the priesthood between deacon and bishop, usually equivalent to the Arabic *qissīs* or *qiss*. The other commonly used term, "priest," translates the Arabic *kāhin*, which could in certain contexts apply also to bishops.

to read portions of the apostolic writings and praises from the psalms. Afterward, a presbyter or a deacon is to read the Gospel while all stand silently.

After the interpretation of the holy Gospel, the bishop is to pray concerning the sick, the strangers, those in captivity, favorable weather, the fruits, the kings, those who have reposed, those who bring the oblations[3] (*qarābīn*) to the church, those who prepare them, the catechumens, the peace of the catholic Church, the bishop, the clergy, and all the people.

Then, the bishop is to lead the prayers while standing at the altar with the veil spread,[4] whereas the presbyters are to be inside and the deacons around him waving fans in the likeness of the wings of the cherubim. Then the people are to kiss one another, but the men ought not to kiss the women. The deacon then is to bring water and the priests are to wash their hands, then [the deacon's response] "to offer (*ibrusfārīn*)" is to be said and the liturgy continues.[5]

3. Employed in the singular, oblation commonly refers to the eucharistic bread offered in the liturgy and believed to be changed to the body of Christ. In the plural, it could also refer to any material offerings donated to the church, such as bread, wine, oil, candles, and the like.

4. Here and elsewhere, consecrating without further qualification refers to the celebrant praying the eucharistic prayer over the bread and the wine, and therefore consecrating them. The context of this statement seems to suggest that the anaphora was prayed while the sanctuary curtain or veil was closed, an otherwise unknown practice in the Coptic tradition. The passage itself is based on a section in Canon 38 of the vulgate recension of the *Didascalia Arabica*, also known as *al-Disqūliyyah*. This version of the *Disqūliyyah* dates to the eleventh century at the latest and relies on an older Bohairic Coptic text. See the publication of this recension, Marqus Dā'ūd's *Al-Disqūliyyah*, 184. See also the text of this passage provided in the appendix of the ancient recension of the *Didascalia Arabica* in William Sulaymān Qilādah, *Ta'ālīm al-rusul al-Disqūliyyah*, 847. On the practice of praying with the sanctuary curtain closed in the Byzantine East, see Robert F. Taft, *The Great Entrance*, 405–416; see also the most updated edition in Italian, Robert F. Taft and Stefano Parenti, *Il grande ingresso*, 645–651.

5. This is an Arabic rendering of the first word of the Greek diaconal command *prospherein* before the anaphora, which O. H. E. Burmester corrects as προσφέρειν κατὰ τρόπον στάθητε κατὰ τρόμου εἰς ἀνατολάς βλέψατε πρόσχωμεν. See Burmester, "The Greek Kīrugmata," 375. The infinitive προσφέρειν (*prospherein*) is usually translated in liturgical books as a command, "offer!" However, the meaning of the command is likely, "Stand with trembling, look toward the east, let us attend, *to offer* according to the custom," a reading supported by comparison to the similar command in the Byzantine liturgy, "Let us stand well, let us stand with fear. Let us attend to offer the holy anaphora in peace." For the latter, see the analysis in Robert F. Taft, "Textual Problems," 340–365.

Those who chant ought not to do so with pleasure but with wisdom.[6] Also, the body is to be divided calmly piece by piece. They should be careful not to allow any part of it to fall. It is to be divided in a way so as to be not too small nor too large, so that it may fill the mouth of the communicant, and that he may be able to move it in his mouth. And let there be a cross on each piece of it.[7]

Once all the prayers have been completed, the presbyters are to confess the Trinity, while all the people cry out accepting the confession.[8] The presbyter is to say through the mouth of the archdeacon,[9] "Whoever is pure, let him approach the mysteries, and whoever is impure, may he not approach lest he burn with the fire of the divinity."[10]

It is also not allowed for a presbyter who did not attend the liturgy from its beginning to approach and break off [a piece of the body], nor to take the body with his hand. Anyone who laughs during the liturgy, if he be a priest, his punishment is to be a week long, and if he be a layman, he ought to depart at this time and not be given the mysteries. Let no one speak in the sanctuary at all, aside from what is called for by necessity, nor around the altar also. Let no one spit while he is at the altar unless he is sick. Let no one speak at all in church, for the house of God is not a place of chitchat, but a place of prayer with fear. No one is to leave the church without necessity after the reading of the holy Gospel, except after the removal of

---

The response in the Coptic liturgy was analyzed most recently in Achim Budde, *Die ägyptische Basilios-Anaphora*, 222–226.

6. This is apparently in reference to chanters employing excessive vocal flourishes in rendering the chants, a practice that may imply deriving too much pleasure from one's own voice and that may also hinder the congregation from participating in these chants.

7. For a description of Coptic eucharistic bread, see O. H. E. Burmester, *The Egyptian or Coptic Church*, 81–82. Small pieces of the eucharistic bread are referred to here and in Arabic sources generally as jewels or gems (*jawharah*), see Georg Graf, *Verzeichnis*, 150.

8. Likely in reference to the Trinitarian response before communion, "One is the Holy Father, one is the Holy Son, one is the Holy Spirit, amen," often assigned to the celebrant in medieval sources, but today proclaimed by the people. See Burmester, "The Greek Kīrugmata," 382; F. E. Brightman, *Liturgies Eastern and Western*, 184.

9. The text has the less frequent form *awwal al-shamāmisah*, or the first among the deacons, i.e., the arch- or protodeacon.

10. This response is unknown in the manuscript tradition of the Coptic liturgy. It appears that Ibn Kabar is simply echoing the similar injunction found in Canon 97 of the Arabic *Canons of Pseudo-Basil*. See Wilhelm Riedel, *Die Kirchenrechtsquellen*, 274.

the oblation,[11] the blessing by the priest, and the dismissal. Anyone who enters the church and listens to the books and does not stand until the prayers are finished must be separated.[12] Likewise, it appeared in some of the laws of the kings (*qawānīn al-mulūk*) that the faithful ought always to stand on their feet during liturgies until they are concluded.[13]

And if the faithful were prevented from going to church, the bishop is to pray the Eucharist (*yuqaddis*) in his house for this purpose. But if there be no need, then he should not, unless there be in that house a consecrated church. Whoever dares and does what should only be done in church in his own home, let him be anathematized. No one is to sit in the sanctuary or to celebrate the Eucharist except after the lamp of the altar is lit or whatever candles are available.[14]

From the holy canons of the offering: The offering of the oblation is obligatory for all Christians and partaking of it is recommended for whoever has first examined his soul, has rectified it, has prepared himself in soul and body, and has become ready internally and externally to partake

11. That is, after the body and the blood have been entirely consumed and are no longer on the altar.

12. That is, he is to be suspended from Church membership and by extension from communion, perhaps only temporarily. The Arabic verb *farraqa* (to separate or to tear apart) is likely a translation of the Greek ἀφορίζω (*aphorizō*), which in Early Church canons commonly refers to excommunication. See G. W. H. Lampe, *A Patristic Greek Lexicon*, 279.

13. It is unclear to which canon of the so-called *Books of the Kings* the author is referring. In the Copto-Arabic canonical literature, these canons attributed to Byzantine emperors are sometimes included after the canons of the Ecumenical Council of Nicaea (AD 325), most famously in the twelfth-century Nomocanon of Macarius (Maqārah) the Monk and in the fifth chapter of the *Lamp of Darkness* itself. On the Arabic canons of the Council of Nicaea, see René-Georges Coquin, "Nicaea, Arabic Canons of," *CE* 6:1789a–1790a. Assuming the author is speaking of the Canons of Nicaea generally by referring to the laws of the kings, a similarity can be noted with the prohibition on kneeling on Sundays and the Pentecost period in Canon 20 of this council. For a discussion of this canon in the eastern tradition, see Gabriel Radle, "Embodied Eschatology, Part 2," 433–461.

14. Likely inspired by Exodus 27:20–21, the requirement for an eastern lamp in the sanctuary appears quite early in some Coptic texts, such as the *Encomium by Celestine of Rome on Victor the General* and the *Miracles of Apa Phoebammon*. See E. A. Wallis Budge, *Coptic Martyrdoms*, 1:57 (Coptic), 310 (English); Kerry E. Verrone, *Mighty Deeds*, 38–39. The requirement appears as a canonical norm in the medieval period, for example in the canons of Pope Gabriel II ibn Turaik (AD 1131–1145). See O. H. E. Burmester, "The Canons of Gabriel Ibn Turaik," 49 (Arabic), 54 (English).

of it with its conditions and obligations. For it is the body and the blood of our Lord, our God, and our Savior Jesus Christ, who said, "Do this in remembrance of me until I come."[15] By means of it, the Holy Spirit, which descends upon it, cleaves to the souls of the communicants thereof. For our Lord—to him be the glory—has granted us rational and spiritual things by means of tangible and bodily things.

Let no one cover his oblation with bread before the dismissal.[16] Likewise, none of the water of ablution (*mā' al-taghṭiyyah*) is to be expelled from the mouth.[17] Also, nothing is to remain from the oblation bread, and whatever remains from it or from the chalice, let all the deacons who are at the altar partake of it.[18] The chalice is not to remain filled after the final thanksgiving to wait for whoever has delayed [in coming] to church at the time of the liturgy.

And let the deacons write the names of those who bring the offering, whether living or reposed, in order to remember them.[19] The entire oblation

15. 1 Corinthians 11:25–26.

16. That is, to consume blessed bread before the dismissal of the service. For more on the blessed bread (*al-ūlūjiyyah*), see note 106.

17. Coptic custom is for the communicants to drink a small amount of water after receiving the body and the blood to ensure that nothing remain in the mouth. This ritual drink of water is often termed in medieval sources *mā' al-taghṭiyyah* or the water of covering. See O. H. E. Burmester, *The Egyptian or Coptic Church*, 87.

18. Like all Eastern and Western traditions, Egyptian Christianity practiced the reservation or keeping of the Eucharist after the liturgy and distributing communion in a later day from this reserved sacrament in a ritual known as the liturgy of the presanctified gifts. The practice was prohibited in the eleventh century by Pope Christodoulus (AD 1047–1077). For early Christian practice, see the discussion in Stefanos Alexopoulos, *The Presanctified*, 7–40. For the history of this practice in the Coptic Church, see Ramez Mikhail, "The Coptic Church and the Presanctified Liturgy," 2–30. The practice of consecrating a chalice of wine from presanctified bread survives in Coptic practice in the form of the *Rite of the Filling of the Chalice*, indicated today only in cases of emergency in which the chalice has been damaged or spilled. For this rite, in addition to the article just cited, see also Īrīs Ḥabīb al-Maṣrī, "The Rite of the Filling of the Chalice," 77–90.

19. Here, Ibn Kabar is repeating an injunction appearing also in many early Church Orders. The earliest of these is the Syriac *Didascalia Apostolorum* 2. See Alistair Stewart-Sykes, *The Didascalia Apostolorum*, 175. This was later incorporated into the Arabic *Disqūliyyah*. See Qilādah, *Ta'ālīm al-rusul al-Disqūliyyah*, 842; Dā'ūd, *Al-Disqūliyyah*, 176. On the question of the reception of the eucharistic offerings by deacons, see Taft, *The Great Entrance*, 11–34; Taft and Parenti, *Il grande ingresso*, 101–127; Adam Łajtar and Grzegorz Ochała, "Two Wall Inscriptions from the Faras Cathedral," 73–102, especially 97–102. By Ibn Kabar's time, the custom of the people bringing their own offerings to

bread is to be sealed, and there should be chosen from it that which is perfect and free of cracks. It is not to be baked outside the church. But if there be no oven in the church and it cannot be prepared there, let the priest or sacristan (*qayyim*) bake it in their house, and let not a woman or anyone else handle it.[20]

Among the liturgies (*quddāsāt*), three have become established in the Coptic Church. One of them, used all the days of fasting and non-fasting, is the liturgy of Saint Basil, the Bishop of Caesarea of Cappadocia.[21] The second is the liturgy of Mark that was completed by Cyril.[22] It has become customary for Egyptians not to use it except in the Great Fast and the month of Kiyahk.[23] The third, exclusive to the days of the divine feasts and joy, is the liturgy of Saint Gregory.[24]

---

church had already ceased, as evident from the canons of Pope Cyril II cited in the following note as well as the remainder of this very passage in Ibn Kabar, in which he seems to paraphrase these canons.

20. Canon 34 of the Arabic *Canons of Pseudo-Athanasius* already forbid the priest from abandoning his duties to bake the bread, implying that the bread was baked in the church's oven rather than in the homes of the faithful. See Wilhelm Riedel and W. E. Crum, *The Canons of Athanasius of Alexandria*, 26 (Arabic), 32 (English). In the same century, Pope Christodoulus *allowed* for people to bake the offering in their own homes, which indicates that the custom was unusual in his time: O. H. E. Burmester, "The Canons of Christodulos," 77 (Arabic), 83 (English). Finally, the subsequent patriarch, Cyril II (AD 1078–1092) insists in his canons that oblations are to be baked in the church's official ovens and are not to be touched by women. Burmester, "The Canons of Cyril II," 269 (Arabic), 282 (English).

21. The Egyptian eucharistic prayer or liturgy of Basil was analyzed and published in a critical edition in Budde, *Die ägyptische Basilios-Anaphora.*

22. The Coptic liturgy of Mark/Cyril still awaits a critical scholarly edition. Brightman's translation is based on the manuscript *Oxford, Bodleian Hunt. 360* (13th c.), supplemented by modern printed editions. See Brightman, *Liturgies Eastern and Western*, 144–188. The study by Geoffrey J. Cuming, *The Liturgy of St Mark*, though very valuable, focuses on the Greek Melkite version of Mark attested in medieval Greek manuscripts.

23. The fourth month of the Coptic calendar (December 10–January 8 in the Gregorian calendar), it concludes with the feast of Christ's Nativity (Kiyahk 29–30) and is thus the Advent season in the Coptic liturgical year. It falls completely within the Nativity fast, which is forty-three days in length, and is marked by particular veneration of the mystery of the incarnation and the Virgin Mary in the form of popular vigils. For more on the Coptic calendar, see Aelred Cody, "Calendar, Coptic," *CE* 2:433a–436a; Burmester, *The Egyptian or Coptic Church*, 12; De Lacy Evans O'Leary, *The Saints of Egypt*, 34–59.

24. For the Coptic liturgy of Saint Gregory, see the critical edition and study in Ernst Hammerschmidt, *Die koptische Gregoriosanaphora.*

And the prevailing custom in the Coptic Church is that there be no eucharistic liturgy (*quddās*) except following a prayer. And it is best if this prayer that precedes it is the *Offering of Incense*, that is, if it is a feast day.[25] But if it is the forty days [i.e., the Great Lent], Wednesdays, Fridays, and the other fasts, the eucharistic liturgy follows the prayer of the hour that precedes it, I mean, the ninth hour in the *Book of Hours* (*ajbiyyah*) and the passages (*al-qiṭaʿ*).[26] However, during the holy forty days, the monks pray before it [i.e., before the liturgy] the two prayers of evening and compline (*al-nawm*).[27]

[Rites of Preparation and the Prothesis]

The order of the liturgy from its beginning:[28] First, the priest advances and makes a prostration toward the sanctuary of the Lord, then to his partners

25. The *Offering of Incense* or *rafʿ al-bakhūr* is the title of the morning and evening daily services. Mostly identical in their structure, the morning and evening incense services are descendants of morning and evening assemblies in fourth- and fifth-century town churches (as opposed to monasteries). It remains the custom to begin the eucharistic service on any given day with the *Morning Raising of Incense*. The entire history of daily prayer traditions in the Early Church, as well as a helpful overview of the Coptic daily prayer cycle can be consulted in Robert F. Taft, *The Liturgy of the Hours*, 31–56, 249–259. For more information on the Coptic *Raising of Incense*, see Hans Quecke, *Untersuchungen*, 2–13.

26. This is in reference to paragraph-length prayers found in the order of every hour of prayer immediately after the Gospel passage. Such pieces are often common with those in the Byzantine tradition. In the latter tradition, as well as in some Coptic manuscripts, they are termed *troparia*. See O. H. E. Burmester, "The Canonical Hours of the Coptic Church," 84–89; Quecke, *Untersuchungen*, 22–29.

27. Ibn Kabar is describing what he believes to be the proper relationship between the prayers of the hours and the eucharistic liturgy. He explains, on feasts—i.e., non-fasting days—the eucharist is to be preceded only by the *Raising of Incense* service. On fasting days, in which the liturgy is customarily delayed to the afternoon, the prayer of the ninth hour is prayed instead, or perhaps in addition to the *Morning Raising of Incense*. An additional discipline is observed by monks, who delayed the liturgy until evening during the Great Fast, and thus prayed the hours of evening and compline (11th and 12th hours) before the liturgy. See Burmester, "The Canonical Hours," 78–100.

28. After the initial introduction summarizing the eucharistic liturgy and providing various canonical observances, Ibn Kabar now begins to explain the unfolding of the Coptic eucharistic service from the very beginning, paying close attention now to ritual details. For this initial section on the preparation and vesting, see O. H. E. Burmester, "Vesting Prayers," 305–306.

[in the priesthood], then to the people. Then he puts on the garments of service, and these are the white tunic and white shawl (*al-ʿarḍī*). And he may wear the sleeves, whether silk or otherwise.[29] Some of the monk presbyters and those from Cairo wear a white wool cope (*burnus*) without a hood and sometimes of silk. But the priests in the Monastery of Saint Macarius do not wear a cope at the time of the service of the liturgy but wear it during the prayers according to their canon.[30]

Then the priest ascends to the sanctuary accompanied by the deacon and they cover the altar together.[31] Every hegumen (*ighūmanus*)[32] or presbyter (*qiss*) who serves the liturgy covers the altar for himself, and it is not for another presbyter to cover it for him, for this has been granted exclusively to the hierarchs.[33] Then the lamb is brought,[34] and the priest washes his hands with water, and he wipes the oblation after inspecting it and choosing what is appropriate as we have said earlier.[35] Whatever is left of

29. U12, fol. 183v adds, "And the epitrachelion, and a *burnus* without a hood, whether silk or wool."

30. For a treatment of the vestments of presbyters as well as deacons and minor orders, see Ramez Mikhail, "Towards a History of Liturgical Vestments I," 55–70.

31. Here, the covering of the altar refers to the set of consecrated cloths accompanying the eucharistic vessels. As part of these preparatory rites, the priest places these cloths in a specific arrangement on the altar. For a useful inventory of these vessels and cloths, see Burmester, *The Egyptian or Coptic Church*, 23–29.

32. Strictly speaking the title of a monastic leader, the term hegumen (*īghūmanus*) has come to be used for protopresbyters, i.e., presbyters who were distinguished by this honorary rank due to age, length of service, or leadership position. For variants of the Arabization of *hēgoumenos*, see Graf, *Verzeichnis*, 18.

33. This means that the celebrant of any given eucharistic service has the responsibility to prepare the altar. On the other hand, a celebrating bishop has the privilege that one of the presbyters may prepare the altar for him in advance.

34. That is, the oblation breads from which one loaf will be chosen to be consecrated as the body of Christ.

35. U12, fol. 183v–184r: "Then the lamb is brought, and he chooses what is appropriate as we have said earlier, and it is placed on the side of the altar. Whatever is left of it from what he has carried is to be removed outside the sanctuary. And he goes to wash his hands while he recites from the psalms secretly. From Psalm 18, 'Purify me, O Lord, from my hidden [sins] and spare your servant from strangers. If they do not have dominion over me,' [Ps 18 (19):13–14].' From Psalm 50, 'Sprinkle upon me your hyssop' [Ps 50 (51):7]. Then he turns to the priests and says, 'Bless.' Then he wipes each oblation bread on its front and back and signs, while saying upon it and upon the blood, 'In the name of the Father and the Son and the Holy Spirit.' And he wraps the oblation bread with a cloth and likewise the deacon wraps the blood. They go with them around the altar once and

it [the oblation breads] from what was offered, is to be removed outside the sanctuary. He wipes every oblation bread on its front and back[36] and says first, "bless." Then he says in the signing of the oblation, "Glory and honor to the Trinity," to its end.[37] He gives the oblation to the deacon who is serving with him, who receives it from his hand on one of the consecrated cloths of the altar and wraps it with its edges. And he proceeds with it around the altar and hands it back to the priest on his left, who places it in the paten on a cloth in the likeness of the wrapping of the body of our Lord Jesus Christ in the graveclothes and bands.

Then the deacon pours the wine in the chalice after inhaling its smell and being careful of any change that may have befallen it, a pouring in the likeness of the cross without haste.[38] He mixes the wine calmly with fresh water the amount of a tenth of it,[39] and begins with unifying the

---

he remembers the name of him who has offered the oblation. Then the priest says, 'Blessed is God the Father, the Pantocrator. Blessed is his only begotten Son. Blessed is the Holy Spirit the Paraclete. Glory and honor, honor and glory.'"

36. A marginal note in P203, fol. 205r in the lower left corner adds: "The correct [way] at the wiping of the oblation with water is to say, 'In the name of the Father and the Son and the Holy Spirit,' and to make the sign of the cross on it and on the wine. The presbyter circles with the body and the deacon with the blood. After their circuit, the priest says, 'Blessed is God the Father, the Pantocrator,' to its end, and he says, 'Glory and honor to the Holy Trinity.' While saying this, he signs three times and he places [it] in the paten. It is done also thus in the presence of the patriarch."

37. The full text of this formula reads, "Glory and honor, honor and glory, to the all-holy Trinity, the Father and the Son and the Holy Spirit, now and forever and unto the ages of ages, amen." See Brightman, *Liturgies Eastern and Western*, 145.

38. Unlike current practice, where only the celebrant may pour the wine into the chalice, medieval sources in Egypt and the East generally are unanimous that the preparation of the chalice was originally a diaconal function. This was a natural extension of the fact that the gifts were prepared in a nearby location by deacons, rather than on the altar directly by the priest, as became the case by the tenth century at the latest. The older practice of assigning the mixing of the chalice to the deacon likely began to diminish by the seventeenth or eighteenth century, as seen in a number of Euchologion manuscripts. See Ramez Mikhail, *The Presentation of the Lamb*, 280–284.

39. The earliest reference to the ratio of water to wine appears in a letter of Bishop Abraham of Hermonthis (6th c.) to one of his priests. Abraham is specific that the wine is to be mixed, "Three parts wine to one part water." See Samuel Moawad, "Liturgische Hinweise," 129. Canon 99 of the Arabic *Canons of Pseudo-Basil* is even more conservative, instructing, "And those who administer the chalice let them know not to allow much water beyond the limit. And let them not exceed a third, and if there were many vessels in the place of preparation, then a tenth suffices." See *Paris, BnF Ar. 251* (AD 1353), fol.

Trinity, and Psalm 116 [117] or another psalm.[40] Then the priest reads the *Prayer of Thanksgiving*[41] and the *Prayer of the Table* [i.e., the *Prothesis Prayer*].[42] Then he covers the altar with the *prospherin* [veil] in the likeness of covering the tomb in which the body of the Lord of glory was placed with a stone and sealing it.[43]

[At this time], *May you be saved, amen* is chanted.[44] Then the priest and the deacon turn to one another, and each makes a prostration to the other. Then they descend and sit before the sanctuary with their heads bowed for the reading of the absolution [prayer]. So, if there is another presbyter serving with them, he reads the absolution over them, but if there is none,

---

188v. Cf. Wilhelm Riedel, *Die Kirchenrechtsquellen*, 277. The current instructions allow for a third, a quarter, or even less. See ʿAbd al-Masīḥ Ṣalīb, ⲡⲓϪⲱⲙ ⲛ̀ⲧⲉ ⲡⲓⲉⲩⲭⲟⲗⲟⲅⲓⲟⲛ, 220.

40. U12, fol. 184r adds, "And the people say *Glory to the Father.*" The expression, "unifying the Trinity," is an interesting way of referring to the diaconal response, "One is the Holy Father, one is the Holy Son, one is the Holy Spirit, amen." That is, the acclamation in which the three persons of the Trinity are affirmed as one.

41. For the text of the *Prayer of Thanksgiving*, ubiquitous throughout the Coptic liturgical tradition, see Brightman, *Liturgies Eastern and Western*, 147–148. The prayer usually serves as an introductory prayer recited by the celebrant in most liturgical services and sacraments, including here near the end of the preparation of the gifts and the beginning of the liturgy proper.

42. U12, fol. 184r adds, "And when he arrives at saying, 'Bless them, sanctify them, purify them,' he bows toward his brothers the priests and returns with his face to sign the bread and the wine together three times." The title *Prayer of the Table* appears also in the manuscripts *London, British Library Or. 8778* (AD 1726), fol. 11r, *Paris, BnF Copt. 28* (13th/14th c.), fol. 10r, and *Yale Beinecke Copt. MS. 20* (19th c.). For the text of the prayer, see Brightman, *Liturgies Eastern and Western*, 148. The *Prothesis Prayer* is a consecratory prayer for the bread and wine that calls upon Christ to shine his face upon the gifts in order to transform them. As such, it is very similar to the genre of epiclesis prayers that come later during the anaphora and that use similar language for the same purpose. This particular prayer in the Coptic prothesis rite appears with a number of variants in the Byzantine, Coptic, Nubian, and Ethiopian liturgies. For more information, see Mikhail, *Presentation of the Lamb*, 315–324.

43. A large white veil that covers the eucharistic gifts on the altar from the conclusion of the prothesis until its removal prior to the anaphora. See Burmester, *The Egyptian or Coptic Church*, 23. The term comes from the Greek προσφέρειν (*prospherein*), see Graf, who lists the Arabic form *abrūsfār* for the veil in question. Graf, *Verzeichnis*, 2.

44. Given in the text as ⲥⲱⲑⲏⲥ ⲁⲙⲉⲛ (*sōthēs amen*), this Greek acclamation is more accurately rendered σωθείης ἀμήν καὶ τῷ πνεύματί σου (*sōtheiēs amēn kai tō pneumati sou*), representing a formulaic greeting and wishing of good health attested in monastic literature. See Andrea Nicolotti, "Forme di partecipazione," 259, and Youhanna Nessim Youssef and Ugo Zanetti, *La consécration du Myron*, 37n150.

then the celebrant priest reads it while standing for himself and for the kneeling deacon. But if the patriarch is present, it is he who reads the absolution over them, and likewise the bishop in his diocese [reads the absolution prayer].[45]

[The Liturgy of the Word]

Then the priest takes the censer and raises it [i.e., he places incense in the censer], and those from among the priests who are serving also raise it with him. And he censes the altar and goes around it, praying the *Prayer of the Apostle* (*ṣalāt al-abusṭulus*).[46] If the patriarch is present, he would be the first to raise [incense].[47] And if he consecrates,[48] we are to praise him [the bishop], and he puts on the vestment of service mentioned in his chapter, and the people are to chant to him what is appropriate.[49]

45. For the text of the *Absolution of the Servants*, see Brightman, *Liturgies Eastern and Western*, 149.

46. U12, fol. 184v has instead, "And he recites the *Prayer of Incense* and it is 'O God the eternal, without beginning and without end.' So, when he has said [the prayer of] *The Peace of the Church*, he goes around the altar and it is the perfection of the prayer up to the completion of three circuits. When the deacon has finished responding the three responses (*ibrūsāt*), the people chant and say *You are the censer*. And he descends and offers incense at the door of the sanctuary." For the complete text of the *Prayer of the Pauline Incense* (*awshiyyat bakhūr al-būlus*), "O God the great the eternal," see Brightman, *Liturgies Eastern and Western*, 150.

47. U12, fol. 184v adds, "And they say what is appropriate in praising him. And he is followed by the bishops and presbyters according to their ranks, then the archdeacon and whoever follows him. And he goes around with incense in the choir and outside it and [to] the people and the women. Then he returns to the sanctuary as was mentioned previously in the chapter on prayer, raising the confession of the people to God (may he be exalted) upon his altar. So, he goes around it once and says the prayer (*al-kalām*) that was mentioned previously in the chapter on prayer. Then he descends to offer incense at the door of the sanctuary, to the patriarch in particular if he is present, or to the bishop in his diocese, then to the presbyters. And he signals with the censer to the people giving them incense then he hangs the censer by the door of the sanctuary and makes a prostration to the sanctuary and to his colleagues and the people."

48. That is, if the bishop presided as celebrant of the liturgy.

49. Likely a reference to the chant *All the Wise Men of Israel*, known by its Coptic incipit ⲚⲒⲤⲀⲂⲈⲨ ⲦⲎⲢⲞⲨ (*nisabeu tērou*), traditionally accompanying the vesting of bishops and the patriarch, which took place at the end of the prothesis rite in medieval sources. For the text of this chant, see the appendix in this volume. For the special rites of the episcopal liturgy in medieval sources, see O. H. E. Burmester, "The Liturgy Coram

After the raising of incense, the chanters sing *This Golden Censer* or *You Are the Censer*, while the presbyter goes around with the incense to the priests, the deacons, the choir, and all the people, the men then the women.[50] Then the lections are read,[51] and they are a passage from the Pauline [epistles], a passage from the Catholic [epistles] and a passage from the Acts. They are to be interpreted in Arabic so that the people may understand their meanings, according to the saying of the apostle, "If there be no interpreter in the church, let the reader be silent."[52] There are prayers (*awāshī*) during these lections, which the priest reads before the veil, one during the Pauline and another during the Catholic [epistle], and they are *O Lord of Knowledge* and *O Lord Our God*.[53] The time of this last prayer is after the second raising of incense.[54]

Before the reading of the Acts, the people chant one of the images from the Sunday *Theotokia*, and it is *Therefore Truly*.[55] After the Acts, the Trisa-

---

Patriarcha," 79–84, and more recently, Ramez Mikhail, "The Liturgy *Coram Patriarcha* Revisited," 279–312.

50. The incensing at the beginning of the Liturgy of the Word is accompanied by the chanting of any of the hymns of the censer. These are short chants, usually linking the censer to the Virgin Mary. For the text of these chants, see Ṣalīb, ⲡⲓϫⲱⲙ ⲛ̀ⲧⲉ ⲡⲓⲉⲩⲭⲟⲗⲟⲅⲓⲟⲛ, 238–239, and the appendix. Although Ibn Kabar makes no distinction between these two alternative chants, current practice assigns the former to all non-fasting days and the latter to the weekdays of the Great Lent.

51. Literally papers (*qarāṭīs*) from Greek χάρτης (*chartēs*). See Wehr, *A Dictionary of Modern Written Arabic*, 757; Henry George Liddell and Robert Scott, *A Greek-English Lexicon*, 1716.

52. 1 Corinthians 14:28.

53. For the text of the *Mystery of the Pauline Incense*, "O Lord of knowledge," see Brightman, *Liturgies Eastern and Western*, 153. For the text of the *Mystery of the Catholic Reading*, "O Lord our God," see ibid., 154.

54. U12, fol. 184v adds, "And at the conclusion of the reading of the Catholic [epistle], the priest ascends to the altar and raises incense once again and says the *Prayer of Incense*, and it is *O God who accepted the offering of Abel*. And he goes around the altar three times, descends, and does what he did previously for the Pauline. He gives incense to the people of the Pauline [?] in particular while the people chant and say verses from the Sunday Theotokia, and it is *Therefore Truly*. And the Acts is read and translated to Arabic. Then the priest returns to the altar and says what was mentioned previously. Then he descends, gives incense to the sanctuary and to his colleagues especially, and he hangs the censer and makes a prostration."

55. The Coptic *Theotokia* (a singular feminine substantive in Coptic usage, the plural of which I render here as Theotokias) are poetic stanzas in praise of the Virgin Mary and the incarnation. There are seven Theotokias in the Coptic repertoire, one for each day of

gion (*ajyūs*) is said.[56] If it is a great feast or a day of celebration, the chanters sing some stanzas (*qiṭaʿ*) in Coptic before it,[57] that is *The Time of Praise* to its end, or a portion of it.[58]

Then the priest prays the *Prayer of the Gospel* and the psalm is chanted in a simple tune and is responded thereto with its melodies.[59] The current custom of the people of Cairo, Old Cairo, and northern Egypt is for one of the younger deacons to chant it while the choir responds to him.[60] In southern Egypt, one or two of the older deacons sings it with the melody

---

the week. Here, the chanters are to select a stanza from the Theotokias to chant during the second incense circuit, containing a symbol (or image) of the Virgin. This particular stanza is identified here as ⲧⲟⲧⲉ ⲁⲗⲏⲑⲱⲥ (*tote alēthōs*) or *Therefore Truly*, which is the first stanza of the sixth part of the Sunday Theotokia. For the full text, see Ṣalīb, ⲡⲓϫⲱⲙ ⲛ̀ⲧⲉ ⲡⲓⲉⲩⲭⲟⲗⲟⲅⲓⲟⲛ, 254–255, and the appendix. For the Coptic midnight praise, see Quecke, *Untersuchungen*, 52–66, and O'Leary, *The Daily Office*, 53–69.

56. The text's *ajyūs* is an Arabic rendering of the Greek ἅγιος (*hagios*), the first word of the famous Trisagion chant, "Holy God, Holy mighty, Holy immortal." For the full text, see Burmester, "The Greek Kīrugmata," 371, and the appendix. Inspired by the "Holy, Holy, Holy, Lord Sabaoth," of Isaiah 6:3, a debate exists among Chalcedonian and non-Chalcedonian communities over its interpretation, whether it is directed to the Trinity or to Christ, respectively. The more ancient text is that used by churches of the Byzantine tradition, i.e., without the Christological additions, "who was born . . . who was crucified . . . who arose." Specifically, sources from both traditions attribute the addition "Who was crucified for us," to the Patriarch of Antioch John Fuller in the mid-fifth century. See Robert F. Taft, "Trisagion," *ODB* 3:2121; Emile Maher Ishaq, "Trisagion," *CE* 7:2278a–2279a; Sebastià Janeras, "Le Trisagion," 495–562.

57. U12, fol. 184v reads, "And if it were a great feast or a day of celebration, the chanters sing a hymn (*wahman*) appropriate for that feast. And on the Sundays of Kiyahk and the [Great] Fast, a hymn is chanted to the lady and its beginning is *Hail Mary*, and after it is said *The Time of Praise.*"

58. The chant is indicated here by the initial words ⲫⲛⲁⲩ ⲙ̀ⲡⲓⲥⲙⲟⲩ ⲡⲉ ⲫⲁⲓ (*phnau ʿmpismou pe phai*), or *This is the time of praise*. For the text, see the appendix. Ugo Zanetti compared the text of this hymn in the Ethiopian liturgy to a number of medieval Coptic sources. In addition to the instance of this chant in chapter 17 of the *Lamp of Darkness*, Ibn Kabar also mentions it in the marriage ritual in chapter 20. See Zanetti, "Voici le temps de la benediction," 25–50.

59. The Coptic liturgical manuscript tradition preserves two alternative prayers before the Gospel, generally titled *A Prayer before/for the Gospel* (*awshiyyat al-injīl*). See the Coptic and Arabic texts of these prayers in Ṣalīb, ⲡⲓϫⲱⲙ ⲛ̀ⲧⲉ ⲡⲓⲉⲩⲭⲟⲗⲟⲅⲓⲟⲛ, 90–95. For the English translation of the first of these prayers, see Brightman, *Liturgies Eastern and Western*, 219.

60. U12, fol. 184v–185r adds, "The first word for the presbyter, the second for him who comes after him, and the third and fourth for all the deacons."

and the congregation responds to them with the first word with the [same] melody. In Alexandria, the archdeacon chants it, and in the Monastery of Saint Macarius (*Abū Maqār*) the chanters intone it in the middle of the church and no one responds to them.

Then the deacon takes the Gospel book and circles the altar with it, following the priest. During the psalm, the priest offers incense, so that when the deacon descends with it [the Gospel] from the sanctuary, the presbyter censes it and kisses it, and the priests kiss it while it is opened according to their ranks. The Gospel is read, either on the *ambo*—which is more appropriate for its honor—or on the lectern.[61] So, if a deacon reads it, he faces east, and the priest is to stand with the censer on the side of the sanctuary [door]. But if a patriarch reads it and likewise the bishop in his diocese, he faces west, standing at the entrance of the sanctuary, while the priest stands with the incense below the sanctuary. Afterward, it is translated into Arabic,[62] except in the Monastery of Saint Macarius (*Abū Maqār*), where they do not translate it to Arabic at all until this day.

Then the priest takes it [i.e., the Gospel book] from the deacon and he venerates it together with the priests who are present. After this, one of the deacons carries it and takes it out to the people to venerate it.[63] Then the presbyter and the deacon bow their heads at the entrance of the sanctu-

61. The *ambo* is a raised pulpit with steps from which, traditionally, the Gospel was proclaimed. Most frequently, it is located in the nave on the northern side. See Alfred J. Butler, *The Ancient Coptic Churches*, 2:64–65; Laskarina Bouras and Robert Taft, "Ambo," *ODB* 1:75–76.

62. U12, fol. 185r adds, "And when the translation has begun, the assisting priest takes the censer from the celebrant priest and says *O Long-suffering*." The latter is a reference to the litanies after the Gospel, which ask on behalf of the sick, the travelers, the harvest, safety for man and cattle, the king, the imprisoned, the reposed, the oblations, those who are in tribulation, and the catechumens. For the complete text of this prayer, titled *The Mystery of the Gospel* (*Sirr al-injīl*), see Brightman, *Liturgies Eastern and Western*, 157–158.

63. U12, fol. 185r adds, "And someone else exits with the Arabic copy to the women to venerate it. And the people chant what is appropriate for this day." The latter is a reference to the *Gospel Response* (*maradd al-injīl*), a genre of variable chants appointed to follow the reading of the Gospel in vespers, matins, and the liturgy. These verses are usually included in chant manuscripts such as *Coptic Patriarchate Lit. 73* and *Lit. 74* (AD 1444) and many others. See the edition of a group of these manuscripts in Samuel, *Tartīb al-bīʿah*.

ary so that the *Prayer of the Veil* is read over them[64] and *May You Be Saved, Amen* is chanted.[65] And they ascend to the sanctuary, so that the presbyter stands toward the east and the deacon toward the west. For the presbyter speaks to God, concerning whom the prophet said, "I hear his voice from the east,"[66] while the deacon receives [cues] from him and proclaims to the people. Likewise, the glorious Gospel witnessed that Mary Magdalene, when she came to the Lord's tomb the morning of the life-giving Resurrection, saw two angels sitting in white clothes, one at the head and one at the feet, where the body of the Lord Jesus was laid.[67] However, in other communities (*ṭawā'if*) such as the Syrians, the Latins (*al-firanj*), and others, the deacon serving the liturgy among them stands beside the presbyter at his right.[68]

64. The *Prayer of the Veil* (*Ṣalāt al-ḥijāb*) is one of a group of prayers before the eucharistic prayer proper and constitutes a priest's expression of his unworthiness to perform his priestly duty. It is particularly ubiquitous in anaphoras of the West-Syrian tradition and their very presence in the Coptic and Ethiopian anaphoras represents one of the many instances of Syro-Antiochene influence on these two traditions. On this prayer in the Byzantine anaphoras and other related eastern prayers, see Taft, *The Great Entrance*, 119–148; Taft and Parenti, *Il grande ingresso*, 257–302. For the text of one such prayer in the liturgy of Cyril, see Brightman, *Liturgies Eastern and Western*, 158.

65. For the chanted acclamation, *May you be saved*, the text in P203, fol. 206v has ⲥⲱⲑⲓⲥⲟⲙⲉⲛ (*sothisomen*), a corruption of the presumed Greek original σωθείης ἀμήν (*sōtheiēs amēn*). See note 44. This acclamation is no longer utilized at this point after the gospel, though it is attested elsewhere in medieval sources, such as the manuscript *BAV Vatican Copt. 27* (15th c.), fol. 7r, containing diaconal responses and chants.

66. This may be a reference to a biblical verse, which according to the Septuagint and Coptic texts reads, "Sing unto God, who has ascended to the heaven of heaven toward the east. Behold he gives his voice with a voice of power" (Ps 67 (68):32–33).

67. John 20:12.

68. U12, fol. 185r adds, "But not among the Copts. And the remainder of those who are serving from the presbyters and deacons ascend to the sanctuary and they stand in line with calmness, serenity, and silence." Medieval Coptic witnesses are unanimous on the custom of the deacon to stand across from the priest. Prior to Ibn Kabar, *The Histories of the Monasteries and Churches* of Abū al-Makārim mentions the practice as an answer to the inquiring Fatimid ruler Al-Āmir bi-Aḥkām-illāh (AD 1101–1130). See B. T. A. Evetts, *The Churches & Monasteries of Egypt*, 182. The thirteenth-century *Guide to the Beginners* explains the practice as the priest and deacon representing the angels at the head and feet of the entombed Christ, where the deacon faces the people to address them with his biddings, and even claims the practice to have been traditional since the time of Mark the Apostle. See *BAV Vatican Ar. 117* (AD 1323), fol. 197v. Cf. Georg Graf, "Liturgische Anweisungen," 121. The likely contemporaneous *Order of the Priesthood* repeats some of the

[The Liturgy of the Eucharist]

Now the priest begins to consecrate the mysteries and says the three prayers: The Peace, the Fathers, and the Assembly.[69] Then the deacon says, "In the wisdom of God, respond."[70] The people recite the Creed entirely, except in the two liturgies of Covenant Thursday and Joyous Saturday[71] according to what will be mentioned in its place.[72] Then water is presented to the presbyter to wash his hands, and from this point forward he is not to touch anything except the consecrated altar vessels, and he is also to incense his hands.[73] So, if there were another presbyter, he is to stand at his right hand with the censer to incense at the times mentioned after this section.[74]

When the *Prayer of the Kiss* (*asbasmus*) has been read, the deacon says, "Kiss one another with a holy kiss."[75] So the men greet the men and the

---

same explanations, adding also that the deacon faces the western doors of the church in order to alert the community to attacks. See Julius Assfalg, *Die Ordnung des Priestertums*, 36 (Arabic), 111–112 (German).

69. For the text of these prayers, see Brightman, *Liturgies Eastern and Western*, 160–161.

70. The Coptic incipit reads: "In the wisdom of God let us attend" (ϩⲉⲛ ⲥⲟⲫⲓⲁ ⲑ̅ⲩ̅ ⲡⲣⲟⲥⲭⲱⲙⲉⲛ, *en sophia theou proschōmen*). The corrected Greek should be Ἐν σοφίᾳ θεοῦ πρόσχωμεν." See Burmester, "The Greek Kīrugmata," 374.

71. Covenant (or Great) Thursday is the day before Christ's crucifixion, on which he shared the Last Supper with the disciples, washed their feet, and was arrested by the Jewish leadership, according to the Gospel accounts. Joyous Saturday is the day following Great Friday, during which Christ was buried in the tomb.

72. U12, fol. 185r–v adds, "And the priest takes the censer and offers incense upon the altar and the body and in front of the altar. Then he turns to the place of the priests to give them incense, then to the people. And he turns again to give incense upon the altar and below it and to the celebrant priest, and he gives it [the censer] to him." On the Creed as an element in the pre-anaphoral rites, see Taft, *The Great Entrance*, 396–405; Taft and Parenti, *Il grande ingresso*, 636–645. On the liturgical use of the Nicene Creed in Egypt, see William F. Macomber, "The Nicene Creed in a Liturgical Fragment," 98–103.

73. U12, fol. 185v adds in red, "Patriarch Benjamin did not approve the incensing of the hand at this time, but rather when the people say, 'According to your mercy, O Lord, and not according to our sins.'"

74. U12, fol. 185v mentions also the archdeacon as permitted to offer incense at the appointed times. On the washing of hands in the pre-anaphoral rites and its early Christian origins, see Taft, *The Great Entrance*, 163–177; Taft and Parenti, *Il grande ingresso*, 319–341.

75. The word *asbasmus* is from the Greek ἀσπασμός (*aspasmos*), for which see Graf, *Verzeichnis*, 7. Here, the term refers to the priestly prayer before the kiss, often referred to by the Arabic *The Prayer of the Kiss* (*ṣalāt al-qublah*) or *The Prayer of Reconciliation* (*ṣalāt al-ṣulḥ*). Many such prayers appear in the manuscripts, while printed editions usually

women greet the women, and some of them kneel to one another. The chanters sing what is appropriate for this day,[76] but in all other days, they are to chant *O Christ Our God* or *Greet with a Kiss*.[77] In the days of feasts and the fifty [days] until the feast of the Nativity, *Rejoice and Be Glad* is to be said.[78] Between the Theophany and the Nativity, [the hymn] *He Was Looking with the Eyes* can be said.[79] But this [type of hymn] is not said in times of brevity, but it can be abbreviated beginning from *Through the Prayers* in the days of the commemorations of martyrs, saints, and angels so that each of their names is mentioned in its day.[80] It can also be shortened to *We Worship*, at which time they all prostrate to God in the days of prostration, or they kneel on the days in which there is no prostrating, but the more common [practice] is to kneel.[81]

---

assign two alternatives for each liturgy (Basil, Gregory, and Cyril). For one such prayer in the liturgy of Cyril, see Brightman, *Liturgies Eastern and Western*, 162–163. The diaconal command for the kiss appears in P203, fol. 206v as ⲁⲥⲡⲁⲍⲉⲥⲑⲉ ⲁⲗⲗⲏⲗⲟⲩⲥ ⲙ̀ⲫⲓⲗⲓⲙⲁⲧⲓ ⲁ̀ⲅⲓⲟⲩ. The corrected Greek text would be ἀσπάσασθε ἀλλήλους ἐν φιλήματι ἁγίῳ (*aspasasthe allēlous en philēmati agiō*). See Burmester, "The Greek Kīrugmata," 374.

76. U12, fol. 185v includes a different list of titles for various chants throughout the year, for Sundays, the feasts of martyrs, saints, angels, the Cross, the Virgin Mary, the apostles, and the feasts of the Lord or dominical feasts.

77. The text here references two alternative chants to accompany the exchange of the kiss, a genre known as *asbasmus adām*. The first chant referenced is *Christ our Savior* (ⲡⲓⲭⲣⲓⲥⲧⲟⲥ ⲡⲉⲛⲥⲱⲧⲏⲣ, *pichristos pensōtēr*). The second chant is *Kiss with a holy kiss* (ⲁⲣⲓⲁⲥⲡⲁⲍⲉⲥⲑⲉ, *ariaspazesthe*). For the texts of these hymns, see Ṣalīb, ⲡⲓϫⲱⲙ ⲛ̀ⲧⲉ ⲡⲓⲉⲩⲭⲟⲗⲟⲅⲓⲟⲛ, 305–308, and the appendix.

78. This chant *Rejoice and be glad* (ⲣⲁϣⲓ ⲟⲩⲟϩ ⲑⲉⲗⲏⲗ, *rashi ouoh thelēl*), is assigned to the eve of the Theophany. For the text, see Albair Jamāl Mīkhā'īl, *Al-Asās fī khidmat al-shammās*, 314, and the appendix.

79. The last chant in this series, though unknown in the current repertoire, is the fourth section of the Monday Theotokia. For the text, see Mīnā al-Baramūsī, *Kitāb al-ibṣalmūdiyyah*, 161–162, and the appendix.

80. Many such *asbasmus* chants conclude with a series of verses asking for the intercessions and prayers of the Virgin, the angels, and saints. Ibn Kabar here is indicating a custom in which, for the sake of time, chanters may chant only the intercessory verses appropriate for the day's commemoration. These verses are formulaic and modeled after the one for the Virgin Mary, "Through the intercessions of the Theotokos Saint Mary, O Lord grant us the forgiveness of our sins." See Ṣalīb, ⲡⲓϫⲱⲙ ⲛ̀ⲧⲉ ⲡⲓⲉⲩⲭⲟⲗⲟⲅⲓⲟⲛ, 307–308, for a number of such verses.

81. The common title *We worship* (ⲧⲉⲛⲟⲩⲱϣⲧ, *tenouōsht*) corresponds to the familiar formula, "We worship you, O Christ, with your good Father and the Holy Spirit, for you came and saved us." While Ibn Kabar here indicates it can be chanted *instead* of any of

Then he removes the veil in the likeness of removing the stone, which was rolled away from the door of the tomb and our Lord's casting off the grave clothes and bands from his pure and honorable body at the time of his Resurrection.[82] After the deacon says, "Those who are seated are to stand" and "Look to the east," he follows this by saying "Respond!"[83] So the people say Holy three times [i.e., the *Sanctus*]. But in the days of feasts, Sundays, the times of feasting [i.e., non-fasts] and celebration, they say *The Cherubim Worship You*.[84] But in the days of the Great Fast, [the month of] Kiyahk, and the Fast of the Disciples, they chant *Come to the Table*.[85] And in the liturgy of Gregory, after "Holy, Holy, Holy," they say *Hosanna in the Highest* to its end.[86]

---

the *asbasmus* chants, current practice has it chanted at all times after the exchange of the kiss. See Ṣalīb, ⲡⲓϫⲱⲙ ⲛ̀ⲧⲉ ⲡⲓⲉⲩⲭⲟⲗⲟⲅⲓⲟⲛ, 310. Regarding kneeling, various church fathers have expressed the notion that prostration is inappropriate at times of joy. The prohibition on kneeling on Sundays was given canonical force as Canon 20 of the Ecumenical Council of Nicaea. On the background and later reception of this canon in various Christian communities, see Gabriel Radle, "Embodied Eschatology, Part 1," 345–371; Radle, "Embodied Eschatology, Part 2," 433–461.

82. U12, fol. 185v adds, "And the priest says after this, 'The Lord with all,' and what follows it. In the beginning of this saying (*al-qawl*) he makes the sign of the cross three times on himself, the people, and the servants."

83. This is the meaning of the Arabic word *ajībū* used in P203, fol. 207r, while the text also provides the Coptic ⲡⲣⲟⲥⲭⲱⲙⲉⲛ (*proschōmen*), let us attend.

84. The title on fol. 207r translates to *The cherubim worship you* (ⲛⲓⲭⲉⲣⲟⲩⲃⲓⲙ ⲥⲉⲟⲩⲱϣⲧ ⲙ̀ⲙⲟⲕ, *nicheroubim seouōsht mmok*), which corresponds to the most commonly chanted hymn at this point today. For the text, see Ṣalīb, ⲡⲓϫⲱⲙ ⲛ̀ⲧⲉ ⲡⲓⲉⲩⲭⲟⲗⲟⲅⲓⲟⲛ, 322 and continued on 317, as well as the appendix. Much literature exists on the history of the Isaian *Sanctus* in Christian worship. For an English treatment, see Bryan D. Spinks, *The Sanctus*.

85. The Coptic title on fol. 207r translates to *Come to the table* (ⲇⲉⲩⲇⲉ ⲛ̀ⲧⲓⲇⲣⲁⲡⲉⲍⲁ, *deude ͤntidrapeza*), which corresponds to the Greek Δεῦτε εἰς τὴν τράπεζαν (*deute eis tēn trapezan*). See Burmester, "The Greek Kīrugmata," 376. This chant occurs as a year-round hymn preceding the *Sanctus* and part of a genre of chants for this point of the service called collectively *asbasmus wāṭus* in Coptic usage. For the text, see Ṣalīb, ⲡⲓϫⲱⲙ ⲛ̀ⲧⲉ ⲡⲓⲉⲩⲭⲟⲗⲟⲅⲓⲟⲛ, 318, and the appendix.

86. The title *Hosanna in the* [*highest*] (ⲱⲥⲁⲛⲛⲁ ⲛ̀ⲑⲏⲓⲥ, *ōsannaͤnthis*) on fol. 207r is a reference to the *benedictus* Ὡσαννὰ ἐν τοῖς ὑψίστοις (*ōsanna en tois hupsistois*), the full text of which reads, "Hosanna in the highest. Blessed is he who came and comes in the name of the Lord. Hosanna in the highest." A feature of the Antiochene version of the *Sanctus*, the presence of the Hosanna in the Coptic Liturgy of Saint Gregory is a testament to this anaphora's Antiochene influence. See the discussion in Hammerschmidt, *Die*

After this, the people are commanded to prostrate themselves. When they have raised their heads, the mentioned litanies are said, which are the peace, the Pope, the hierarchs, the priests, the deacons, the seven ranks of the Church, the salvation of the world, the city, the districts, villages, and every monastery, the fruits, the trees, the vineyards, and for the holy oblation and the sacrifice.[87] Then the celebrant points to the deacons to remember the names of the patriarchs and the fathers [i.e., the saints], so they begin first by remembering the Virgin, Saint John the Baptist, Stephen the head of the deacons, and the patriarch seated at that time on the throne of Mark. If the throne was vacant, he [the celebrant] is to mention the name of the reposed patriarch until someone else is enthroned, so the name of the reposed patriarch is added to the end of the names of the fathers [i.e., the previous patriarchs]. At the end, the name of Saint Severus the patriarch of Antioch is mentioned.[88]

koptische Gregoriosanaphora, 119–120. After this, U12, fol. 186r adds the following commentary on the rites of the anaphora: "And when the people say Holy, Holy, Holy, the priest signs himself, the servants, and the people three times. Then the assisting priest goes around the altar with the censer and returns to stand in his place until the celebrant priest says, 'And he will reward each one according to their deeds.' So, he gives to him the censer to cense his hands again and he places both hands on the paten and says, 'He established for us this great mystery.' When he says, 'He took bread on his hands,' he is to remove the veil from the paten and lift the oblation bread on his hands. When he says, 'And he gave thanks,' he is to turn toward the priests and sign upon the oblation three times at the mentioning of thanksgiving, blessing, and sanctification. When he says, 'He broke it,' he is to signal as though dividing it and he breaks the oblation from the middle then from the top with his thumb. Then the priest holds [the chalice] when he says, 'Likewise the cup after supper he mixed it with wine and water,' so he turns it and signals to the priests and signs it three times. And when he says, 'Every time you eat of this bread and drink of this cup,' he points with his hands toward the body and the blood and signals to the people to prostrate. So, when they have raised their heads, he motions toward the priests and signs over the body three times saying, 'And this bread you make into a holy body.' Likewise, he signs the chalice three times, saying, 'And this cup also,' and he bows down kneeling before them. And when he says, 'Our Lord, our God, and our Savior Jesus Christ,' he no longer makes the sign of the cross upon it, for the bread and the wine have become one holy body and precious blood united by the Holy Spirit and the whole world is sanctified by it."

87. For the text of the post-epiclesis litanies, see Ṣalīb, ⲡⲓϫⲱⲙ ⲛ̀ⲧⲉ ⲡⲓⲉⲩⲭⲟⲗⲟⲅⲓⲟⲛ, 343–352.

88. U12, fol. 186r adds, "And when the commemoration of the reposed (*al-tarḥīm*) is read, the assisting priest is to go around with the censer, then he is to hand it to someone to remove it and none shall remain of it." Ibn Kabar here is essentially paraphrasing the Greek diaconal response *Through the prayers and intercessions* (Εὐχαῖς καὶ πρεσβείαις,

In the liturgy of Gregory, there are litanies additional to those of the liturgy of Basil, and they are prayed before the litany on behalf of the world. These are four: for the ruler, the palaces and soldiers, the oblation, and those in captivity.[89] Then they are to say, "Worship God in fear."[90] And when they had raised their heads, they all say with one tongue, "Have mercy on us, O God the Pantocrator."[91] After this is the prayer for the fruits, the salvation of the world, and the commemoration of the reposed. This is the order in the liturgy of Gregory in particular.[92] After this is also said in it [i.e., the liturgy

euchais kai presbeiais), a commemoration of saints that transitions into a listing of all the reposed Coptic patriarchs and Severus of Antioch. For the corrected Greek text, see Burmester, "The Greek Kīrugmata," 380, and the appendix. See also the brief discussion in Budde, *Die ägyptische Basilios-anaphora*, 516–517.

89. For the text of the particular post-epiclesis litanies of the Liturgy of Saint Gregory, see Hammerschmidt, *Die koptische Gregoriosanaphora*, 46–49 and the discussion on 137–142 of the same work.

90. The Coptic on fol. 207v translates to "Bow to God in fear" (ⲕⲗⲓⲛⲁⲑⲉ ⲑ̅ⲩ̅, *klinathe theou*) corresponding to the Greek, Κλίνατε θεῷ μετὰ φόβου (*klinate theō meta phobou*). See Burmester, "The Greek Kīrugmata," 379.

91. The title on fol. 207v translates to *Have mercy on us* (ⲉⲗⲉⲏⲥⲟⲛ ⲓⲙⲁⲥ, *eleēson imas*) corresponding to the Greek, Ἐλέησον ἡμᾶς ὁ θεὸς ὁ πατὴρ ὁ παντοκράτωρ (*eleēson hēmas ho theos ho patēr ho pantokratōr*), "Have mercy on us, O God the Father the Pantocrator." See Burmester, "The Greek Kīrugmata," 378.

92. U12, fol. 186v adds, "Then he turns to the people and says the blessing. And he completes what he is to recite. So, when he says, 'The holy body,' he is to dip the tip of his finger in the blood and sign with it the body in its center, its back, and side. Then he gives the peace (*yusallim*) and breaks. In the liturgy of Gregory, when the priest says, 'He who blessed at that time blesses now,' it was said that no one of the high priests ought to bless with his hand, but he is to take the holy oblation that has become the body of Christ on his hand, raises his face upward, and makes the petition that was just mentioned. And when he says, 'He who sanctified at that time,' he is to place the tip of his finger in the precious blood. When he says, 'Now he blesses,' he signs with it upon the oblation on its front, back, and side. And when he says, 'He who broke at that time,' he breaks the oblation, so that when he says, 'He now breaks,' he completes the breaking of the oblation with his hands, and he gives thanks and continues the fraction. Then the servants begin to exit from the sanctuary to the choir one after the other until there remains only the presbyter and the deacon alone. He completes the *Prayer of the Fraction* (*ṣalāt al-qismah*) and the people say *Our Father*. And the priest says the absolution: If it were [the liturgy] of Gregory, he says the *Absolution to the Son*, but if it were [the liturgy] of Basil, he says the *Absolution to the Father*. Then he turns to the people and blesses them. And he returns and raises the *despotikon* with both hands and says, 'The holy [gifts].' The deacon says, 'With fear,' and the people say Lord have mercy three times [and] 'One is the holy Father, one is the holy Son, the holy Spirit, amen.' Then he signs with the *despotikon* in the pre-

of Gregory], "Worship the Lamb, the Word of God," *Absolve and forgive*,[93] and after it, *Just as it was*,[94] then the blessing on the body and the blood.

Then the holy body is fractioned, and the deacons descend from the sanctuary.[95] After this, the presbyter greets the people, and they respond to him and say *Our Father*. Then the liturgy is completed, and the confession is said, which is, "We believe, we believe, we believe and confess to the last breath that this is the life-giving body of the only begotten Son, our Lord, our God, and our Savior Jesus Christ. He took it from our lady, the Mother of God, Saint Mary, and made it one with his divinity without mingling, confusion, or change. He confessed the good confession before Pontius Pilate and gave it up for us by his will alone for salvation upon the holy wood of the cross on behalf of us all. I believe that his divinity did not depart from his humanity for one moment nor even a twinkling of an eye. He gave it up as salvation, remission of sins, and eternal life to those who partake of it. This is in truth, amen."[96]

---

cious blood and signs with it upon the body and places it back in the chalice. Then the priest gives the peace (*yusallim*) and completes the order of the fraction." On the *Fraction Prayer* mentioned here, see chapter 2, note 111.

93. The title on fol. 207v, ⲃⲱⲗ ⲉⲃⲟⲗ (*bōl ebol*) refers to the congregational chant unique to the liturgy of Saint Gregory, *Absolve and forgive.* For the text, see Ṣalīb, ⲡⲓϫⲱⲙ ⲛ̀ⲧⲉ ⲡⲓⲉⲩⲭⲟⲗⲟⲅⲓⲟⲛ, 524–525, Hammerschmidt, *Die koptische Gregoriosanaphora*, 60–61, and the appendix.

94. The incipit on fol. 207v reads, ⲱⲥⲡⲉⲣⲓⲛ (*ōsperin*) corresponding to the chant *Just as it was* ("Ὥσπερ ἦν, *hōsper ēn*). For the Greek text, see Burmester, "The Greek Kīrugmata," 381. For the English, see the appendix.

95. An analogous command for the deacons to descend appears also in the Melkite liturgy of Saint Mark, pronounced by the archdeacon. In the context of this Byzantinized Alexandrian liturgy, this command takes place immediately after the second epiclesis—a feature of anaphoras of the Alexandrian type—and before the *Our Father*, since the fraction in the Byzantine Rite takes place immediately before communion. The response in the manuscripts of Melkite Mark is, "Descend, O deacons. Pray together, O presbyters," which suggests ideas of concelebration by the presbyters at specific key points, such as the epiclesis. See Cuming, *The Liturgy of St Mark*, 48. A similar command for the deacon(s) to descend and for the presbyter(s) to ascend to the sanctuary appears also in the Sahidic diaconal parchment fragment *London, British Library Or. 3580A (11)* (= Crum 154) from the White Monastery. Judging from the limited surviving text of that fragment, the command seems to come in the context of an anaphora around the time of the epiclesis prayer and before the post-epiclesis litanies. See W. E. Crum, *Catalogue*, 41.

96. The text of the confession given by Ibn Kabar is identical to the received text except in the introductory affirmation, "we believe," given as a first-person plural (*nu'min*), on fol. 207v. The received text has a first-singular "I believe." See Brightman, *Liturgies*

[Communion]

Then the deacon descends and makes a prostration to the people. The priest turns to them and bows to them a small bow. Then he takes the oblation bread together with the priest who served with him.[97] And if there be another chalice, or two, or more upon the altar, he consecrates the second chalice. So, he takes the spoon, takes with it from the chalice of the liturgy, and pours three spoonsful into the chalice that has not been consecrated, saying, "Blessed" to its end,[98] while the people respond and say, *One is the Holy Father*,[99] and this is repeated three times from this to that.[100] Then, he places the *despotika* according to the number of additional chalices in the first chalice,[101] and he transfers them [the *despotika*] from the chalice and distributes them to the remaining chalices.

Eastern and Western, 185. U12, fol. 187r adds here, "Then the deacon says, 'Pray for the Christians,' and the priest says, 'This is he through whom.'"

97. In chapter 12 of this same work on the canons and regulations for priests, Ibn Kabar has this to say concerning the communion of multiple priests, "The celebrant priest (*al-kāhin al-muqaddis*) communes (*yataqarrab*) first. Then to those who have served with him from among the presbyters, he is to give to them the body. And they take the chalice and give to him (*yunāwilūnahu*). Then they give communion to each other [from the chalice]. Then the celebrant presbyter gives communion [i.e., the body] to the presbyters in the church who have not served, and he or those who served with him give them the chalice." It is unclear to me if receiving the chalice in this context implies using a communion spoon to do so or drinking directly from the chalice. See P203, fol. 174r. Cf. Villecourt, "Les observances," 201. Alternately, U12, fol. 187r reads, "And the assisting priest takes the chalice in his hand from the throne and gives it to the celebrant priest, so he drinks from it and gives it back to the assisting priest, who communes and puts it back in place." The latter's order seems to emphasize that each priest receives communion from the other's hands rather than taking it himself from the altar.

98. The incipit P203, fol. 208r is given as ⲉⲩⲗⲟⲅⲓⲑⲟⲥ (*eulogithos*) from the Greek εὐλογητός (*eulogētos*), "Blessed," and likely refers to the blessing formula from the precommunion rite, "Blessed be the Lord Jesus Christ the Son of God. The Holy Spirit is sanctification, amen."

99. See note 8.

100. That is, the process of transferring blood from the original chalice to the new one is done three times.

101. The *despotikon* (pl. *despotika*) rendered in Arabic *isbādīqūn* is the central portion of the eucharistic bread bearing a seal consisting of four small square crosses. Before communion, the *despotikon* is placed in the chalice. For the term and its attested Arabic variants, see Graf, *Verzeichnis*, 7. For more information on the eucharistic bread in the Coptic tradition, see Burmester, *The Egyptian or Coptic Church*, 81–82.

He gives communion to the deacon who served with him and to the remainder of the deacons.[102] At that time, Psalm 150 is chanted, for which there are two melodies: A melody for the fast, and a melody for all other days. [There is] a third abbreviated melody said during the month of Kiyahk and in whatever [season that] follows its order.[103] And the chanters sing whatever is suitable for that day from the Theotokia and hymns.[104]

After the conclusion of communion, the presbyter removes whatever of the body may have remained with him, whether a small or a large amount, and distributes it among those who served with him. The deacon elevates the chalice and the presbyter partakes of it with the *despotikon*; then he consumes the remainder of the blood. The majority of presbyters consume the chalice and give it empty to the deacon in order to wash it. However, to do so is not for them, but only for the deacon who has carried it.[105]

Then the presbyter washes his hands and the paten. He pours a small amount of it over the vessels, says the *Prayer of Dismissal* (*awshiyyat al-tasrīḥ*), and blesses the people. He signs their foreheads and the deacon prays likewise, dismisses the people, and distributes the blessed oblation bread.[106] It is not lawful to distribute it before this time. As for the water of the paten, the priest consumes it all by drinking it. But if someone comes and asks to drink it or a portion thereof, let him be given to drink if he has not yet placed anything else in his mouth, otherwise no. It is also unseemly for anyone who has served the mysteries to drink water before the lifting [of the mysteries], lest something from the body remain with the presbyter, [since]

102. U12, fol. 186r adds, "Then he gives communion to any presbyters who are present and have not served."

103. U12, fol. 187r reads, "And it has melodies according to their seasons: A melody for the weekdays, and for Sundays, and the feasts, a melody for the middle of the week (*wasaṭ al-jum'ah*), a melody for the forty days of the Holy Fast, and an abbreviated melody said in Kiyahk and whatever follows its order."

104. For the Coptic Theotokia, see note 55.

105. That is, the deacon who has distributed the blood at this liturgy.

106. That is, the bread baked for the Eucharist that day but not chosen for the consecration, known and referenced in the text as *al-ūlūjiyyah*, from the Greek εὐλογία (*eulogia*). See Graf, *Verzeichnis*, 17. For a discussion of the use of this term in a variety of ways including the blessed but unconsecrated bread, see Robert F. Taft, *The Communion, Thanksgiving, and Concluding Rites*, 708–711.

he should not consume it alone.[107] This may perhaps occur in the liturgies of our companions the Jacobite Copts, but not so among the others.[108]

It may also occur that someone, who was prevented by necessity or has come from a far place arrives to the church after the middle of the liturgy. Let there be read for him another Gospel at the end of the liturgy and let him be given communion, especially in the major feasts of the Lord. But if he is late [in arriving] until after communion has begun, the priest is not to give him communion, if he learns that he has not attended the liturgy nor has heard the passages that were read, nor has prepared himself properly to receive the mysteries.

A Chapter on the Order of Incense Offering

It was said that [incense] must be made of sandarac (*ṣandarūs*) because it is a pure tree.[109] Nothing remains of it [after being burned] in the fire, and it has not been defiled by being offered as incense to demons and idols or in sorcery. [Incense] can also be [made] of frankincense (*lubān*), because the Magi offered it to Christ the Lord when they came to worship him in Bethlehem and were informed that he is an incarnate God.[110] Some of the

107. On the practice—and later the prohibition—of eucharistic reservation, see note 18.

108. "*wa-rubbamā ya'riḍu hadhā fī qarābīn aṣḥābinā al-qibṭ al-ya'āqibah, wa-ammā man siwāhim fa-lā.*" The meaning of this sentence is not entirely clear. Ibn Kabar designates the Jacobite Copts as companions (*aṣḥābinā*), which could imply that he is not a member of this group. Alternatively, the author may be simply implying that only among the Jacobite Copts is this strict requirement observed, namely, that the elements must be entirely consumed and that those who have already drunk water may not assist in consuming the remainder of the Eucharist. The term Jacobite ultimately refers to the person of Jacob Baradaeus (Syr. Burd'ānā), a Syriac sixth-century bishop, generally understood to be responsible for strengthening the Miaphysite Church in the Syriac East through the ordination of clergy and the consecration of churches. Though strictly speaking the term Jacobite refers to Miaphysite Syriac Christians (i.e., the Syrian Orthodox Church), the term was also applied in the medieval period to all Miaphysite Christians, including Copts. For more on the term "Jacobite," see H. G. B. Teule, "Ya'ḳūbiyyūn," *EI*[2] 11:258–262.

109. Here begins an addendum to chapter 17 of the *Lamp of Darkness* explaining in greater detail the ritual of incense offering and, further below, the times during the service in which the priest is to make the sign of the cross. This section is given here from manuscript P203. While no exact parallel appears in manuscript U12, similar sections on incense and blessing with the sign of the cross are scattered in chapter 16 in the context of morning prayer and in chapter 17.

110. Matthew 2:11.

earlier fathers used to avoid offering [frankincense], since it used to be offered to idols, [but] Paul the apostle says that an idol is nothing and a sacrifice to an idol is nothing.[111] Incense is also offered using the Indian aloe tree (*al-ʿūd al-hindī*) and Javanese resin (*al-Jāwī*). It has been said that incense, by its very nature, casts out evil spirits and overturns the plots of sorcerers. The use of any other type of incense has been forbidden, [though] storax is also [allowed].

Incense is an offering, a holy sacrifice, and [a sign of] obedience to the God of glory. It is to be offered in a specified amount without excessiveness. The charcoal used in [burning incense] is to be from burned vine branches (*aṭrāf al-zarjūn*). During prayer, the priest is to offer incense after the *Prayer of Thanksgiving* (*al-shibihmāt*) and he censes the altar, going around it three times, followed by the door of the sanctuary (*bāb al-ḥijāb*). Then [he gives incense to] the patriarch, asking [God] for his protection, security, and for the suppression of his enemies, then kisses the cross from [the patriarch's] hand. After that, he gives incense to the bishops who are present, asking [God] for them in a manner nearly equal to entreating for the patriarch. But if [the bishops] are in their dioceses, they are to be honored more than that. After them, the hegumens (*al-qamāmiṣah*), presbyters (*al-qusūs*), the archons, and the deacons [receive incense in turn]. The deacons are to kiss the priest's hand while he blesses them.

It is also preferable that one confesses his sin and asks for forgiveness secretly in a few words at the time of censing [the laity]. For some have said that the [act of] bringing out the incense to the people is of the same significance as the sacrifice of the Old Testament that used to be brought outside. The person who was able [to do so] would confess their sin in the [animal's] ear, and it would be offered on that person's behalf.[112]

111. 1 Corinthians 8:4.

112. Here, ibn Kabar seems to have in mind the Old Testament practice of burning animals as a sin offering outside the camp, mentioned in Hebrews 13:11 and in Leviticus 4:12. The curious Coptic medieval practice of offering one's confession secretly during the priest's incense round was the subject of fierce controversy in the twelfth-century polemics between Metropolitan Mīkhāʾīl of Damietta and the controversial reformer and blind Coptic priest Marqus ibn al-Qunbar. The practice was defended by the former as the official and accepted Coptic custom on the grounds that neither oral tradition nor Scripture explicitly enjoin private confession to a priest. This position was spelled out by the metropolitan as a rebuttal of Marqus's claims that private confession of sins to a priest is a necessary aspect of a successful spiritual life, among other reforms Marqus sought to promote among his disciples. The arguments in defense of confession over the censer are

When the priest has finished incensing the entire people—men and women—as well as the places of the sanctuaries,[113] and the icons of martyrs and saints, then he returns to the sanctuary and ascends to the holy of holies[114] as though he were raising the sins of the congregation up to God. After this, he censes the sanctuary and the patriarch only. But if the patriarch is not present, the priest gives incense to the bishop or to whoever is present from among the priests. Then, he motions with the censer toward the people. The offering of incense the first time should be in a copious amount, the second time should be in a moderate amount, and the final time in a small amount, so that it completely runs out when it should and none of it remains beyond what is needed. But if some of the incense remains [in the censer], it is to be removed, and the ashes are to be kept and thrown in the sea.[115]

The second incense round of the priest is just like the first. He is to go around to the people during the prayer when they say *Grant O Lord.*[116] When the Gospel is venerated, if there is no other priest with the celebrant

---

to be found in the treatise by Mīkhā'īl of Damietta titled *The Customs That Distinguish the Copts*, for which text see O. H. E. Burmester, "The Sayings of Michael," 101–128, and the German discussion and translation in Georg Graf, *Ein Reformversuch*, 38–71, 147–180. It appears that Ibn Kabar in the early fourteenth century still echoes the same arguments of Mīkhā'īl of Damietta in defense of confessing during the incense round. For the main primary source on the controversy between Mīkhā'īl and Marqus, see Evetts, *The Churches & Monasteries of Egypt*, 12–22, 65–66 (Arabic), 20–43, 152–153 (English). See also the summary of this episode in medieval Coptic Church history in Mark N. Swanson, "Marqus ibn al-Qunbar," *CMR* 4:98–108; Swanson, "Michael of Damietta," *CMR* 4:109–114.

113. That is, the other altars available within the same church. Since at least the tenth century, it became increasingly common to outfit Coptic churches with three altars, likely due to governmental restrictions on the building of separate churches as well as a desire to honor more saints by dedicating altars to them. See Peter Grossmann, *Christliche Architektur*, 96n323; Emmanuel Fritsch, "The Preparation of the Gifts," 99n3.

114. That is, he ascends to stand at the altar.

115. Louis Villecourt points out that in this case, "sea" is likely in reference to the water basin available in church, used for certain liturgical functions such as the blessing of the water on Theophany. See Villecourt, "Les observances liturgiques," 260n1. For more on the basin as an architectural feature of Coptic churches, see chapter 3, note 4. Villecourt's suggestion fails to explain how a basin of still water intended for ceremonial ablutions can be the receptacle for disposing of burnt ashes. Alternatively, the text's *baḥr* (sea) could also refer to any body of water, such as a pond, lake, or even the Nile River.

116. The prayer *Grant O Lord* is part of the evening prayer, signaling that Ibn Kabar in this section is discussing the offering of incense generally, and not just during the eucharistic service.

priest to hold the censer [and stand] at [the entrance of] the sanctuary, the most senior deacon serving with the celebrant is to carry it. The times of placing incense in the censer during the liturgy are the following: First, during the *Prayer of the Apostle* (*ṣalāt al-abusṭulus*), and then when [the incense] has decreased or diminished during the reading of the lections (*al-fuṣūl*), and during the *Prayer of the Gospel* (*awshiyyat al-injīl*), and then when [the priest] ascends to the altar and says *The Sacrifices*.[117] The celebrant priest is to take [the censer] during the Creed and give incense to the body [of Christ] from underneath the *prospherin* veil,[118] as well as above the altar and in front of it. He then returns the censer to the person who carries it, since after washing his hands, he is not to touch it. Instead, the bearer of the censer is to give it to him to fumigate his hands only when he says, "And he recompenses each one according to their deeds."[119] When the deacon says, "Holy and honorable gift,"[120] the bearer of the censer—if he is a presbyter—goes around to the corners of the sanctuary and censes the body and the blood and toward the east. Then the censing presbyter gives the censer to the one who will dispose of the incense remaining in it.

A Chapter on the Times to Bless the Oblations in the Sign of the Cross

When the oblation bread is wiped with water before its offering, the priest signs it with the cross, three times on each oblation bread, and says, "Glory

117. The title on P203, fol. 209r is the Coptic *nithusia*, indicating the *Prayer of the Oblations*, said during the morning service, but also in this context during the Liturgy of the Word. For the text, see Ṣalīb, ⲡⲓϫⲱⲙ ⲛ̀ⲧⲉ ⲡⲓⲉⲩⲭⲟⲗⲟⲅⲓⲟⲛ, 68–72.

118. At this point before the eucharistic prayer and during the Creed, the eucharistic gifts are covered with the large veil called the *prospherin*. For the priest to give incense to the bread and wine, he must lift the veil, holding it to slightly expose the gifts and give them incense.

119. The quotation from the anaphora is given in P203, fol. 209v as an insertion written diagonally and upside down on the top margin. This sentence appears in the anaphora of Basil immediately before the words of institution. See Ṣalīb, ⲡⲓϫⲱⲙ ⲛ̀ⲧⲉ ⲡⲓⲉⲩⲭⲟⲗⲟⲅⲓⲟⲛ, 329.

120. Given in the text in P203, fol. 209v as *agion dimion dōron*, this corresponds to the deacon's response to the prayer of the oblations in the Liturgy of Basil. The response in full reads, "Pray for these holy, honorable gifts, our sacrifices, and for those who offer them," which Burmester corrects to: Προσεύξασθε ὑπὲρ τῶν ἁγίων τιμίων δώρων τούτων καὶ θυσιῶν ἡμῶν καὶ προσφερόντων. See Burmester, "The Greek Kīrugmata," 370.

and honor to the Holy Trinity, the Father, the Son, and the Holy Spirit."[121] During the *Prayer of the Mystery*, when he says, "Bless them, sanctify them, purify them, and change them," he makes the sign of the cross upon the oblation and the chalice a total of three times.[122] When he says,[123] "He took bread after supper and he gave thanks," the priest takes the oblation on his hands, removes the cloth from the paten, and makes the sign of the cross upon the oblation three times.[124] In the same manner, he [blesses] the chalice, when he places his finger on it and says, "Likewise, he mixed the chalice after supper with wine and water," and he makes the sign of the cross on it three times. Also, when he cries out saying, "This bread becomes the holy body," he signs upon it three times, and [when he says,] "This

121. Descriptions of the number of crosses to be performed during the liturgy became a sort of common liturgical genre in medieval sources. Witnessed in the Coptic tradition at least since the thirteenth-century *The Guide to the Beginners*, the Euchologion *Oxford, Bodleian Hunt. 572* (13th/14th c.), and Ibn Kabar's the *Lamp of Darkness* (14th c.), it was often copied in later Euchologia as an additional section. For this section in *The Guide to the Beginners*, see *BAV Vatican Ar. 117* (AD 1323), fol. 198r–199r; Graf, "Liturgische Anweisungen," 122–123. The same genre is attested much earlier in the Syriac tradition, where it appears in the *Synodicon* of Jacob of Edessa (AD 633–708), and the commentary on the liturgy by Moses bar Kepha (AD 813–903). See Arthur Vööbus, *The Synodicon I*, 367:225–226 (Syriac); Vööbus, *The Synodicon I*, 368:209–210 (English); R. H. Connolly and H. W. Codrington, *Two Commentaries on the Jacobite Liturgy*, 70 (English), 64 (Syriac).

The syntax makes it difficult to locate this action in the unfolding of the ritual preparation of the gifts (prothesis rite). It is possible that Ibn Kabar implies that more than one oblation bread can be offered and consecrated, a practice not entirely unique in late antiquity, and certainly clear below in the context of breaking the body before communion. Alternatively, a similar blessing of all the oblation breads presented, and from which the priest is to select only one, survives even in current practice. For this blessing formula, see Brightman, *Liturgies Eastern and Western*, 146.

122. The *Prayer of the Mystery* (*ṣalāt al-sirr*) is an alternative title to the *Prothesis Prayer*, in which the priest prays for the consecration and changing of the bread and wine to the body and blood. For more information, see note 42. For the text of the prayer, see ibid., 148.

123. This section, where Ibn Kabar describes the blessings performed over the bread and wine during the anaphora, appears in the other manuscript U12, fol. 186r in a more logical place during the description of the liturgy in chapter 17. See note 86.

124. Ibn Kabar here conflates the words pronounced over the bread with those prayed over the cup. According to the account of the institution common to all three Coptic anaphoras, the priest says over the bread, "He took bread . . . looked up to heaven, when he had given thanks," and over the chalice, "Likewise, also the cup after supper, he mingled it of wine and water. When he had given thanks . . ." See Brightman, *Liturgies Eastern and Western*, 176–177.

chalice becomes the honored blood of the new covenant," he signs upon it three times.[125] When he has said, "of our Lord, God, and Savior Jesus Christ," he no longer makes the cross over it, for the bread and the wine have become the holy body and the precious blood, united by the Holy Spirit, and the whole world receives sanctification from them.

Another Chapter Appended to the Previous One

When the priest desires to break the holy body, he dips the tip of his finger in the precious blood without making the sign of the cross in it, and he blesses the body, each oblation bread on its front, back, and side, signifying their union in having been consecrated.[126] When he has raised the *despotikon* and has cried out saying, "The holy [gifts] for the saints," he makes the sign of the cross with the *despotikon* on the precious blood three times, on the body three times, and then places it in the chalice.

In the Liturgy of Saint Gregory, when the priest says, "He who blessed at that time blesses now," it is said that none of the high priests ought to bless with his hand, but he is to take the holy oblation that has become the body of Christ in his hands, raise his face upward, and make the petition that was just mentioned. And when he says, "He who sanctified at that time sanctifies now," he is to place the tip of his finger in the precious blood and make the sign of the cross with it on the holy oblations, on their front and back. And when he says, "He who broke at that time, breaks now," he gives the peace (*yusallim*) and begins the breaking [of the bread] (*al-qismah*) to its end and completes the liturgy.

The chapter on the liturgy has been completed.

125. That is, during the consecration of the gifts after the *Epiclesis Prayer*, so called because in it the Holy Spirit is *called upon* (from the Greek ἐπικαλέω, *epikaleō*) to descend on the bread and wine and complete their consecration into the body and blood of Christ. Each anaphora possesses its own version of the *Epiclesis Prayer*. For the one in the Liturgy of Basil, see Ṣalīb, ⲡⲓϫⲱⲙ ⲛ̀ⲧⲉ ⲡⲓⲉⲩⲭⲟⲗⲟⲅⲓⲟⲛ, 339–342; Budde, *Die ägyptische Basilios-Anaphora*, 161–163. Scholarship on the epiclesis prayers is rich. Two helpful references are Robert F. Taft, "From Logos to Spirit," 489–502, and John H. McKenna, *The Eucharistic Epiclesis*.

126. With some variation, this section appears in U12, fol. 186v. See note 92.

CHAPTER

2

The Precious Jewel on the Ecclesiastical Sciences

(AL-JAWHARAH AL-NAFĪSAH FĪ ʿULŪM AL-KANĪSAH)

By Yūḥannā ibn Abī Zakariyyā ibn Sabbāʿ

CHAPTER 58
REGARDING AGREEMENT ON THE THREE LITURGIES

The liturgies, which the opinion of the early fathers has agreed upon, are three.[1] The first liturgy is from Basil the Great, Bishop of Caesarea. He dedicated it to the hypostasis (*uqnūm*) of the Father Almighty. The second liturgy is the liturgy of Saint Gregory, and it is specific to the hypostasis of the eternal only begotten Son, and the narrative of his incarnation, his crucifixion, his sufferings, his burial, his Resurrection from the dead, his ascension to the heavens, and his coming to judge the living and the dead, which is the second coming after the first. The third is the liturgy of Saint Cyril, and it is also specific to the hypostasis of the Father, following what Basil has established in devoting the liturgy to the hypostasis of the Father.[2]

1. Here and throughout, the Arabic *quddās* (pl. *quddāsāt*) is rendered as "liturgy." The root of the Arabic means "to consecrate" or "to hallow" (Arabic *qaddasa*), while the term liturgy derives from the Greek *leitourgia*, an act of public worship, especially the Eucharist. Though the two terms are not etymologically equivalent, they are essentially synonymous in usage, which justifies this translation choice.

2. Ibn Sabbāʿ is referring here to the explicit addressee of each of these eucharistic prayers or liturgies. While most prayers of the Eucharist explicitly address the Father, the liturgy attributed to Gregory of Nazianzus addresses the hypostasis of the Son. For more information on the three anaphoras of the Coptic liturgical tradition with references to scholarly publications, see chapter 1, notes 21, 22, and 24.

[The liturgies] have been limited to these three, which were agreed upon over other liturgies preserved in the Church, said to be twelve in number.[3]

CHAPTER 59
ON THE ABBREVIATION OF THE PRAYERS OF THE LAITY AND THE LENGTHENING OF THE PRAYERS OF MONKS

As for the prayer of the laity, it must be abbreviated on account of their occupation with worldly livelihood. They ought to arrive to church early in the morning with prostration, kneeling, and a mind free of thoughts. Likewise, also in the evening as explained.

As for the prayers of the third, the sixth, and the ninth hours,[4] they ought to pray therein without delay while they are engaged in their occupations or traveling by land or sea, in any condition they may be in. They should pray [standing] if the body is free to stand. Otherwise, one ought to persevere in prayer in whatever condition the body may be in.

The definition of prayer is to elevate the mind to God (may he be exalted) (*Allāhi tʿālā*) and to be engaged in picturing one standing before the throne of greatness. Thus, if someone is in church, he ought first to fasten the girdle (*zunnār*), second to straighten his feet, third to lift his hands, and fourth to elevate the mind to God (may he be exalted) and to request of him remission and forgiveness, uttering the words of prayer properly.

But if one is not in church, he must be diligent in prayer, whether standing or lying down or while eating or traveling or in any other activity. One

3. The liturgical tradition of southern Egypt in particular seems to have known a large number of eucharistic prayers. The tenth-century *Great Euchologion*, a book of prayers for a priest or bishop produced in the White Monastery near Suhāj, witnesses to at least nine eucharistic prayers in addition to the three standard ones in use today in the Coptic Orthodox Church. Some of these prayers are incomplete and/or of an unknown attribution. For the Sahidic Coptic text with French translation, see Emmanuel Lanne, *Le grand euchologe du Monastère Blanc*. On the regional liturgical tradition of southern Egypt in particular, see Diliana Atanassova, "The Primary Sources of Southern Egyptian Liturgy," 47–96.

4. The reference here is to the daily prayers of the Coptic tradition. For a comprehensive treatment of the subject in East and West with references throughout to the so-called little hours of third, sixth, and ninth, see Robert F. Taft, *The Liturgy of the Hours*, esp. 249–259 on the Coptic office. For more specialized treatments of the Coptic liturgy of the hours, see O. H. E. Burmester, "The Canonical Hours of the Coptic Church," 78–100; Burmester, *The Horologion of the Egyptian Church*; Hans Quecke, *Untersuchungen*, 13–52.

must not miss his prayer in its appointed time. But if he misses the time, he is to perform it at a different time and not to neglect it. For prayer is a proper duty and a necessary obligation.[5]

But regarding the lengthening of the prayer of the monks, they have renounced the things of the world, they have freed themselves for worship, and they have taken rest from occupation with the worldly livelihood that used to occupy their minds. Thus, since they have become free to seek after eternity after they have ceased from seeking after the world and its means of subsistence and have put on themselves the likeness of the heavenly angels, they have become obliged to acquire what befits the likeness of the heavenly angels. That is, [they ought to] persevere in praising and hallowing the Creator (may he be exalted) at all times. Nor was this order restricted to particular times, but they ought to continue praising and hallowing while breathing in and breathing out. Nothing is to separate them from praying except sleep for bodily rest. For they have become angels on earth and heavenly men.

CHAPTER 60
ON THE PRIEST'S EXAMINING OF HIS BODY AND HIS SOUL BEFORE THE SERVICE

As for the priest, when he has intended to prepare himself for the service of the liturgy, he ought first to consider the condition of his body with

5. The text reads: *ḥaqqan wājiban wa-farḍan lāziman*. The fact that Ibn Sabbāʿ here employs the Islamic language of *farḍ* (obligation, religious duty) to encourage prayer is significant as an example of speaking about Christian religious practice using the terminology of religious obligations in Islam. As such, *al-Jawharah* shows how such Islamic terminology had become integrated into Coptic religious language by the fourteenth century. Although we should not read too much into Ibn Sabbāʿ's expression as indicative of a sophisticated knowledge of Islamic law, it is interesting that he seems to consider *farḍ* and *wājib* essentially synonymous. This perspective was shared with the Shāfiʿī school of Sunnī Islamic interpretation, in contrast to the Ḥanafī position, which distinguished between actions considered obligatory and those considered a duty. For more on this, see T. W. Jyunboll, "Farḍ," *EI*², 2:790. For the legal distinction according to the Ḥanafī school between *farḍ* and *wājib*, see A. Kevin Reinhart, "Like the Difference between Heaven and Earth," 205–234. For the use of the term *farḍ* to stress the necessity of making the pilgrimage to Jerusalem in Ottoman Egypt among the Copts, see Febe Armanios, *Coptic Christianity in Ottoman Egypt*, 99. For the broader topic of incorporating Islamic terminology in Coptic religious discourse, see Tamer el-Leithy, "Coptic Culture and Conversion" 434–444. I am grateful to Liran Yadgar and Febe Armanios for providing me with references to this topic.

respect to the weakness that forbids him from service.[6] Second, he is to consider examining the elimination of bodily necessity.[7] Third is his consideration of his soul, that it be free of rancor toward anyone, or else no intercession would be acceptable from him. Thus, if he were resentful of someone and knew this about himself, he ought not to approach the service at all. Otherwise, he would depart [from the service], and rather than having received grace and mercy, he would find perdition and vengeance, on account of the saying of the Holy Scripture, "If you are offering your oblation at the altar, and remember that your brother has something against you, leave your oblation on the altar and go first and be reconciled to your brother, and then come and offer your oblation."[8]

He is also to take heed in what he recites with respect to pronouncing the priestly words, lest he pause or commit an error and thus lose his people and cause them to resort to responding to him.[9] Thus, this would be an offense against the priest of God, the Exalted One, and the priest would be the cause of it through negligence on his part.

Then when the priest begins to offer the liturgy, the archdeacon—head of the deacons—grants permission to one of the chanters to sing alleluia with an appropriate melody for this time and season. If it is a fast, a sad [melody], and if it is one of the feasts of the Lord,[10] it should be with a

6. This is most likely a reference to nocturnal emissions. The issue of approaching the altar or communion following a nocturnal emission was treated by Dionysius of Alexandria in his canonical epistle to Basilides, albeit without pronouncing any rigid ruling on the matter. For the Greek text, see Charles Lett Feltoe, *Διονυσίου λείψανα*, 91–105. An English translation is available in Alexander Roberts and James Donaldson, *The Ante-Nicene Fathers*, 6:96.

7. This is perhaps a reference to using the toilet. That is, the priest should take care of such bodily necessities before beginning the service rather than interrupting the service later to do so.

8. Matthew 5:23–24.

9. That is, in case the priest happens to forget the words of the prayer he is to recite—or otherwise loses his place when reading from a book—the congregation would have to interfere to assist him with the words.

10. Lordly feasts are days in the liturgical year commemorating events in the life of Christ. According to Ibn Sabbā''s own listing of these feasts in *The Precious Jewel*, these are the annunciation of the birth of Christ, the nativity or birth of Christ, the theophany or the baptism of Christ, Palm Sunday, the Resurrection, Thomas or New Sunday commemorating the appearance of Christ to the Apostle Thomas along with the disciples, the ascension of Christ to heaven, and Pentecost. See *Pretiosa margarita*, 308–357 (Arabic), 553–581 (Latin).

joyous melody. Thus, the minds of all attending the church may be occupied with listening to it and taking pleasure in it, in order to keep them from the gossiping of the devil, which is exchanged by the nations outside the Church of God (may he be exalted).

During the chanting, the subdeacons advance, they who are appointed for the door of the sanctuary (*iskinā*),[11] who prevent the one who is not a priest and has no share among the clergy from entering it. The subdeacon advances and takes the head covering of the deacon, who is appointed for service in this liturgy, and hands him the vestment of the diaconate.[12] When the deacon has been vested in the vestment special to his rank, he then proceeds to the priest, takes his head covering, and hands him the vestment specific to the rank of the priesthood.

CHAPTER 61

CONCERNING THE VESTMENT AND THAT IT IS OF SEVEN PIECES AND ITS EXPLANATION

As for the vestment of the priesthood, it is of seven pieces as are the number of the ranks of the Church. That is, first, the tunic (*tūniyah*). The interpretation of the tunic is "of the sanctuary." Second, the turban (*ṭaylasān*), in the likeness of Aaron the priest, for God commanded him to put on the turban in the tabernacle of witness (*qubbat al-zamān*).[13] Then the third piece, and that is the girdle, with which the priest fastens his waist. Then [fourth and

11. From the Coptic ϯⲥⲕⲏⲛⲏ (*tiskēnē*) itself a loan word from the Greek σκηνή (*skēnē*). See Graf, *Verzeichnis*, 9.

12. In this section, head covering (Arabic *ʿimāmah*) likely refers to the turban or head covering men wore as street clothes and not to a type of liturgical headgear. The vestment of deacons consists of a white tunic, *tūniyah*, and a long thin band, most often referred to as *baṭrashīl*, wrapped under the right arm and going over the left shoulder to flow freely on the front and back of the wearer. For more information on deacon's vestments, see Karel C. Innemée, *Ecclesiastical Dress*, 29.

13. Although in all likelihood priests in Egypt, as elsewhere in the East, celebrated bareheaded, they soon came to adopt a variety of head coverings in the Islamic period. The *ṭaylasān* in its modern shape is a crown-shaped stiff hat usually with a band of cloth extending from the bottom and draped over the back of the wearer. On this and other vestments of presbyters, see Ramez Mikhail, "Towards a History of Liturgical Vestments I," 55–70. The Arabic *qubbat al-zamān* is a literal rendering of the Syriac expression *mashkan zabnā* found in the Syriac Peshitta, which translates to the tabernacle of time or assembly. The equivalent expression in the Septuagint is the σκηνή τοῦ μαρτυρίου (*skēnē tou martyriou*) or tabernacle of witness, for example in Numbers 17:7.

fifth are] the two sleeves, which free the hands of the priest to carry the holy mysteries. After this is the sixth piece, which is the stole (*baṭrashīl*), which the priest hangs on his neck. The explanation of the stole in Greek is a thousand stones.[14] Then, the seventh piece is the robe (*burnus*). If he is the high priest, the robe is to be [worn] with a hood (*qaṣlah*) on his head, but if he is someone other than a high priest, the robe is to be without a hood.[15]

The wearing of the vestment for the priest is to be before the ascent to the sanctuary. If he is a high priest, his wearing of the vestment is to be after the offering of the oblation, that is, before the absolution, in order for the high priests to be distinguished in this way from the priests with respect to their position of leadership.

CHAPTER 62
ON THE CLEANSING OF THE FEET OF THE PRIEST BEFORE HIS ASCENT TO THE SANCTUARY

Then the celebrant priest—whether a hierarch or a subordinate—ought only to wash his feet before putting on the vestment and ascending to the holy sanctuary.[16] For he is pure on account of baptism, and on account of the saying of the Lord in the holy Gospel, "He who has bathed does not need except to wash his feet only, for he is entirely clean."[17] Thus, no one ought to ascend to the holy of holies unless he is wholly clean, first by baptism, and second by washing his feet.

And the reason for this is that God (may he be exalted) commanded Moses the prophet in the Torah, at the end of the second book, the book of Exodus, to build the tabernacle (*qubbat al-zamān*) and its furnishings. He was to set up a bronze basin among the furnishings of the tabernacle between the veil of the sanctuary and the second veil, which is the holy of

14. Here, Ibn Sabbā‘ has misjudged the etymology of *epitrachelion* as coming from χίλιαι πέτραι (thousand rocks) rather than the more likely ἐπί and τράχηλος (on the neck).

15. Here and throughout, high priest is a direct translation of the term *ra's kahanah* (head of the priests) and similar derivatives, i.e., a bishop, metropolitan, or the patriarch. On the distinctive hood of the episcopal robe or *burnus*, see Julius Assfalg, "Arabisch qaṣla," 133–139.

16. That is, the priest whose service that day is to pronounce the prayer of consecration or *Epiclesis* and a number of other central roles throughout the eucharistic service, culminating in him administering the consecrated body of Christ. For any given eucharistic liturgy, only one priest is to assume such a role as celebrant. Cf. Youhanna Nessim Youssef and Ugo Zanetti, *La consécration du Myron*, 32.

17. John 13:10.

holies. In the basin would be water, so that Moses, Aaron, and all the priests might wash their feet before entering the holy of the holies. For just as the church is analogous (*naẓīr*) to the tabernacle of assembly, and in it is the lampstand, the vessel of manna, the ark of the covenant, and cherubs of gold overshadowing the altar, likewise there must be in the church a bronze basin, in which there would be water for the washing of the feet of everyone who ascends to the sanctuary of God, to become completely purified, as the Savior has said, "He who has bathed does not need except to wash his feet only."[18]

Furthermore, after washing his feet—as we have said—and putting on the priestly vestment, he is to come forward and prostrate once before the sanctuary of God (may he be exalted) if it is a day other than a Sunday. But if it is a Sunday or a feast of the Lord, there shall be no prostration but a submission and a bowing three times.[19] After this, he is to prostrate toward the people of God, for whom he has become an overseer and an intercessor, so that his soul may not be magnified over them, and likewise the deacon [is to prostrate to the people] after him.

Moreover, when the priest ascends to the sanctuary, he ascends with his right foot before the left, for he has become of the people of the right.[20] Then he is to cross his arms [before his chest], kiss the altar, and say, "One thing have I asked the Lord, this will I seek after; that I may dwell in the house of the Lord all the days of my life, to see the joy of the Lord, and to observe his holy temple."[21]

CHAPTER 63

ON HIS RECEPTION OF THE COVERING OF THE ALTAR, ITS COVERING, AND THE CARRYING OF THE OBLATION

Then the priest places before him the covering of the altar,[22] and raises his hands and says the first prayer of the covering [of the altar], without [in fact] covering it, with his mind collected and his hands raised to the

18. Ibid.

19. On regulations and prohibitions on kneeling at certain times, see chapter 1, note 81.

20. Cf. Matthew 25:33, where at the final judgment the sheep are placed on the right side of God, whereas the goats are placed on his left. The association between the right side and holiness is prevalent throughout Coptic ritual. Another example is that the curtain of the sanctuary is to be opened from the left to right and never vice versa.

21. Psalm 27 (28):4.

22. See chapter 1, note 31.

end of the first prayer.[23] After it is finished, he covers the altar with an attentive mind. When he is finished covering the altar and has placed the vessels, with everything in its place, he says the second prayer.[24]

Afterward he goes to the small sanctuary of offering and takes from it the lamb.[25] He examines it, lest it be cracked, for a crack is a defect, and it is written that it must be an unblemished lamb.[26] That is because this oblation is the lamb of one year of age in the Old Testament, in which there is no blemish. For whenever the oblation is cracked it is a defect, for it is supposed to be a male without blemish. Also, whenever the oblation is cracked from the force of the fire itself, and its crack is from itself, it shall be an offense to the celebrant priest, for whom there would be no opportunity to break the bread, according to the saying of the Gospel concerning the companions of Christ on the road to Emmaus, "We knew him at the breaking of the bread."[27] Also, broken bread on the carnal table would be a sign of disrespect toward the priests, but even more so on the spiritual table.

23. The prayer referenced here is the so-called *Prayer of Preparation of the Altar*, among other titles in the manuscript tradition. For the text of the prayer, "O Lord who knows the hearts," see F. E. Brightman, *Liturgies Eastern and Western*, 144.

24. For the *Prayer After the Preparation*, "You, O Lord, have taught us," see ibid., 145.

25. In a eucharistic context, the lamb refers to the oblation bread that will become the body of Christ during the liturgy. The exact meaning and location of this so-called sanctuary of offering is unclear. It seems to echo the more ancient and universal practice of keeping the eucharistic offerings in a dedicated space from which it would be brought to the altar by deacons before the eucharistic prayer or anaphora. In Egypt, Syria, and Ethiopia, this designated space was a room within the church adjacent to the sanctuary and termed *pastophorion*. See Marcel Metzger, *Les constitutions apostoliques*, 3:210–211. In Constantinople's cathedral of Hagia Sophia, the location was an external round structure called *skeuophylakion* in the sources. On the latter as well as the Byzantine rite of the Great Entrance to transfer the eucharistic gifts, see Robert F. Taft, *The Great Entrance*, 185–191; Robert F. Taft and Stefano Parenti, *Il grande ingresso*, 353–359; Taft, "*Quaestiones disputatae*," 1–35, and the earlier study, Thomas F. Mathews, *The Early Churches of Constantinople*, 158–162. In Egypt particularly, the practice of placing the gifts in a dedicated space away from the altar until the anaphora likely began to decline ca. the seventh century and was certainly completely extinct by the tenth century, as seen in the *Letter of Macarius of Manūf*. See Louis Villecourt, "La lettre de Macaire," 34–35. Elsewhere, I term the arrangement described by Ibn Sabbā' here as the *intermediate ordo* of the Coptic prothesis rite, in which the priest personally retrieves the gifts from the adjacent sanctuary and brings them to the altar before the beginning of the service. See Ramez Mikhail, *The Presentation of the Lamb*, 117–119.

26. Exodus 12:5.

27. Luke 24:35.

Thus, according to the law, bread that is cracked, that is, broken, ought not to be offered. For whenever all the oblation breads are cracked, and the wine [has become] vinegar, that is, corrupted, they are not to be offered. For he has said that the wine is to be precious in smell, free of souring. Thus, if the priest has transgressed and put on the vestment without inspecting the integrity of the oblation bread and the quality of the wine in a pleasing and acceptable manner, he is to remain in his vestment fasting until the next day as a rule (*qānūn*) upon him for his negligence regarding these things.

So, when he has found what he needs of oblation bread, wine, incense, charcoal, and all the equipment of the liturgy, when he has found them all in good order, he takes the bread offering, and anoints it just as the Lord—to him be the glory—was anointed with water before his presentation to Simeon the priest. Then he turns it around in his hands, as Simeon the priest went around the sanctuary with Christ. Then the priest receives it, places it in the paten, which is the manger, and wraps it with the cloths as the Virgin did at the birth. For the paten is first in the likeness of the manger, and last in the likeness of the tomb.[28]

CHAPTER 64
CONCERNING THE EXPLANATION OF THE SERVICE OF THE DEACON

At that time, the deacon says by permission from the priest, while all the people are listening, *īsbātīr ajyiūs īsiyūs ajyiūs abnūmā ajyiūn amīn*,

28. The theme of seeing the altar and the sanctuary as variably representing the birth and suffering of Christ is fairly common in this period. The thirteenth-century treatise *The Guide to the Beginners and the Disciplining of the Laity* likens the sanctuary to the tomb of Christ and the altar cloths to the burial shrouds. See the oldest manuscript of this text, copied in AD 1323, *BAV Vatican Ar. 117*, fol. 197v. Cf. Georg Graf, "Liturgische Anweisungen," 121. Also, the thirteenth-century anonymous *Order of the Priesthood* adds to this passion symbolism the idea that the altar cloths symbolize also the swaddling clothes in which Christ was wrapped in the manger. Cf. Julius Assfalg, *Die Ordnung des Priestertums*, 15 (Arabic), 84 (German). The Syriac author Moses bar Kepha sees the altar solely as the tomb citing the authority of John Chrysostom. R. H. Connolly and H. W. Codrington, *Two Commentaries on the Jacobite Liturgy*, 34–35. Both the Byzantine prothesis table and the altar have been interpreted as referring to the tomb. See Germanus of Constantinople (8th c.) in Paul Meyendorff, *St Germanus of Constantinople on the Divine Liturgy*, 60–61; Nicholas Cabasilas (14th c.) in J. M. Hussey and P. A. McNulty, *A Commentary on the Divine Liturgy*, 41.

whose translation is, "One is the holy Father, one is the holy Son, one is the Holy Spirit the holy,"[29] as he pours the wine in the chalice.[30] And after the wine a little water, so that it becomes mixed, as the Virgin Mary used to drink it during her pregnancy.[31]

After this, the deacon says, "Praise the Lord, all nations. Bless him, all peoples. For his mercy is abundant upon us, and the truth of the Lord endures forever, alleluia."[32] The intention behind appointing this psalm apart from all other psalms is that it mentions the abundance of mercy that the priest began to request for the people and that it mentions the truth of the Lord and its endurance forever. For the Lord—to him be the glory—said in his holy Gospel from the mouth of John the Evangelist, "My body is food in truth, and my blood is drink in truth."[33] For that which is now placed in the paten is the truth, as the Gospel has said, and it is the truth that endures forever.

Furthermore, the deacon stands facing the presbyter, contrary to all the other confessions.[34] For among all the confessions the deacon stands to the right of the presbyter during the liturgy, except among the Copts, and that is for a specific reason among them. For all were originally of the same arrangement. However, when the heretics bore the Satanic hatred and would raid and attack the churches of those who believe in the one nature

29. Brightman, *Liturgies Eastern and Western*, 146. The author gives the response above in a transliteration of the Greek followed by an Arabic translation. The text of this response, corrected orthographically, reads, Εἷς Πατὴρ ἅγιος, εἷς Υἱὸς ἅγιος, ἓν Πνεῦμα ἅγιον ἀμήν. For the full text in Greek, see O. H. E. Burmester, "The Greek Kīrugmata," 370. For the English text, see the appendix.

30. On the deacon's role in pouring the wine into the chalice, see chapter 1, note 38.

31. The tradition that the Virgin Mary drank wine and water during her pregnancy makes a number of appearances in the Copto-Arabic literary tradition and goes back at least to *Kitāb al-īḍāḥ* or the *Book of Elucidation* falsely attributed to the tenth-century Bishop Sāwīrus of Ashmunein. The idea seems to be that Christ's own flesh and blood, which he took of the Virgin Mary, were formed by the mixture of bread, wine, and water, which she drank, an idea that attempts to explain how sacramentally bread, wine, and water can change into Christ's own body and blood. For the relevant passage in the *Book of Elucidation*, see Marqus Jirjis, *Al-durr al-thamīn*, 97–100. For an English translation, see Stephen J. Davis, *Coptic Christology in Practice*, 297–298, as well as Davis's discussion of this passage on pages 194–197.

32. Psalm 116 (117):1–2.

33. John 6:55.

34. By this is meant that the deacon is to stand across the altar opposite the priest, i.e., facing west. See chapter 1, note 68.

and one will,[35] slay their priests as they stood at the altar consecrating the oblations, and take their oblation and trample it with the feet, the Copts arranged for the deacon to stand facing the presbyter to watch for anyone of the transgressors who might come from behind him intending harm. Thus, he would carry the oblation bread and the chalice and place it in the cavity beneath the altar to the east. This custom has lasted until now.

Then the deacon admonishes the people and says, *abi-brāsaw shi-ṣṭātīdā*, the interpretation of which is, "Stand up for prayer."[36] As for his saying, "stand," it means to rise up from sitting, and his saying "for prayer," it means, the prayer which the priest will begin on your behalf. Thus, it is incumbent upon the people at this time to rise from their seated position, and to have their palms raised and their feet aligned, ready to respond to the priest.

At that time, the priest turns to the west after he has faced the east, and says to the people, *irīnī bāsīn*, the interpretation of which is "Peace to you all."[37] So the people respond to him with an alert mind, *kā-ṭubnūmā tī-sū*, the interpretation of which is, "And with your spirit," that is, may peace like that which you gave us be with your spirit.[38] Then, the priest begins the *Prayer of Thanksgiving* to its end.[39] At its conclusion, if the high priest was present, he says, "This is he through whom."[40] And the reason for designating the patriarch, metropolitan, or bishop for the conclusion of the *Prayer of Thanksgiving*,[41] which is, "This is he through whom," and in all

35. That is, the Copts, who adhere to the non-Chalcedonian theology of Miaphysitism and Miatheletism.

36. Corrected orthographically, the response would be Ἐπὶ προσευχὴν στάθητε (*epi proseuchēn stathēte*). See Burmester, "The Greek Kīrugmata," 366.

37. Εἰρήνη πᾶσιν (*eirēnē pasin*). See ibid. The translation in the text is Ibn Sabbāʿ's own, which noticeably adds the second-person personal pronoun *you*, where it does not appear in the Greek.

38. καὶ τῷ πνεύματί σου (*kai tō pneumati sou*). See ibid.

39. For more information on the *Prayer of Thanksgiving*, see chapter 1, note 41.

40. The concluding doxology of the *Prayer of Thanksgiving* reads as follows: "This is he through whom the glory, the honor, the dominion, and the worship are due unto you, with him and the Holy Spirit, the giver of life, who is of one essence with you, now and at all times, and unto the age of all ages, amen." See ibid., 148. Here and throughout this section, the text provides the beginning of this doxology in Coptic transliterated into Arabic script as follows: *bā īdā ūūl hī ḍudf.*

41. The text reads *al-shibihmāt,* an Arabic rendering of the initial verb in the Coptic text of the prayer: ⲙⲁⲣⲉⲛϣⲉⲡϩⲙⲟⲧ (*marenshepehmot*). See Graf, *Verzeichnis*, 65.

prayers with the same conclusion is thus: The earthly Church resembles the heavenly Jerusalem in that the minds of the luminous angels praise and hallow the Holy Trinity, the Father and the Son and the Holy Spirit.[42] There are ranks among the luminous angels, and for each rank a leader, who raises its praise to the leader of the rank who is higher than him, the sublime and the infinite, unto the throne of greatness. Satan, leader of all the angelic hosts, who fell because of haughtiness, was designated for this function, for he used to take the praise of the exalted angels and present it to his Creator. But when he thought that it was due to him and refrained from offering it to its rightful owner, this necessitated his fall. Then, God created humans in order to compensate for Satan with them and to populate by them the empty rank.[43] Thus, the high priest, who is of the earthly priestly rank, whose members are angels of earth and heavenly men, became the one to conclude the *Prayer of Thanksgiving* offered by the subordinates, and to conclude himself by his own mouth and say, "This is he through whom." That is, he resembles the leader of the exalted angels in taking the praises of his subordinates and elevating them to the Holy Trinity—the Father, the Son, and the Holy Spirit—while they are praising and hallowing. This is the reason for especially designating the high priest to conclude the *Prayer of Thanksgiving* and all prayers.

When the priest has finished the *Prayer of Thanksgiving*, the deacon also notifies the people, "Stand up for prayer." In every prayer, the deacon says,

42. A ubiquitous theme throughout the *Precious Jewel* is the analogy between the Church's assembly and hierarchical nature and the heavenly ranks of angels, who constantly stand before God's throne in praise and adoration. This ongoing theme shows the work's dependency on the works of Pseudo-Dionysius the Areopagite. See, for example, the *Celestial Hierarchy* 1.3, where one reads, "The sacred institution and source of perfection established our most pious hierarchy. He modeled it on the hierarchies of heaven." See Colm Luibheid, *Pseudo-Dionysius*, 146. According to Georg Graf, the works of Pseudo-Dionysius were known to Copto-Arabic authors of the thirteenth century, such as Al-Mu'taman ibn al-ʿAssāl. See Georg Graf, *GCAL*, 1:370–371. See also the numerous references to Pseudo-Dionysius throughout Milad Zakhary's study of the *Precious Jewel*: Milad Sidky Zakhary, *De la Trinité à la Trinité*, 178.

43. The notion that God created humans to replace with them the rank of the fallen angels appears also in chapter 9 of the famous medieval catechetical work *The Book of Elucidation* (*Kitāb al-īḍāḥ*), likely from the eleventh century. The chapter in question was deliberately omitted from the popular Egyptian edition of this work. Jirjis, *Al-durr al-thamīn*. For a discussion of the contents of this chapter, see Mark N. Swanson, "The Specifically Egyptian Context of a Coptic Arabic Text," 220–221.

"Stand up for prayer." Have they sat down, so that the deacon should command them to stand in every prayer? [No], rather, the command to stand, first, is to have them rise up from sitting, but the second and third reason is to prevent the mind from roaming around in every prayer, and to have them listen attentively to the recitation of the priest, so that the people may assent to everything that the priest entreats and asks from Christ the Lord at the time of consecration.[44]

Furthermore, if the celebrant is a high priest, he is to wear the vestment at this time in the likeness of Aaron, while the chanters sing what is appropriate to the putting on of the priestly vestment.[45] But if he is not a high priest, he is to go around the altar and the deacon prostrates before him at this time. The reason for this prostration by the deacon to the priest at this time is that the deacon was standing higher than the priest because of his proximity to the east, toward which they looked. Thus, it is necessary for the deacon to recompense the priest by prostrating to him, for the truths of the doctrine are built upon humility.

Then, the priest and the deacon veil Christ, who is present, who is the oblation that is placed [upon the altar], with the veil of the *prospherin*,[46] in order to conceal Christ from the minds of the people until the recitation of the Creed. Thereafter, when the priest has descended from the sanctuary, he bows together with the celebrant deacon, and a hegumen[47] or the high priest who is present comes forward to read the absolution upon them.[48] [This is] not as though they were bound that they might be set free, but because this is submission to the one who is higher than they. For they [the priest and the deacon] were above in the holy of holies, close

44. P208, fol. 88v adds, "I mean ⲁⲙⲏⲛ ϯⲛⲁϩϯ (*amēn tinahti*, amen I believe)." It seems that the text here provides an example of when the people assent to the prayers, since this response is not in fact said at this time.

45. See chapter 1, note 49.

46. That is, the large veil that covers the gifts on the altar. For more information, see chapter 1, note 43.

47. That is, a priest holding the honorary rank of *hēgoumenos*, often translated as *qummuṣ*. For more information, see chapter 1, note 32.

48. A class of priestly prayers usually appearing at the end of services and having in common a request by the presider for the forgiveness of sins of the people. The term comes from the Arabic root *ḥalla*, to unbind, undo, or to set free, which acquired the Christian sense of absolving from sins. Thus, the term is related to the Greek *apolysis*. See the explanation of the term in Burmester, "The Canonical Hours of the Coptic Church," 91n2; Hans Quecke, "Zum 'Gebet der Lossprechung des Vaters,'" at 68n1.

to God, unlike those who were lower in the church. Thus, they desired—in order for their souls to be saved from pride—to bow with their heads, while someone else is to recite [the absolution] upon them, lest they think within themselves that they are superior.[49]

Some priests sit together with the deacon, and this is inappropriate, but what is intended is for them to bow and submit with their heads. This submission is twofold; one is to God (may he be exalted), and the other is humility toward him who is to recite [the absolution] upon them, as love toward God first and the neighbor second.

Moreover, the reader of the absolution recites the *Absolution to the Son*.[50] After it, [there is] a request that these servants may be absolved from the mouth of the Holy Trinity, from the mouth of the catholic and apostolic Church, from the mouth of the three councils that were assembled to issue the Creed, from the mouth of the patriarchs of old, from the mouth of the patriarch who is present, and from the mouth of the one who is reciting this absolution.[51]

Then the priest ascends to the sanctuary and presents the box of incense to him who is higher in rank to bless the incense before it is placed in the censer. But if there be none higher than him, he himself is to bless and sign with the cross on the box of incense before he places it in the censer.

CHAPTER 65
CONCERNING THE EXPLANATION OF THE CENSER

This censer has numerous meanings that must be explained. First, it contains three chains of the same metal, indicating the trinity of the hypostases (*aqānīm*) and the oneness of the essence (*jawhar*), since the metal is one. Second, it has a rounded dome like the heavens. Third, the hook that

49. In other words, since the bishop remained outside the sanctuary during the prothesis, ascending only at the end to vest, the lower clergy are now to prostrate before him while he reads the absolution, lest they think themselves higher or more important than the bishop.

50. For the text of the *Absolution to the Son*, "O Master, Lord, Jesus Christ, the only begotten Son," see Brightman, *Liturgies Eastern and Western*, 148–149.

51. Ibn Sabbā' is essentially paraphrasing the *Absolution of the Servants*, "May your servants, the ministers of this day." See ibid., 149. CM15 adds: "from the mouth of the catholic and apostolic Church, from the mouth of the apostles, and from the mouth of the three councils."

is hanging down indicates the Son, who has condescended.[52] Fourth, the rounded bowl of the censer resembles the roundedness of the womb of the Virgin Mary, and the coal that is in it corresponds to the dense body taken from our nature, while the fire that is in the coal indicates the union of the divinity with the humanity. All these are signs of the unity and the trinity, and the condescension of the Son for the union that is contained in the censer.

Furthermore, the offering [of incense] in it is to be performed three times in the name of the Holy Trinity, the Father, the Son, and the Holy Spirit. Likewise, an offering performed three times is in the likeness of the oblation of Abel, the incense of the righteous Noah, and the sacrifice of Isaac. For these three are types that have been provided beforehand in the Old Testament before the New Testament; thus, the priests do not follow other than this example.

Every time he transfers incense from the box to the censer, he is to make the sign of the cross upon it before taking it. After the three times, he says, "Glory and honor to the Holy Trinity, the Father, the Son, and the Holy Spirit."

After this, the priest recites the prayer of the acceptance of this incense.[53] After he finishes its recitation, the deacon says, "Pray for these oblations, and the sacrifices that are offered," and the people respond saying, "Lord have mercy." The people also ought to add to the phrase Lord have mercy, "Lord accept from your priest this rising incense for the forgiveness of our sins."[54]

After the *Prayer of Incense*, the priest recites a prayer for the peace of the one, only, catholic, and apostolic Church. Then, the deacon calls to the people to pray for the one, catholic, apostolic Church, so the people

52. A reference to the incarnation of the Son, often described as an act of humility or condescension, ultimately from the Greek συγκατάβασις (*synkatabasis*), condescension or accommodation. See Henry George Liddell and Robert Scott, *A Greek-English Lexicon*, 1446.

53. For the text of the *Prayer of Incense* at the beginning of the Liturgy of the Word, "O God the great the eternal," see Brightman, *Liturgies Eastern and Western*, 148–149, 150.

54. Beginning here and throughout the remainder of the commentary, Ibn Sabbā' adds these short prayers for the people to accompany the response "Lord have mercy" in each litany. These short prayers are not part of the received text of the Coptic liturgy but are provided here as a tool for private devotion.

respond saying, "Lord have mercy." The people ought to add to Lord have mercy, "O Lord protect this your one, only, catholic, apostolic Church," assenting to the priest's supplication for it.

Then the priest says a prayer for the protection of the head of the confession (*ra'īs al-ṭā'ifah*), that is, the patriarch or the metropolitan or the bishop. So, the deacon says, "Pray for our father, and our head, and our leader, the father the patriarch Abba so-and-so, and likewise the metropolitan and the bishop," and the people say, "Lord have mercy." The people ought to add to the response Lord have mercy, "O Lord, keep for us and upon us the head of your priests, the father Abba so-and-so, to shepherd us in protection and safety."

Then the priest prays for the assembling of the people in the holy church. So, the deacon calls out and says, "Pray for the assembling of this congregation in this holy church," and the people say, "Lord have mercy." The people ought to add to the response Lord have mercy, "O Lord, maintain our assembly in this holy church and all our care [for it]."

Then the priest begins to go around the altar with the incense three times.[55] Each time, at the place of the bread and wine that is offered, he is to make the sign of the cross with the censer.[56] When he has finished the three rounds, the priest descends with his left foot before the right, just as he ascended with his right foot before the left.

CHAPTER 66

CONCERNING THE INCENSING BY THE HIGH PRIEST NINE TIMES

He [the presbyter] censes the altar three times, each time of the three, threefold, that is, nine times. Then [he gives incense] nine times to the high priest like the number of the angelic ranks, and the nine are three ranks each. And there is to be a [sign of] the cross at the end of each three, as a demonstration of the three crosses of him who was crucified for them at the appointed time. Otherwise, the high priest would not have given the presbyter the cross to kiss it.

55. In current practice, the priest recites the preceding prayers for the Church, the hierarchs, and the assembly while already circling the altar and offering incense. This current practice appears to be contradicted even by the standard Euchologion of ʿAbd al-Masīḥ Ṣalīb. See ʿAbd al-Masīḥ Ṣalīb, ⲡⲓϫⲱⲙ ⲛ̀ⲧⲉ ⲡⲓⲉⲩⲭⲟⲗⲟⲅⲓⲟⲛ, 237.

56. That is, the priest is to wave the censer in the sign of the cross each time he arrives to the western end of the altar and faces east.

By this sign, the incense offered to God (may he be exalted) by the high priests can be distinguished from incense to idols. For when idol worshippers used to offer incense to them [the idols], their incense did not include the sign of the cross. Likewise, at the conclusion of the three times, the presbyter kisses the cross, received from the bishop. Likewise, also the presbyter incenses his brothers the presbyters three times in the likeness of the Holy Trinity.

And he says to the noncelebrant priest, "I ask you, my son, to assist me by your prayers," so the noncelebrant priest places his two open hands on the censer and bows slightly toward it. The meaning of this is, "Just as you offered this incense as an offering to God (may he be exalted) in your service, here I am also partaking with you in offering it." While he is bowing slightly with his hands, he says, "May the Lord preserve your priesthood like Aaron and Zachariah."

Then, he incenses the people one by one according to their ranks while he goes around the church. The purpose of his going around the church is multifold: first, to raise those who are seated and to awaken those who are asleep; second, to accept everyone who has brought votive offerings, whether incense, candles, or otherwise; third, to take note of who was present in church at that time, in order to know at the time of communion who is a true believer and who is a heretic; and fourth, to admonish those who delay their coming after that time so that they may cease from this.

Furthermore, it is necessary for every one of the people of God to whom the censer comes at the hand of the priest of God (may he be exalted), to say, "I have sinned, my Lord Jesus Christ, and I know my guilt and my sin."[57] Then he is to kiss the hand of the priest for his humility and his coming to receive his confession, and if he has a votive offering, he is to hand it to the priest at that time.

After the priest has gone around to the people of God with the incense accepting their confession and receiving their votive offerings, he ascends to the sanctuary of God once more with his right foot first as was said previously, and he says, "Receive, O Lord, the confession of your people and your pasture, O good shepherd. Remember, O Lord in your kingdom all those who have bidden us to remember them."

57. For the curious Coptic medieval practice of offering one's confession secretly during the priest's incense round, see chapter 1, note 112.

Then he circles the sanctuary one time and descends with his left foot first, as was explained previously, and incenses the high priest who is present three times three. At the end of each three times, [he makes] the sign of the cross. If the high priest is not present, but another presbyter is present, he incenses [the other presbyter] three times, and at their conclusion [he makes] the sign of the cross, and says to him, "I ask you, my son, to assist me with your prayers, and to remember me." The noncelebrant priest answers him and says, "May the Lord preserve your priesthood like Aaron and Zachariah."

CHAPTER 67
CONCERNING THE ARCHDEACON'S SUPERVISION OF THE DEACONS ACCORDING TO THEIR RANKS AND DEGREES

Then, the archdeacon—the head of the diaconate—grants permission to one of the readers[58] to read the epistle of Saint Paul (*al-būlus*) and read its translation,[59] according to the saying of the apostle Matthew, if there is no interpreter in the church, let him who speaks a foreign tongue be

58. The text has *al-aghnusṭusiyyīn*, Arabic derivation from the Greek ἀναγνώστης (*anagnōstēs*). By the late fourth or early fifth century, the term had acquired a technical usage for a member of the rank of readers designated to proclaim scriptural and other readings in liturgical services. See Socrates, *Historia ecclesiastica* 5.22, in Pierre Périchon and Pierre Maraval, *Socrate de Constantinople*, IV–VI, 230–231 and *Canons of Hippolytus* 7 in René-Georges Coquin, *Les canons d'Hippolyte*, 358–361. In Egypt specifically, ecclesiastical readers are attested in documentary papyri since the late fourth century. For this body of evidence, see Ewa Wipszycka, "Les ordres mineurs," 246; Georg Schmelz, *Kirchliche Amtsträger*, 38–39.

59. Cf. 1 Corinthians 14:28. The northern Egyptian Coptic Liturgy of the Word includes four lections from the New Testament: from (1) the epistles of Paul, (2) the catholic epistles, (3) the Acts of the apostles, and (4) the four Gospels. The emphasis on interpreting the epistle after reading it indicates the practice of reading the lection first in Coptic, indicated here as a foreign language (!), then translating it to Arabic, which by this period was the more easily understood language by the majority of Egyptians. The literature on the fate of Coptic and the spread of Arabic among Egypt's Christians is immense. For the language shift in Egyptian society during the transition from Byzantine to Islamic Egypt, see Maged S. A. Mikhail, *From Byzantine to Islamic Egypt*, 79–105. The Arabization of patristic literary heritage in particular is discussed in Samuel Rubenson, "Translating the Tradition," 4–14.

silent.[60] [He may read in a foreign language only] if he is proficient in translating well and has mastered it in a house of learning outside the church, for the church is a house of prayer and asking for forgiveness, not a house of learning and inquiry.

Every reader of a passage of the readings of the Church, from whichever rank he may be of the seven mentioned previously,[61] ought to prostrate to God (may he be exalted) after he has read that passage before the door of the sanctuary, and after this to prostrate to the congregation in the two choirs. As for prostrating to God (may he be exalted), it is to him who has given the reader the grace of his Holy Spirit to become a member of the clergy (*iklīrus*). The interpretation of the word *iklīrus* is "the heir," that is, he has inherited the grace of the Holy Spirit, for no one inherits except him who is someone's own [i.e., natural] son.[62] As for prostrating to the people, it is as though he were saying to them in meaning, behold, the mouth that has catechized and instructed you, here it is placed beneath your feet. Thereby he imitates the humility of the pre-eternal Son and is worthy of the inheritance of his Father.

60. According to the scheme proposed by Samuel Rubenson for the Arabization of the Coptic heritage, Arabic lectionary manuscripts would have begun appearing already during the first phase, ca. the tenth century. See Rubenson, "Translating the Tradition," 6–8. In the thirteenth century, the canons attributed to Pope Cyril III ibn Laqlaq described the liturgical reading of Scripture in Arabic as, "not a rite (*ṭaqs*) in the Church, for it is for everyone to know what he (the reader) is saying." See O. H. E. Burmester, "The Canons of Cyril III ibn Laḳlaḳ (Part II)," 125 (Arabic), 144 (English). Among the lectionaries listed in Ugo Zanetti's study of Bohairic lectionaries, only one (*Cairo, Coptic Museum Lit. 26*) is an Arabic thirteenth-century witness. Nine other witnesses are from the fourteenth century. See Zanetti, *Les lectionnaires coptes annuels*, 285–335.

61. In chapters 45–51, Ibn Sabbā‘ discusses the following seven ranks of the ecclesiastical hierarchy: reader, subdeacon, deacon, archdeacon, presbyter, hegumen or archpriest, and patriarch, metropolitan, and bishop. The latter three are considered as one rank for a total of seven ranks altogether. For more information on each rank, see O. H. E. Burmester, *The Egyptian or Coptic Church*, 154–174. This is supplemented by the detailed discussion of minor orders in Egypt between the fourth and eighth centuries in: Wipszycka, "Les ordres mineurs," 225–255. The rites of ordination of these various ranks were published by Burmester from the manuscript *Cairo, Coptic Museum Lit. 253*, copied in AD 1364 and considered the oldest surviving manuscript of these rituals. See Burmester, *Ordination Rites of the Coptic Church*.

62. That is, a clergyman has been allotted a share in the grace of the priesthood; hence, he is an heir. Cf. G. W. H. Lampe, *A Patristic Greek Lexicon*, 757; Graf, *Verzeichnis*, 12.

After this, the priest stands before the altar after the reading of [the epistle of] Paul and the deacon [is to stand] with him on his right. The deacon says, "Stand up for prayer," then the priest says *irīnī-bāsīn*, which is "Peace to you all." The people say responding to him, *kā-ṭu-bnūmātī-sū*, that is, "May this peace be with your spirit."[63] Then the priest says the special prayer for the Pauline reading while the entire people listen attentively,[64] for whenever the priest speaks in the church, no one ought to speak. When the prayer has ended, the people assent to it by saying with one mouth, "Lord have mercy."

Then the archdeacon of the church commands one of the subdeacons to read the catholic reading (*al-qatālīqūn*), since the catholic reading is higher in position than the Pauline reading, because catholic means "comprehensive," that is, it was gathered from Peter, James, John, and Jude.[65] Thus, since the catholic reading is higher in position than the Pauline reading, its reading has been [assigned] to the subdeacon, since he is higher in position than the reader. Then he who is proficient in translation interprets it. Afterward, the priest reads a prayer after the [reading] of the catholic, after the deacon has alerted the people to rise for prayer according to the custom.[66]

After this, the priest ascends to the sanctuary of God and presents the box of incense to the high priest who is present to bless it. If the high priest who is present is the patriarch, it would be for the patriarch to say together with the blessing, "In the name of the Father, and the Son, and the Holy Spirit," and the priest then is not to bless nor say anything, but he is to raise the incense [to the censer] in silence. After raising the incense [to the censer] in the name of the Holy Trinity three times as explained previously, he is to say the prayer of God's acceptance of the sacrifice of Abraham and [God's act of] preparing a lamb for him, and for the two mites of the widow.[67]

63. Here, Ibn Sabbāʿ clearly elaborates on the literal meaning of the response, which is simply, "And to your spirit."

64. For the complete text of the *Mystery of the Pauline Incense* (*Sirr bakhūr al-būlus*), "O Lord of knowledge and provider of wisdom," see Brightman, *Liturgies Eastern and Western*, 153.

65. From καθολικόν (*katholikon*) meaning general or universal, used to refer to the general epistles attributed to Peter, James, John, and Jude. See Graf, *Verzeichnis*, 95.

66. For the text of the prayer the *Mystery of the Catholic* (*Sirr al-kāthūlīkūn*), "O Lord our God," see Brightman, *Liturgies Eastern and Western*, 154.

67. Mark 12:41–44; Luke 21:1–4. By contrast, the actual prayer in the Euchologion titled the *Mystery of the Praxis* (*Sirr al-ibraksīs*) only references the sacrifice of Abraham.

Then the priest goes around the altar three times following the first example as was mentioned, and then he descends with his left foot before the right and incenses the high priest who is present just like the previous arrangement. He goes around to the people a second time, for the first time was to awaken the people and raise those who were seated, while this second round is [like] preaching during the reading of the narratives of the apostles, since they used to roam the lands and preach the Lord Christ.

Then the archdeacon grants permission to one of the deacons to read the reading from the Acts (*al-ibraksīs*), since it is higher in position than the two books, the Pauline reading and the catholic epistle. Thus, the archdeacon grants permission to the deacon to read it, since he is higher in position than the reader and the subdeacon, and it is then interpreted as was done previously. Then the deacon says, "Christ is risen."[68]

CHAPTER 68

CONCERNING THE REASON FOR UNIQUELY PRIVILEGING THE HIGH PRIEST WITH ONE *HOLY* OF THE NINE *HOLIES* AND THE REASON FOR ITS APPEARANCE

Then the highest-ranking one present from among the priests, whether presbyter or bishop—being the head of the earthly angelic rank and heavenly men—begins the *Trisagion* and says the first *Holy*.[69] This is for two reasons. First, since the *Holies* are in the likeness of the Holy Trinity. Second, they are in the number of the three passages [of Scripture] that are read to the people of God for instruction and consolation. Meanwhile, the remaining ranks of the church say the other two *Holies*.

The text of the *Trisagion* is, "Holy is God, Holy is the mighty one, Holy is the immortal one, who was incarnate of the Virgin Mary. Have mercy on us." This is the first *Holy*, and it is the privilege of the high priest alone.

It seems that Ibn Sabbāʿ here is conflating this prayer with a separate prayer that follows, known as the *Prayer of the Sacrifices*. See Brightman, *Liturgies Eastern and Western*, 154.

68. The Greek Resurrection chant *Christ is risen* has been part of the received chant repertoire of the Coptic tradition since the medieval period at least. In current usage, it is indicated only from Easter until the feast of the Ascension, and thus its mention here is somewhat unusual at what is otherwise a nonfestal liturgical celebration. See Burmester, "The Greek Kīrugmata," 389, and Sameh Farouk Soliman, "Re-Translating the Byzantine Paschal Troparion," 232–235. For the text of the chant, see the appendix.

69. On the Trisagion chant, see chapter 1, note 56.

The second *Holy* is, "Holy is God, Holy is the mighty one, Holy is the immortal one, who was crucified for us. Have mercy on us." The third *Holy* is, "Holy is God, Holy is the mighty one, Holy is the immortal one, who rose from the dead and ascended to the heavens. Have mercy on us."

These three *Holies* are the three hypostases (*aqānīm*), and they are three times three, nine *Holies*, three *Holies* in each stanza. These nine *Holies* are in the number of the nine ranks, which are the angels, archangels, principalities, authorities, thrones, lordships, powers, the cherubim, and the seraphim. Thus, the nine ranks are completed in the number of the nine *Holies*, which are attributed to the praising of the nine ranks, so that it may be known that human beings resemble the ranks of the heavenly ones in their assembling in church.[70]

Furthermore, the reason for the existence of this sanctification at this time is that the deacon says, *ikhrisṭās anāstī* before the sanctification, that is, "Christ is risen."[71] Thereby, they recall what took place before the Resurrection and the burial. Namely, after Joseph and Nicodemus had anointed the Lord—to him be the glory—they carried him to the tomb to be buried. This tomb was a cave, as the Gospel witnessed. It was a new tomb, and no one had been placed therein. When they had lowered him in the tomb, they received confirmation concerning his death, [which happened to him] just as to the rest of humankind. They did not yet know that he would rise on the third day according to the Scriptures, so they mourned and lamented him [saying], "Who has remained in order to console and deliver us, O you whom all of us had hoped would be the consolation of Israel and its Savior?" But, while they were weeping, the angels appeared saying, "Holy is God, Holy is the mighty one, Holy is the immortal one." And when they said, "the immortal one," and Christ the Lord opened his eyes before their faces, the angels offered him this praise. [Christ] saw the angel, who appeared to him the night of the crucifixion and who gave him the praise of power and victory. Thus, they ascertained that he did not die involuntarily, but willingly. So, Joseph and Nicodemus said, "O you who was crucified for us, have mercy on us."[72]

70. On the nine ranks of angels, cf. Pseudo-Dionysius, *Celestial Hierarchy* 6.1. Luibheid, *Pseudo-Dionysius*, 160–161.

71. The text's *ikhrisṭās anāstī* is an Arabic transliteration of the Greek Χριστός ἀνέστη (*christos anestē*), Christ is risen.

72. As Sebastià Janeras points out in his extensive study of the Trisagion, the tradition ascribing the birth of the Trisagion to the burial of Christ—one of many such miraculous

Thus, when the Church was organized according to the best order, and the liturgy was arranged in it, the Resurrection of Christ came to be proclaimed [in it]. [The fathers of the Church] recalled what took place also at the burial before the Resurrection and they imitated the sanctification of the angels, when they were praising, "Holy," at the time of the burial of Christ. Thus, they chanted three *Holies* in the number of the three hypostases, which are "Holy is God, Holy is the mighty one, Holy is the immortal one, who was incarnate of the Virgin. Have mercy on us. Holy is God, Holy is the mighty one, Holy is the immortal one, who was crucified for us. Have mercy on us," and in imitation of Joseph and Nicodemus, "Holy is God, Holy is the mighty one, Holy is the immortal one, who rose from the dead and ascended to the heavens. Have mercy on us."

After the recitation of the nine *Holies*, they glorify the Father, the Son, and the Holy Spirit, which is, "Glory to the Father,"[73] in order that glorification may be fulfilled after the sanctification to the Father, the Son, and the Holy Spirit.

Afterward, the deacon announces to the people that they should rise for prayer, and the priest beseeches God (may he be exalted) to prepare the people to listen to the holy Gospel, to fulfill its commands, and to refrain from its prohibitions. Then, the deacon says, "Pray for the holy Gospel," so the people say, "Lord have mercy." In addition to this, it should be added, "O Lord, make us worthy to listen to the pure Gospel, and open the ears of our hearts to heed and to understand your life-giving teachings, so that our souls may live thereby."[74]

Then, the archdeacon commands one of the chanters to read two verses from the Old Testament, and they are from the Davidic Psalms. The text [they read] is to match the time appointed for the assembly. Whether it is a feast of the Lord, a feast of the lady Saint Mary (*al-sayyidah mart-maryam*), or a feast of a martyr, the verses of the psalm are to agree with the meaning of the Gospel [passage] designated for that occasion.

---

origin stories in the eastern heritage—goes back to West Syrian author David bar Paulos (8th/9th c.) in a dialogue with a Melkite Christian on the Trisagion. See the discussion in Janeras, "Le Trisagion," 551–552. For the text of the dialogue, see François Nau, "Opuscules maronites," 328–332.

73. Given in the text as *dhukṣā-batrī*, an Arabic transliteration of the Greek δόξα πατρὶ (*doxa patri*).

74. For the *Prayer of the Gospel*, see chapter 1, note 59.

After singing the appropriate chants, whether mournful, joyful, annual, of the month of Kiyahk, or of the Paschal season,[75] the priest and the deacon go around the altar with the glorious Gospel book, while the servants cover it over with candles, and the deacon carries it until they descend from the sanctuary. Meanwhile, the people chant and say, "Cause me to hear your mercy in the morning, for in you have I trusted."[76] As for the deacon, he says privately, "Teach me, O Lord, the way wherein I should walk."[77] This single circuit around the altar corresponds to the spreading of the Gospel to all the world, the journey that encompassed the entire inhabited world.

After the priest has gone around the altar with the Gospel book in the likeness of its dissemination to the whole world, as we said, and before reading it, he is to open it and place it upon the altar, as a sign that this text proceeds from the sayings of Christ, who is placed upon this altar.

CHAPTER 69
CONCERNING THE OPENING OF THE GOSPEL FOR THE PRIESTS TO BE KISSED WHILE IT IS OPENED AND THE ASSENTING TO IT

Then he [the priest] summons the priests who are present to inspect the words written in it [the Gospel], and to verify and witness that this opened

75. The designation *khamsīniyyah* literally means "belonging to the fifty," in reference to the fifty days between the Resurrection and Pentecost. The term annual (*sanawiyyah*) refers to normal time, i.e., standard services not falling within any particular fast or feast to which other designated melodies would apply.

76. Psalm 142 (143):8. This is a reference to verses from the psalms chanted during the procession of the Gospel around the altar, termed in Arabic *ṭawwāf* (pl. *ṭawwafāt*) in Coptic liturgical usage, from the Arabic *ṭāfa*, to encircle or go around. The psalm verse given in the text is the standard *ṭawwāf* for the morning incense throughout the year. The analogous verse(s) for the evening incense is "Lord I have cried to you, hear me, attend to the voice of my supplication when I cry out unto you. Let my prayer be set forth as incense before you, the lifting up of my hands as an evening sacrifice" (Ps 140 (141):1–2). See Ṣalīb, ⲡⲓϫⲱⲙ ⲛ̀ⲧⲉ ⲡⲓⲉⲩⲭⲟⲗⲟⲅⲓⲟⲛ, 97–98. Additionally, manuscripts preserve a number of these *ṭawwafāt* for various occasions and classes of saints, such as major feasts of the Lord, the Virgin Mary, angels, martyrs, and monastic saints. For a collection of such psalm selections in printed editions, see Raphael al-Ṭūkhī, ⲡⲓϫⲱⲙ ⲛ̀ⲧⲉ ⲡⲓϣⲟⲙⲧ ⲛ̀ⲁⲛⲁⲫⲟⲣⲁ, 158–162.

77. Psalm 142 (143):10. CM15 adds: "since the Gospel is a way unto the people, and the deacon carries it and walks with it."

book is indeed the Gospel. After this examination and verification, they venerate it while it is open, to distinguish the priests on account of their priesthood in kissing it [while it is] opened unlike the rest of the people.

After this, if the priest chooses to read the Gospel, it is his rightful privilege apart from anyone else, for he is a successor of the apostles, who preached the Gospel. But if the priest does not choose to read the Gospel, he may permit the deacon to read it. To this deacon is granted a special status: He is styled *a deacon of the Gospel* (*shammāsun injīlī*), meaning that he reads the Gospel, and he is distinguished by this from the rest of the deacons, who have not mastered the reading of it. For reading it ought to be restricted to an appointed elder, who knows the correction of the text,[78] and knows the explanation of the meaning of the text. Thus, [the older deacon] may read the Gospel and satisfy the hearing of those present as regards to both the text and its meaning.

Furthermore, the reading of the Gospel is to be from the *ambo*, the interpretation of which is: a means of ascent, according to the saying of the Lord, to him be the glory, "What you have heard with your ears, preach upon the housetops."[79] The housetop is this *ambo*, which the savior has indicated, since it is elevated like the housetops.[80]

Then, after the one who has read the Gospel and interpreted its text and meaning has descended, the rest of the priests who are present come and venerate it by way of agreeing and assenting. [This is] not a witnessing like the first veneration when it was open, but as an assent, agreement, and confirmation, so that the people would imitate them in venerating it.

CHAPTER 70

CONCERNING THE SUBDEACON'S GOING AROUND WITH THE GOSPEL TO THE PEOPLE TO VENERATE IT

Afterward, the subdeacon carries the Gospel book and covers it with a silk veil, and he goes around with it to the people to venerate it while it is closed. This is that they may consent to what they have heard, conforming to the veneration by the priests in agreement and confirmation.

78. That is, is skilled in vocalizing the text correctly.

79. Matthew 10:27.

80. For the ambo, see chapter 1, note 61.

The going of the subdeacon to the people is preferable to the people coming to him. This is because the Gospel, when it was preached at first, went out to the people, and they agreed and believed in it. Thus, if all the people had come to it, the preachers of the Gospel would have remained in one place and the people would have come to them. In addition, the benefit in this [practice] is to avoid crowdedness and disturbance of mind.

CHAPTER 71
CONCERNING THE PRIEST'S STANDING AND BOWING OUTSIDE THE DOOR OF THE SANCTUARY

After this, the priest and the deacon come to stand before the sanctuary, and the deacon says, admonishing the people, "Stand up for prayer." Then the priest says, "Peace be to you all." So, when the people have responded to his peace, he says, "O long-suffering one, who is plenteous in mercy, remember, O Lord, those who are sick among your people." The deacon says, "Pray for the sick who are among the people." Then the people say, "Lord have mercy."[81]

Then the priest says, "Remember, O Lord, the travelers. Cause them to return safely." The deacon says, "Pray for the travelers, so that Christ our God may cause them to return safely," and the people say, "Lord have mercy."

Then the priest says, "Remember, O Lord, the seeds of the earth and its plants." If it is the season of fruits, they say, "The fruits of the earth," and if it is the season of the Nile, they say, "The Nile, so that he may raise it according to its measure." The deacon says, "Pray for the Nile and its rising, the growth of all the fruits, the seeds of the earth, and its plants." The people respond saying, "Lord have mercy."[82]

81. For the complete text of this prayer, titled the *Mystery of the Gospel* (*Sirr al-injīl*), see Brightman, *Liturgies Eastern and Western*, 157–158.

82. Prayers in the Coptic liturgy related to the yearly cycle of seasons are changed throughout the year to match the three phases of agricultural life. Consecutively, these are a prayer for the waters of the Nile from 12 Ba'ūnah to 9 Bābah (June 19 to October 19/20), for planting from 10 Bābah to 10 Ṭūbah (October 20/21 to January 18/19), and for the fruits from 11 Ṭūbah to 11 Ba'ūnah (January 19/20 to June 18). The Nile in particular occupied a significant place in the life and pious practices of Egyptians. Not only does the Coptic liturgy pray for a timely inundation season, but an entire liturgical service existed in the medieval period to bless the rising of the Nile both among Copts and

Then the priest says, "Remember, O Lord, the king of the land, your servant. Establish in his heart the peace of the Church." The deacon says, "Pray for the king," so the people say, "Lord have mercy."

Then the priest says, "Remember, O Lord, those who have reposed and departed." The deacon says, "Pray for those who have reposed and died in the Christian faith," and the people respond, "Lord have mercy."

Then the priest says, "Remember, O Lord, those who have offered these oblations." The deacon says, "Pray for those who have offered these oblations from their hard labor," so the people respond and say, "Lord have mercy."

Then the priest says, "Remember, O Lord, your servants the catechumens," that is, [those who are] under the canons, whether before baptism or after and have committed sin and are under penance by a spiritual teacher. The deacon says, "Pray for the catechumens," so the people respond, "Lord have mercy."[83]

Then the priest says, "Remember, O Lord, the safety of this place and those who stand therein." The deacon says, "Pray for the safety of this place and all those standing therein," so the people say, "Lord have mercy."

Then the priest says, "Remember, O Lord, your servants who are captives in bitter slavery." The deacon says, "Pray for those who are captives in bitter slavery." The people say, "Lord have mercy."

When these entreaties have been concluded and the people have assented to them, they ask for mercy. Then the priest bows his head and reads a secret prayer outside the veil before ascending to the sanctuary.[84] He is to

---

Melkites. See Hieronymous Engberding, "Der Nil," 56–88; Roshdi Wassef Behman Dous, "Ο Αγιασμός των υδάτων του Νείλου Ποταμού." For the cultural aspects of Coptic Nile celebrations, see Boaz Shoshan, *Popular Culture in Medieval Cairo*, 40–51; Huda Lutfi, "Coptic Festivals of the Nile," 254–282. For the text of the prayers referenced here, see Ṣalīb, ⲡⲓϫⲱⲙ ⲛ̀ⲧⲉ ⲡⲓⲉⲩⲭⲟⲗⲟⲅⲓⲟⲛ, 112–116; Brightman, *Liturgies Eastern and Western*, 167–168.

83. A system of catechumenate whereby those seeking entry into the Christian faith were instructed for some time prior to Baptism was common in the fourth and fifth century. While the decline of the catechumenate has not been studied extensively for Egypt, it likely declined by the seventh century and the Arab conquest. Robert Taft similarly concludes that the catechumenate also had declined in Constantinople by the seventh century. See Taft, "When Did the Catechumenate Die Out in Constantinople?" 288–295.

84. For the *Prayer of the Veil*, see chapter 1, note 64.

stand bowing the head, as a sign of submission, and not remain seated squatting!

CHAPTER 72
CONCERNING THE PRIEST'S ASCENT TO THE SANCTUARY FOR THE CONSECRATION AND THE EXPLANATION OF THE LITURGY

Afterward, the priest is to ascend to the level of the sanctuary and the deacon ascends with him from the right side and stands facing him [across the altar] as explained at first. The deacon says, "Stand up for prayer," so the priest turns to the west and says, *irīnī-bāsīn*, that is, "Peace to you all." The people say responding to him, "And with your spirit."

Then the priest begins to pray, ask, and beseech on behalf of the peace of the one catholic and apostolic Church.[85] The deacon says announcing to the people, "Pray for the peace of the one catholic and apostolic Church." The people say, "Lord have mercy."

Then the priest supplicates in prayer and beseeching for the sake of preserving the leadership of the father the patriarch Abba so-and-so, and the maintaining of his leadership, and for the placing of his enemies under his feet. The deacon says, "Pray for our father, the great one among the patriarchs, Abba so-and-so," and the people say, "Lord have mercy." After "Lord have mercy," the people [also] ought to say, "O Lord, keep for our sake and upon us the leadership of the father the patriarch Abba so-and-so, so that we may live and be nourished by his teachings that vivify our souls."

Then the priest says in supplication, "Remember, O Lord, our assemblies in this your holy catholic and apostolic Church." The deacon says, "Pray for our assemblies in this, the holy church of God, and all our care for it," and the people say, "Lord have mercy." After "Lord have mercy," the people [also] ought to say, "O Lord, preserve our assemblies in this holy church, and increase our care for it."

When these three great prayers have concluded, as well as the people's assent to them—a "Lord have mercy" each time—the deacon says to the people, "In the wisdom of God, respond!" And the wisdom of God is the

85. At this point, the priest begins to pray the so-called *Three Great Litanies*. For the text of these prayers, see Brightman, *Liturgies Eastern and Western*, 160–161.

recitation of the orthodox Creed (*al-amānah*).[86] So the people say the correct and orthodox Creed word by word to its end, all with one mouth. When the Creed has been completed and the people have correctly confessed the Holy Trinity, the incarnation of Christ, his crucifixion, burial, Resurrection from the dead, his ascension to the heavens, his sitting at the right hand of the Father, and his second coming as mentioned in the Creed, the priest says, "Peace to you all." All the people respond to him, "And with your spirit."

CHAPTER 73
CONCERNING THE KISSING OF ONE ANOTHER WITH THE PURE KISS

The priest begins the prayer of the holy kiss [and recites it] to its end.[87] Then the deacon says, "Pray for the perfection of peace, love, and the holy kiss." The people respond saying, "Lord have mercy." After this, the deacon says proclaiming to the people, "Let everyone kiss each other with the holy pure kiss." Thus, the whole people kiss one another with a holy and pure kiss, [a kiss that is] free of dishonesty or the mere appearance of a kiss. Let each one kiss the other on the right side of the neck, and the other reciprocates with a similar kiss on the neck.

CHAPTER 83
[THE COMPLETION OF THE LITURGY][88]

When he [the newly-consecrated patriarch] has arrived at the point of removing the *prospherin* veil,[89] he demands of the servants and says, "Stand

86. On the use of the Creed of Nicaea-Constantinople in the eucharistic liturgy during the pre-anaphoral rites, see chapter 1, note 72.

87. On the kiss as a liturgical act in preparation for the eucharistic prayer, clearly inspired by Christ's injunction in Matthew 5:24 to reconcile with others before making one's offering, see Taft, *The Great Entrance*, 374–396; Taft and Parenti, *Il grande ingresso*, 605–635.

88. The commentary on the liturgy of the Eucharist is resumed here after the conclusion of the rite of consecration of the patriarch of Alexandria. Chapter 83 itself begins with the remainder of this rite, not included here. The original title of the chapter is *Concerning Handing Him [the Newly Consecrated Patriarch] the Pastoral Staff from the Hand of Christ—to Him be the Glory—and the Completion of the Liturgy.*

89. On the *prospherin* veil (*ibrūsfārīn*), a large cloth that covers the bread and the wine on the altar, see chapter 1, note 43.

well, stand in awe, stand in supplication in the fear of God, and respond."[90] The people respond saying, "Peace, mercy, and sacrifice."[91]

Then the priest turns his face to the west and says, "The Lord be with you all," so they say to him, "And with your spirit." Then the priest says to them, inquiring of them, "Are your minds [elevated] on high?" so they say, "They are with the Lord." Thus, if their minds were with the Lord at that time as they have said, [it is well], otherwise, they would all be lying, having said with their tongues what is not in their hearts. Then the priest says to them, "Give thanks to the Lord," so they respond to him saying, "It is worthy, befitting, and right." Then the priest begins and says, "Worthy and right, worthy and right, in truth it is worthy and right," to its end.[92]

Then the deacon notifies the people and says, *iqātī mānī anāstītā*, that is, "Let the seated arise!"[93] Then the priest narrates the [act of] standing

90. In the received text of the Coptic liturgy, this inquiry appears as a diaconal command in the liturgy of Saint Gregory the Theologian, which Engberding and Hammerschmidt concluded is of Antiochene origin, combined usually with the Egyptian version of this command, "Stand according to the pattern, look toward the east, let us attend in order to offer." See Ṣalīb, ⲡⲓϫⲱⲙ ⲛ̀ⲧⲉ ⲡⲓⲉⲩⲭⲟⲗⲟⲅⲓⲟⲛ, 470. For this diaconal command in particular, see ibid., 99. Cf. Engberding, "Ein Problem in der Homologia," 150; Ernst Hammerschmidt, *Die koptische Gregoriosanaphora*, 99–100. See also the discussion of this diaconal command linguistically and in comparison with parallel texts in other eastern liturgies in Achim Budde, *Die ägyptische Basilios-Anaphora*, 222–226.

91. See Budde, *Die ägyptische Basilios-Anaphora*, 226–228. The standard text of this pre-anaphoral people's response reads, "A mercy of peace, a sacrifice of praise" as seen for example in Brightman, *Liturgies Eastern and Western*, 164. The nominative pair "mercy, peace" appears in one Sahidic witness, the diaconal responses in *Paris, BnF Copt. 129 (20)* (9th/11th c.). However, the text given here is unlike any known variant of this response and could even be a paraphrasing rather than a literal quotation. For variants of this response in the Byzantine tradition, see Robert F. Taft, "Textual Problems in the Diaconal Admonition," 340–365.

92. At this point, manuscript CM15, fol. 93v omits the remainder of the eucharistic liturgy until the Our Father, including instead the following explanation, "Now the celebrant high priest begins the remainder of the liturgy according to the text that is explained in the book of the liturgy [the Euchologion] and it is superfluous to write it here." On the introductory dialogue between celebrant and people in the anaphora, see Budde, *Die ägyptische Basilios-Anaphora*, 228–239. Cf. Robert F. Taft, "The Dialogue before the Anaphora I," 299–324; Taft, "The Dialogue before the Anaphora II," 47–77; Taft, "The Dialogue before the Anaphora III," 63–74.

93. Curiously, ibn Sabbāʿ provides no commentary on the preface of the anaphora of Saint Basil (i.e., the priestly prayer between the introductory dialogue and the deacon's command to stand). For the text of the anaphora after the introductory dialogue, see

by the ranks of angels and describes them as standing before God. They are the angels, the archangels, the principalities, the authorities, the thrones, the lordships, and the powers. Then, the deacon says, "Look to the east," and the priest says, "You are the one whom the cherubim and the seraphim praise saying, Holy, Holy, Holy." The deacon says to the people, "Respond!" Thereupon, all the people say, "Holy, Holy, Holy, Lord of hosts. Heaven and earth are full of your holy glory," analogous to the sanctification by the lofty angels.[94] After this, the priest says, "Holy, Holy, Holy is the Lord our God, who fashioned us, created us, and placed us in the paradise of comfort." At its end, he says, "who recompenses everyone according to his work," so everyone in the church cries out, "According to your mercy, O Lord, not according to our sins."[95]

Afterward, the priest says, "And he has left for us this great mystery."[96] Immediately at this moment, the priest inclines toward the oblation bread that is in the paten before stretching his hands over the [smoke] of the censer. Then he places his hands over the censer and turns them three times in the number of the Holy Trinity.[97] After this, he removes the cloth that is below the oblation bread and says, "He took bread in his pure hands, raised his eyes to heaven and said." At this time, he carries the oblation bread in his hands and says as Christ has said, "Take, eat, this is my body, which is sacrificed for you for the remission of your sins."[98] The people

---

Ṣalīb, ⲡⲓϫⲱⲙ ⲛ̀ⲧⲉ ⲡⲓⲉⲩⲭⲟⲗⲟⲅⲓⲟⲛ, 314–316. The Coptic text with a German translation is in Budde, *Die ägyptische Basilios-Anaphora*, 145. The corrected diaconal response reads, Οἱ καθήμενοι ἀνάστητε (*hoi kathēmenoi anastēte*). See Burmester, "The Greek Kīrugmata," 375.

94. The division of the dialogue before the *Sanctus* is different in the received text. The priest says, "You are he around whom stands the cherubim full of eyes and the seraphim of six wings praising continuously and unceasingly saying." The deacon says, "Let us attend." The people say, "The cherubim worship you and the seraphim glorify you, crying out and saying, Holy, Holy, Holy . . . etc." See Ṣalīb, ⲡⲓϫⲱⲙ ⲛ̀ⲧⲉ ⲡⲓⲉⲩⲭⲟⲗⲟⲅⲓⲟⲛ, 316–317; Budde, *Die ägyptische Basilios-Anaphora*, 145–147.

95. For the full text of the prayer of commemoration of the divine economy of the liturgy of Basil, see Ṣalīb, ⲡⲓϫⲱⲙ ⲛ̀ⲧⲉ ⲡⲓⲉⲩⲭⲟⲗⲟⲅⲓⲟⲛ, 324–329; Budde, *Die ägyptische Basilios-Anaphora*, 147–151.

96. Here begins a commentary on the prayers and actions accompanying the words of institution. See Ṣalīb, ⲡⲓϫⲱⲙ ⲛ̀ⲧⲉ ⲡⲓⲉⲩⲭⲟⲗⲟⲅⲓⲟⲛ, 329–337; Budde, *Die ägyptische Basilios-Anaphora*, 153–157.

97. That is, he is to place both hands over the smoke of the censer then move them over the oblation on the altar, repeating this action three times.

98. Matthew 26:26; Mark 14:22.

say, "We believe, we confess, and we glorify," that is, "We acknowledge and confirm and confess what you have said, O priest, in relating to us the Gospel narrative of Christ having taken the bread on his hands."

Afterward, the priest carries the chalice in his hands and says, "Likewise, after the supper, he mixed the chalice with wine and water and said, 'Drink from this, all of you. This is my blood of the new covenant, which is shed for all of you for the forgiveness of sins.'"[99] When he has uttered the word *shed*, he tilts the chalice to the right side as a sign of the shedding but does not disturb it as the other priests do.[100] Just like the first time, the people also say, "We believe, we confess, and we glorify."

Then the priest says, "Every time you eat of this bread and drink of this cup, you proclaim my death and preach my Resurrection until the time of my coming."[101] So, the people respond saying, "Your death, O Lord, we proclaim, and your holy Resurrection we preach, and your ascension we confess. We praise you, we bless you, we give thanks to you, and we entreat you, O Lord our God."

Moreover, the priest also recalls the crucifixion of Christ, his sufferings, his burial, his rising from among the dead, his ascension to heaven, his sitting at the right hand of the Father, and his second coming that is full of glory. At this time, the deacon commands the people and says to them, "Prostrate to God with fear and trembling!" Behold, my beloved one, the beauty of this rite full of grace, how when the priest recalled the second coming of Christ to judge the living and the dead, the deacon said, "Prostrate to God with fear and trembling." Behold, how he mentioned the prostration and the glorious coming, [the time] when he will come!

Then the priest says a silent prayer,[102] which is, "We ask you, we your unworthy servants, and we bow down before you and entreat you, so that your Holy Spirit may descend upon your people and upon these oblations to purify them and to make them holy [gifts] for your saints."[103] Behold,

99. Matthew 26:28; Mark 14:24.

100. That is, he is to tilt the chalice to the right while being cautious not to allow the contents of the chalice to be excessively shaken or spilled.

101. 1 Corinthians 11:25–26.

102. Here begins the *Epiclesis Prayer*, so called because in it the Holy Spirit is *called upon* (from the Greek ἐπικαλέω, *epikaleō*) to descend on the bread and wine and complete their consecration into the body and blood of Christ. See chapter 1, note 126.

103. The Arabic reads "*quds li-qiddīsīk*." The first word is a substantive meaning holiness, sacredness, or sanctity. The expression in part hearkens to the Old Testament's holy

O beloved brother, how the priest asks and entreats for the descent of the Holy Spirit of God (may he be exalted) upon his people before his descent upon the oblations, so that he would sanctify [the people], purify them, and make them into an abode well disposed to receive the oblations!

Then the deacon says as loudly as he can, "Attend, O people!" to be prepared to respond to the priest. Then the priest cries out and says, "This body becomes the body of our Lord, our God, and our Savior Jesus Christ," at which point the people say, "We believe that this is true, amen." Then the priest says, "And this cup becomes the blood of our Lord, our God, and our Savior Jesus Christ," so the people say, "The blood of Emmanuel our God, this is in truth, amen," and, "Lord have mercy," three times.

Then the priest says, "O our King, make us worthy of purity of soul and body. Remember, O Lord, the peace of your one and only, catholic and apostolic Church,"[104] so the deacon says, "Pray for the peace of the Church," and the people say, "Lord have mercy." One also ought to say, "O Lord, grant peace to your Church and accept the entreaty of your priest therein."

Then the priest says, "Remember, O Lord, the blessed head of your priests, Abba so-and-so" The deacon says, "Pray for our blessed father, the high priest, Abba so-and-so," so the people say, "Lord have mercy." One also ought to say, "Preserve, O Lord, over us and for our sake, the shepherding of our father Abba so-and-so, and hearken to the entreaty of your priest on his behalf."

Then the priest says, "Remember, O Lord, the priests, deacons, all the servants of the Church, and all your faithful people." The deacon says, "Pray for the priests, deacons, and all the seven orders of the Church," so the people say, "Lord have mercy." And they ought to say, "Preserve, O Lord, the servants of your Church and its priests, who intercede therein."

Then the priest says, "Remember, O Lord, the salvation of this holy place, and every place, and every monastery, and those who dwell therein." So, the deacon says, "Pray for this holy place, and every Orthodox place,

---

of holies, the innermost room of the Jewish temple. The common liturgical expression uses a neuter plural *qudsāt* derived from the Greek text, which has *hagia*, or holy things, in reference to the body and blood.

104. At this point, the commentary transitions to the post-epiclesis litanies, where Ibn Sabbā' once again inserts his own suggestions for the people's private devotion as seen in the Liturgy of the Word (see note 54). For the text of the litanies, see Ṣalīb, ⲡⲓϫⲱⲙ ⲛ̀ⲧⲉ ⲡⲓⲉⲩⲭⲟⲗⲟⲅⲓⲟⲛ, 343–352; Budde, *Die ägyptische Basilios-Anaphora*, 165–179.

every monastery, every city, and all who dwell in them," and the people say, "Lord have mercy." After "Lord have mercy," they ought to say, "Preserve them, O Lord, in the upright faith to the last breath."

Then the priest says, "Remember, O Lord, the seeds of the earth and its plants, its Nile, its fruits, and the fairness of its weather. Raise them according to their measure this year." The deacon says, "Pray for the seeds of the earth, its plants, its fruits, its Nile, and the fairness of its weather," so the people say, "Lord have mercy, Lord have mercy, Lord have mercy."[105] These three [utterances] from the mouth of the people are for the plants, the fruits, and the Nile, for each season [there is] one *Lord have mercy*. Another reason also is that these seasons of planting, the Nile, and the fruits are the cause of the vigor of the body, which perfects the soul, and reaches to its place.[106] Thus, for this reason they arranged for this crying out of *Lord have mercy* three times apart from all other litanies.

Then the priest says, "Remember, O Lord, these oblations and those who offer them to you, and those who have brought them. Give them their reward in the heavens." The deacon says, "Pray for these oblations and the offering," so the people say, "Lord have mercy." After Lord have mercy, the people ought to say, "Accept, O Lord, these oblations from those who have offered from their labor and increase your mercy upon them."

Then the priest says, "Remember, O Lord, all your saints, who have pleased you from the beginning, our holy fathers the patriarchs, the prophets, the apostles, the martyrs, the confessors, the preachers, the evangelists, and all who have been perfected in the orthodox faith. Rather, and most of all, [remember] the Lady the Virgin, full of glory, the mother of God, Saint Mary; and Saint John the Baptist, Saint Stephen, Saint Mark the Evangelist, our father Severus, Dioscorus, John Chrysostom, Saint Cyril, Saint Basil, and Saint Gregory; and our righteous father Antony the Great, our father Abba Macarius, Abba John, Abba Bishoi, and our Roman fathers Maximus and Dometius; and the forty-nine martyrs, Abba Moses, and John Kame; and our father Pachomius and our father Shenoute the leader of the solitaries (*ra's al-mutawaḥḥidīn*),[107] and all the ranks of

105. For the prayers on behalf of agricultural life in Egypt, see note 82.

106. *wa-ḥatta yaṣilu ilā maḥallihā*. The final word can mean place or location. The phrase is certainly ambiguous, but perhaps the author meant that water and produce ensure the body's growth to its proper stature or measure.

107. On P207, fol. 156v, above the Arabic title "head of the solitaries," the following appears in Coptic: ⲁⲣⲭⲏⲙⲁⲛⲑⲣⲓⲧⲏⲥ (*archēmanthritēs*) a corruption of the Greek

your saints." Then the deacon says at this point, "Let the readers say the names of our fathers the patriarchs. May the Lord repose their souls." Thereupon, the servants who have served the readings of the liturgy are to read the intercessory prayer for those who have reposed (*al-tarḥīm*), distributed among them in its entirety. The deacon says, "And all the orthodox fathers, who discern the word of truth, the bishops, the presbyters, the deacons, the laymen, and everyone. Pray for our fathers and brothers, the departed. May the Lord repose their souls."[108]

Then the priest beseeches and says, "Those whose souls you have taken, repose them in that place. And we too the strangers in this place, preserve us [having] faith in you unto the end in perpetuity." Then the people say, "May it endure and remain from generation to generation, forever and ever, and unto the age of the ages."[109] And this enduring and remaining is [said] here particularly of the faith that the priest has mentioned.

Then the priest says, "Guide us to your kingdom, so that through this also and in all their deeds we may be blessed with Jesus Christ your beloved Son, and the Holy Spirit."[110] Then the priest says, "Peace to you all," and the people respond to him, "And with your spirit."

Then the priest says and beseeches and gives thanks to God the Almighty, the Father of our Lord, our God, and our Savior Jesus Christ, "For he has made us worthy of the partaking of and preparation for his divine and immortal mysteries, the holy body and the precious blood of

---

ἀρχιμανδρίτης (*archimandritēs*, archimandrite). Strictly speaking, an archimandrite is the head of a monastic community (Gr. μάνδρα, *mandra*, literally a sheepfold). In the Copto-Arabic tradition, Shenoute became known as the head of the solitaries, a slightly inaccurate title, since he was an abbot of a communal (cenobitic) group of monasteries rather than a group of hermits as such.

108. Ibn Sabbāʿ here is quoting—in near perfect fidelity—the text of the respective prayer in the liturgy of Basil. For a discussion of the text of the commemoration of the saints of the liturgy of Basil, see Budde, *Die ägyptische Basilios-Anaphora*, 478–504.

109. This appears to be a paraphrasing of the anaphoral concluding doxology, whose Greek text more accurately translates to, "As it was, so it is and will be from generation to generation and to all the ages of ages, amen." See Ṣalīb, ⲡⲓϫⲱⲙ ⲛ̀ⲧⲉ ⲡⲓⲉⲩⲭⲟⲗⲟⲅⲓⲟⲛ, 382; Budde, *Die ägyptische Basilios-Anaphora*, 538–541.

110. The syntax of this sentence is unclear in the manuscript as well as in Vincentio Mistrīḥ's edition *Pretiosa margarita*, 255 (Arabic), 525 (Latin). The Coptic text of this prayer in the Euchologion reads, "So that as in this so also in all things your great and holy name may be glorified, blessed, and exalted in everything that is honored and blessed with Jesus Christ your beloved Son and the Holy Spirit."

his Christ." The deacon says, "Again, pray." Then the priest says the *Prayer of the Fraction*, which is the portioning of the body into parts, "O God, the begetter of light, author of life, who granted knowledge, the creator of light, the beneficent to the souls, the treasure of wisdom, the essence of purity, who accepts the pure prayers."[111]

At the conclusion of the *Prayer of the Fraction*, the people say, "Our Father who is in heaven," to its end. So, behold your stature at this time, O man! The only begotten Son is placed on the altar, while you are standing, saying to his Father who is in heaven, "Our Father who is in heaven." Know now that you have become a partaker with him in sonship, [first] in word and afterward in deed, seeing that you will receive him in your body, and his divinity will unite with your soul.[112] Behold this great stature, and do not despise it, and do not forsake your own soul and deny it this glory.

Afterward, the priest says, "Yea, O good Father, who loves goodness, do not lead us into temptation, and may transgressions not rule over us," so the deacon says to the people, "Bow your heads to the Lord in fear," and the people say, "Before you, O Lord," and everyone bows their heads.[113]

Then the priest says, "The grace of the beneficences of your only begotten Son, our Lord, our God, and our Savior Jesus Christ has overflown. We confess his salvific sufferings, we preach his death, and we believe in his holy Resurrection unto the perfection of the mystery. We give thanks

111. The *Prayer of the Fraction* (*Ṣalāt al-qismah*) is a prayer introducing the Our Father, which the celebrant recites while he manually divides the body. A large number of *Fraction Prayers* is found in the manuscripts. Such prayers form a distinct genre of euchological prayers that ultimately originated in the Syrian tradition. Each anaphora of the three of the Coptic Rite has its own *Fraction Prayer*, but many more are often found appended to Euchologion manuscripts and printed editions. Of these additional ones, some were written for specific seasons of the liturgical calendar, making the *Fraction Prayer* the only prayer of the celebrant with this seasonal quality. Recently, Ugo Zanetti has compiled an inventory of sixty-eight such prayers from a variety of sources. The particular prayer referenced here by Ibn Sabbāʿ is prayer Zanetti 13. Although it is not the prayer typically included in the Basil formulary in printed editions, it is widely attested in manuscripts of the northern Egyptian Coptic liturgy, the earliest of which is *BAV Vatican Copt. 17* (AD 1288). For Zanetti's inventory, see Zanetti, "Inventaire des prières de la fraction," 780. See also the Greek text in Geoffrey J. Cuming, *The Liturgy of St Mark*, 50, and the Coptic text in Ṣalīb, ⲡⲓϫⲱⲙ ⲛ̀ⲧⲉ ⲡⲓⲉⲩⲭⲟⲗⲟⲅⲓⲟⲛ, 723–725.

112. That is, the assembled people first declare their sonship to God in praying Our Father, then affirm this verbal declaration by their act of receiving the Eucharist.

113. For the text of the *Prayer After Our Father*, see Ṣalīb, ⲡⲓϫⲱⲙ ⲛ̀ⲧⲉ ⲡⲓⲉⲩⲭⲟⲗⲟⲅⲓⲟⲛ, 392–393.

to you, O Lord the Almighty."[114] The deacon says, "Attend with the fear of God." The priest says the absolution prayer with his face to the east as usual. But if there is a high priest on his throne,[115] he is to read it with his face to the west, as though drawing his people closer, so that they may be worthy to receive the holy body and the blood. At the end of the absolution prayer, the priest remembers those who have offered the oblation, and everyone who has asked him to remember him, each one by his name.

After this, he turns to the east with reverence and submission, and takes the part of the fractioned holy body, which is in the center of the oblation bread. He raises it upward, raising with it candles and the cross, and keeps it elevated for half an hour![116] Then the priest cries out as loudly as he can while it is raised, "This is the holy [gifts] for the saints!"[117] All the people of the church cry out with one mouth, "Lord have mercy," with their heads uncovered and their necks bowed if it is a Sunday. If it is [a day] other than Sunday, they are to be prostrate with their foreheads to the ground and without a head covering.

Then the priest alone says, while all the people are silent, "One is the holy Father, one is the holy Son, the Holy Spirit, amen."[118] This is the true consecration and it is a privilege of the priest at this time. For just as the deacon said this at the beginning of the liturgy and no one participated with him in it, likewise the priest says it at the end of the liturgy, and it is not for anyone to participate with him in it.

Then the priest makes the sign of the cross in the chalice with the [piece of the] body, which is the center of the oblation bread that was offered. When the piece has been dipped in the blood, and the blood has mingled with the flesh, he makes the sign of the cross with the blood upon the body

114. For the text of the *Prayer of Inclination* (*ṣalāt al-khuḍūʿ*), see ibid., 394–396.

115. That is, if a bishop were in attendance at the service but not himself celebrating, in which case he is to remain outside the sanctuary on the bishop's throne.

116. The expression is almost certainly an exaggeration, since no other known source—ancient or modern—attests to the literal practice indicated here.

117. For the call to communion and its response, see Robert F. Taft, *The Precommunion Rites*, 230–248. As written in note 103, the text employs the singular *quds*, whereas the standard liturgical text uses the plural *qudsāt*, holy things.

118. The text is given in Arabic transliteration of the original Greek as: *isbātīr ajiyūs īsīyūs ajiyūs ibnūmā ajiyun amīn*. For more information on this response, see note 29. In current practice, this response is proclaimed by the people in response to the priest's call to communion, the holies for the saints. See Brightman, *Liturgies Eastern and Western*, 184.

that is in the paten, so that the flesh may mingle with the blood. Thus, the body and the blood become one, and the priest says, "Blessed is the Lord God forever, amen."[119]

CHAPTER 84
CONCERNING HIS CONFESSION PROCLAIMED AT THE END OF THE LITURGY

[The priest says,] "The body and the blood of Jesus Christ our God," the people say, "Amen," that is, the truth. Then the priest says also, "The body and true blood of Jesus Christ our God." The people say, "Amen," that is, the truth. Then the priest says, "The holy body and precious blood of Emmanuel our God. This is in truth, amen." The people say, "We believe," that is, we confirm.[120]

Then the priest says, "I believe, I believe, I believe, and confess to the last breath that this is the life-giving body of your only begotten Son, our Lord, our God, and our Savior, Jesus Christ, which he took from the lady of us all the Mother of God the pure Saint Mary.[121] And he made it one with his divinity without confusion, or mingling, or change, since [he

119. Regarding the rite of commixture in the Byzantine liturgy, see Taft, *The Precommunion Rites*, 381–435. For a brief description of this ritual in Coptic practice, see Burmester, *The Egyptian or Coptic Church*, 75–77.

120. At this point, P208, fol. 119r abruptly concludes the chapters on the eucharistic liturgy with the following note: "This is what was found in the copy. They have abbreviated from it here the remainder of the chapters since they appear in the *Book of the Canon* and they are sixteen chapters in total." The designation the *Book of the Canon* is uncommon, though it appears to refer to the Euchologion.

121. Rather than include the text of the confession formula, the later manuscript CM15, fol. 94v has the following instead: "Then he says the confession completely with [. . .] and fear and weeping while the body is in his right palm and his other left palm under his right palm. When he says, 'he made it one with his divinity,' he is to take one of the thirds that are in his hand and recites the confession upon it. Then he places it in the paten and takes in its place from the paten [another third], over which he has said, 'He divided and gave to his disciples,' until there be in his hand another third of the honorable body. When the priest has finished the confession, and the deacon has said the petition for the forgiveness of the sins of the people of Christ, and the people have said 'A thousand years,' the priest is to cover the honorable body and the deacon covers the precious blood. That is, this body and blood are wrapped with pure grave cloths."

has][122] confessed the good confession before Pontius Pilate, and he gave it up for us upon the holy wood of the Cross by his will alone. I believe that his divinity did not separate from his humanity for one moment nor a twinkle of an eye. [There is] salvation, forgiveness of sins, and eternal life for those who partake of it. I believe, I believe, I believe that this is so in truth, amen."[123] The deacon says, "With the peace and love of Jesus Christ, chant, O chanters!"[124]

Afterward, the priest says, "This is that concerning which all glory, all honor, and all worship is due unto you, with the Son and the Holy Spirit, who is consubstantial with you, now and at all times, and unto the age of the ages, amen."

Thereafter, the priest covers the paten, while the deacon covers the chalice, that is, this body is shrouded with these grave cloths. Now, if the priest so chooses, he preaches to the people about that which they [will receive].[125]

122. The text in P207, fol. 159v clearly has the second-person *iʿtarafta,* "you have confessed." The text above was adjusted to match the pronouns in the remainder of the passage. The use of the second person is perhaps under influence of the text as it occurs in the Liturgy of Saint Gregory, which addresses Christ directly.

123. On the history of the confession formula of the precommunion rites, see Engberding, "Ein Problem in der Homologia," 145–154.

124. The current text of this diaconal command to the chanters reads in the nominative, "The peace and love of Jesus Christ [is] with you. Chant!" (Ἡ εἰρήνη καὶ ἀγάπη Ἰησοῦ Χριστοῦ μεθ' ὑμῶν. ψάλλατε). See Ṣalīb, ⲡⲓϫⲱⲙ ⲛ̀ⲧⲉ ⲡⲓⲉⲩⲭⲟⲗⲟⲅⲓⲟⲛ, 408–409. This is however not supported by the majority of early sources, which transmit the dative reading, "Chant with the peace and love of Jesus Christ with you." (Ἐν εἰρήνῃ καὶ ἀγάπῃ Ἰησοῦ Χριστοῦ μεθ' ὑμῶν ψάλλατε). See Brightman, *Liturgies Eastern and Western*, 185. Many sources transmitting the dative variant are contemporaneous with Ibn Sabbāʿ. See for example one of the earliest extant northern Egyptian Euchologia, *Oxford, Bodleian Hunt. 360* (13th c.), fol. 114v and the diaconal manuscript *BAV Vatican Copt. 28* (AD 1306), fol. 41v. This dative reading is also found in related traditions, such as the Melkite Alexandrian liturgy of Saint Mark in the manuscripts *Greek Orthodox Patriarchate of Alexandria 173/36, Pegas Manuscript* (AD 1586), the Greek text of the Coptic liturgy of Saint Basil preserved in *Paris, BnF Gr. 325* (14th c.), fol. 45v and the Greek liturgy of Saint James. See Cuming, *The Liturgy of St Mark*, 57; Eusèbe Renaudot, *Liturgiarum Orientalium Collectio*, 1:80; B. Charles Mercier, *La liturgie de Saint Jacques*, 232–233.

125. The reading of the final word is unclear in P207, fol. 160r, but could be reasonably assumed to be *yanālūnahu* (they receive it).

In the Name of the Father and the Son and the Holy Spirit, One God, Amen

A Homily on the Meaning of the Holy Oblation

He [David] said,[126] "Listen to this, all you nations, and hearken, all you inhabitants of the earth. My mouth speaks wisdom."[127] Know that you are the chosen and purchased people of God, the kingdom that is pure and the Church that was bought.[128] Its price was the honored and precious blood, which the Lord Christ shed in delivering you. Every one of you ought to listen to my wretchedness. Here I am, placing my sinful head beneath your pure feet, that you may be patient with regard to my weakness concerning what I am about to tell you, in which there is the salvation of my sinful soul and your righteous souls.

Listen, O my fathers, brothers, and children, to the one whom this holy place has contained; [this place] which resembles the heavenly Jerusalem, and in which we dwell as earthly angels and heavenly men. Listen to my weakness with a pure disposition and a soul longing to accept the seeds of instruction. Listen to what the blessed David, the great prophet, the joyous one among the prophets, has said. He said, "Praise the Lord, all you nations; bless him, all you peoples. For his mercy is abundant upon us, and the truth of the Lord endures forever."[129]

Know that it is incumbent upon my wretchedness to correct you by way of reminder as long as I am in this house, although you are adhering to the present truth. Nonetheless, I see it as an obligation and duty upon me to go to great lengths in instructing you and in interpreting the meaning of the books of God to you. For the hand of the priesthood [has been laid] upon me, and [I am] in fear of the word, which God (may he be exalted) has said to Ezekiel the prophet, "O son of man, I have made you a watchman for my people, to teach it the fear of God and to guard it. If one of

126. The text of this homily is entirely omitted from the manuscript P208. In CM15, fol. 94v–99v, the text of the homily has some minor additions and omissions compared to P207. For reasons of space, the text provided here is only that of P207, the principal manuscript used in this edition.

127. Psalm 48 (49):3.

128. Acts 20:28.

129. Psalm 116 (117):1–2. Ibn Sabbāʿ chooses to begin his homily on the Eucharist by commenting on the psalm proclaimed by the deacon during the prothesis rite while filling the chalice.

them perished in sin, I will require their blood from between your eyes. Warn the sinner to return from their sin. If they return, you and the sinner will be saved for the sake of you having instructed them, but if he does not return, you will save your soul, while the sinner will die in his sin."[130]

My wretchedness is now calling upon you, begging your piety, beseeching you, and exhorting your love, to stand firm first in repenting to God (may he be exalted) of all sins and filthiness, and in spiritual love for both the relative and the stranger, in not harboring malice, in forgiving the offender, in humility, by which man reaches to the level of perfection, in mercy upon the poor, according to the saying of the Lord—to him be the glory—"Blessed are the merciful for they shall obtain mercy,"[131] and in persisting in obtaining this jewel, which is to pardon when one is able.

Concerning the saying of David the prophet, the joyous one among the prophets, "Praise the Lord, all you nations,"[132] it is obligatory upon them to praise him, since he brought them into being out of nothing. "Bless him, all you people,"[133] for you are one of the peoples, whom God (may he be exalted) has chosen. Thus, it is requisite upon us and upon you to praise him, to glorify him, and to continuously bless him for what he has done for us out of his beneficences.

As for his saying, "The truth of the Lord endures forever,"[134] know that the truth of the Lord is this pure body and this precious and honorable blood. For he said from his own pure and holy mouth, "My body is food indeed, and my blood is drink indeed."[135] It is this truth that endures forever, which David, the joyous one among the prophets, meant. He who eats me will live for me.[136] "I am the bread that came down from heaven; if anyone eats of this bread, he will live forever."[137] David also said, "Taste and see that the Lord is good."[138] By this saying, David demonstrated that the Lord can both be seen and be tasted, delightful to the taste. And noth-

130. Ezekiel 3:17–21.
131. Matthew 5:7.
132. Psalm 116 (117):1.
133. Ibid.
134. Psalm 116 (117):2.
135. John 6:55.
136. John 6:57.
137. John 6:51.
138. Psalm 33 (34):9.

ing can be seen or tasted unless it is edible, according to the saying of Christ our Lord, "My body is food indeed, and my blood is drink indeed."[139]

Thus, if our Lord—to him be the glory—has permitted us to eat his body and to drink his blood as the means for binding our eternal life to him, why then do we refrain from eating his body and drinking his blood so that he would remain in us and we in him as he promised, and we would live for him? Know this, O children of the Christian Church, who are firm upon the rock of the upright faith in him, that whoever eats worthily of this bread, which has become flesh by means of my wretchedness, and drinks worthily of this chalice, which has become blood through the descent of the Holy Spirit upon it and through its change from the nature of wine to the essence of the blood of Christ, [that one] has become firm in Christ, and Christ in him.[140] He who has become firm in Christ, and in whom Christ has become firm, it is he whom the heavenly angels praise—the cherubim and the seraphim—and they give the hymn of victory over his enemy, just as they gave to Christ the Lord the hymn of victory over Satan our enemy, when he overpowered him and ruled over him.

Thus, if God has prepared this provision for us, why then are we found slothful and lax in receiving this life, occupying ourselves instead with ephemeral matters, which keep us from receiving it so that we may live an eternal life thereby?

Therefore, know, understand, incline your minds, and be confirmed in your souls that this oblation that is now placed on the holy of holies is the body of our Lord and his blood. [This is that which] was first in the manger, second on the Cross, third in the tomb, and fourth has ascended to heaven and seated on the throne of his glory.

Paul the apostle said, "Whoever eats the bread or drinks the cup of the Lord unworthily has sinned against the body of our Lord and his blood. That is why the sick have multiplied among you, and some have

139. John 6:55.

140. Here, the author appears to imply that the change of the eucharistic gifts to the body and blood of Christ takes place at a specific moment, namely, the descent of the Holy Spirit during the *Epiclesis Prayer*. Although a traditional eastern position, such specificity in identifying a single and unique moment of consecration is not always expressed in Coptic and eastern sources. On the topic of the moment of consecration in eastern thought, see Taft, *The Precommunion Rites*, 211, 214, 227–228; and more recently Michael Zheltov, "The Moment of Eucharistic Consecration," 263–306.

died suddenly."[141] Thus, let everyone examine and correct himself before he approaches this fearful table. Let him search himself. If he is prepared to approach it, let him come forward to receive eternal life. But if he knows within himself that he is neither worthy nor prepared, neither alert nor ready to approach it, let him not approach, lest he receive destruction for his soul and sentence himself to eternal death and everlasting hell.

For no one ought to approach this spiritual table and divine sacrifice, in whose heart is found deceit and cunning, nor one who hates his brother, nor one who is malevolent, a reviler, a robber, a fornicator, a drunkard, a slanderer, nor one who lies with men, nor one who persists in an abominable sin.[142] He who has known himself to abstain from what we have listed, let him approach this fearful table, but he who has taught himself [to abstain] from only some of what we have said, let him not approach, lest he destroy himself. My wretchedness is innocent of his sin. His transgression and blood are upon his head, and I am innocent of him. Christ is a witness against him of all that I have said to him. The righteous judge will judge between me and him on the day of judgment, for I have admonished him, instructed him, and placed the silver of my master upon the table, according to his word.[143] Whoever transgresses these words of mine and transgresses the instruction of my wretchedness, has the one who will judge him in the last day.

The oblation is noble and its rank is great for pure and righteous souls. Thus, the one who has purified himself from impurities let him now come to the sanctuary of the Lord and proceed to approach him. But the one who recognizes in himself an impurity, let him delay and not approach, lest he perish, while I am innocent of his sin.

Thus, my wretchedness has warned you with what is of benefit to your souls and the divesting of it of all impurities. May God aid my weakness to continue preaching and instructing you to understand and to do what you have heard with your ears, and may he aid you to obey according to [your] ability, so that you and I may be delivered from the dreadful place.

For my wretchedness has exhorted you with what is of benefit to your souls. By means of this preaching, I am [now] innocent of your sin and transgression, as Pontius Pilate was made innocent of the crucifixion of

141. 1 Corinthians 11:27, 30.
142. 1 Corinthians 6:9–10.
143. Luke 19:23.

Christ our Lord.[144] Thus, he who transgresses the preaching of my wretchedness, and dares to partake of this holy oblation, which is the body of our Lord Jesus Christ, with shamelessness, unworthiness, and unpreparedness, may he know that he is like one of those who crucified Christ our Lord, transgressing the orders of Pilate. Though hearing with his own ears Pilate's absolving of himself of the crucifixion of Christ our Lord, he went and convinced himself of his own opinion. What strange wonder it would be, if someone among you accepts upon himself this condition, and rather than receiving forgiveness for himself, becomes as one who has crucified Christ—may God forbid!

Therefore, understand, know, ascertain, confirm, assent, and believe, that Christ the Lord, the one who is present, is the lamb slain for the sins of the world for its salvation.[145] It is he who formed the two worlds, the heavenly and the earthly. It is he who is sacrificed, laid, and distributed through his compassion, mercy, and tenderness, in my hands, I the sinner and the one unworthy of the rank of the priesthood. His blood is shed in the mouths of his beloved ones who receive him. Let no one then approach him, except the one who has loved him and sacrificed himself in keeping his commandments, just as he [Christ] has sacrificed himself for his sin to deliver him therefrom.

Know that one of the saints exhausted himself in asceticism for a long period, and he asked God (may he be exalted) that he might partake of the holy oblation. Then, a great pillar of light appeared to him [stretching] from earth to heaven, and he heard a voice calling and saying, "If you know yourself to be like this pillar of light, come and partake of the holy oblation." It was also said concerning one of the saints, that when he partook of the holy oblation, he remained sixty years thereafter without spitting on the ground in reverence to it. Thus, everyone here, my beloved, ought to know himself and the measure of that which he approaches.

May God (may he be exalted) render you righteous and honest. May he write all your names in the book of life and make you as the fruitful tree that is planted by the streams of water[146] and hinder you from being heedless. May he seat you at his right hand on the day of judgment and include you among the band of the saintly fathers and honorable martyrs, amen.

144. Matthew 27:24.
145. John 1:29.
146. Psalm 1:3.

[Communion and Related Rites]

After this, the priest uncovers the body and partakes of it before anyone else, and likewise from the blood. Then, he administers communion to the metropolitan before the bishops, and the bishops according to their ranks.[147] To everyone whom he gives the oblation with his hand, he says, "This is the body of Emmanuel our God." So, the communicant makes the sign of the cross on his own mouth before partaking, that is, he has struck his enemy with this rod that is in his hand before partaking of the lamb of God, which he is commanded to eat. Then, he says, "I believe that this is in truth, amen." The same goes for the hegumens (*al-ighūmanusīyyīn*) and after them the presbyters according to their ranks.

But if the patriarch is not celebrating the liturgy, he ascends to the sanctuary after the fraction and says the absolution and confession to complete the liturgy. Then he communes, administers communion to whoever desires, washes his hands, and descends. As for the bishop, he may do all of this in his diocese. However, in someone else's diocese, whether the patriarch's or another bishop's, he is not to do so. Instead, he is to walk up to the altar after washing his hands in the sanctuary. Then he approaches and partakes of the oblation bread with the spoon and covers it, and likewise [he partakes of] the chalice and covers it also and descends. As for the hegumen (*al-ighūmanus*), he may hold the spoon with his hand so that the celebrant priest may place for him [a piece of] the oblation bread to commune, without he himself taking anything from the paten with the spoon.

As for the presbyter, it is for him to receive the oblation from the hand of the celebrant priest without handling any of the oblation with his hand if he assisted in the service. But once the first absolution prayer has been read and no presbyter had come,[148] but rather [a presbyter] came to the church after the absolution and wished to commune, let him do so below the sanctuary as a form of disciplining and chastisement for his absence. It is the same also for the deacon. If the deacon is not present for the first absolution prayer, he is not to participate in the service. As for the remain-

147. For the order of communion in Byzantine and other eastern sources, though not mentioning Ibn Sabbāʿ's *al-jawharah*, see Robert F. Taft, *The Communion, Thanksgiving, and Concluding Rites*, 94–96. The text seems to imply that the homilist and celebrant is the newly consecrated patriarch, since he is said to give communion to the metropolitans and bishops.

148. That is, after the *Absolution of the Servants*. See notes 48 and 51.

ing ranks, the celebrant priest is to place [the oblation] in their mouths with his hand, so that the distinguishing of the high priests in their [order of] vesting and also in their [manner of] communing may be made manifest.

And if the multitude in the church is large and in need of another additional chalice, the patriarch, the metropolitan, the bishop, the celebrant presbyter, and his partners the servants, who are bareheaded in the service in particular, are to approach to partake [of it].[149] After the bareheaded servants have received the precious body and blood, the patriarch—or whoever was serving from among the bishops or presbyters—is to proceed to consecrate the chalice that is needed to offer communion to the people, assisting the celebrant priest. At the time of consecrating it, he is to say *isbātīr ajiyūs* three times, that is, "One is the holy Father, one is the holy Son, one is the Holy Spirit, amen," while he removes [blood] from the consecrated chalice to the assisting chalice (*al-ka's al-musāʿid*), and from the assisting chalice to the consecrated chalice. Likewise, he is to place a *despotikon* in the chalice in the same manner as the chalice that was initially consecrated.[150]

And the reason for consecrating the chalice is that it is a practice introduced in addition to the original custom. That is, the chalice that was in the hand of Christ the Lord the night of his crucifixion was sufficient for twelve souls, but when the faithful increased by the Lord and became thousands and myriads in the one Church, they maintained the arrangement of having the serving priest and his partners in the service commune from the original chalice following that which was in the beginning, and afterward they would fill other chalices to be consecrated by the priest from the original chalice. These all become the blood of Christ and are distributed to the multitude of the crowd.

After this, the deacons and the subdeacons who served are to commune while they are below the sanctuary step, then the readers and afterward all the people. And when the priest turns around to the west to commune the people, two servants are to stand carrying a long veil under the paten from

149. It would seem that a distinction is being made here between higher clergy who are permitted to wear a variety of head coverings and so-called bareheaded servants, i.e., anyone of the rank of subdeacon and below. For more information on head coverings as part of clerical vestments in the Coptic tradition, see Mikhail, "And They Shall Stand Bareheaded," forthcoming.

150. For more information on the *despotikon*, see chapter 1, note 101. Compare to the similar instructions for providing additional chalices in chapter 1.

its four corners, lest anything fall from the communicant. Likewise, there is to be another deacon with him who is carrying the chalice with cloths for wiping. He is to wipe the mouth of everyone who communes and is not to come at all near the cloth of the chalice.[151]

Afterward, the head of the priests (*ra's al-kahanah*) alone is to say alleluia, and the archdeacon alone [says], "Praise God," then the chanters [say], ". . . in all his saints. Praise the Lord in the firmament of his power," to its end.[152] Then, in every season the chanters sing whatever is suitable to it, as the occasion demands.

After the people have finished receiving the oblation, the priest is to wipe and clean the paten and the chalice well. Then the deacon is to say, "Pray for the worthiness and the elevation of the heavenly and undefiled mystery."[153] Then the deacon says, "May the grace of our Lord, our God, and our Savior Jesus Christ be with you. Go in peace, and again, go in peace."[154] And the priest is to dismiss the people and is to read the blessing over them. He is to say after this, "O king of peace, grant us your peace. O God, forgive our sins."

151. This is noticeably different from current practice, in which communicants carry their own small veils to cover the mouth after receiving the body. No such cloth is used after receiving the blood. For the small communion cloths, or *lifāfah*, see Graf, *Verzeichnis*, 102. For the prohibition on wiping the mouth with a cloth after receiving the blood, see Burmester, *The Egyptian or Coptic Church*, 87.

152. Psalm 150 is the sole communion psalm throughout the liturgical year in the received Coptic tradition. It is often followed by a variety of other chants and hymns, many of recent composition, based on need and the duration of communion. The custom described here in which the priest and archdeacon begin the chanting of the psalm is unlike usual practice in which chanters execute the entirety of the psalm from the beginning.

153. The received text of this diaconal command is, "Pray for the worthy *partaking* of the pure, heavenly, holy mysteries" (προσεύξασθε ὑπὲρ τῆς ἀξίας μεταλήψεως ἀχράντων καὶ ἐπουρανίων τῶν ἁγίων μυστηρίων). The Greek μετάληψις (*metalēpsis*, partaking) is consistently mistaken for ἀνάληψις (*analēpsis*, ascension) in Arabic translations of the Coptic liturgy, which may explain the text given here. Alternatively, given the place of this command in the unfolding of the communion rites in this text, it is possible the elevation intended may be the removal of the mysteries and their return to the sanctuary. See Burmester, "The Greek Kīrugmata," 383.

154. The diaconal dismissal, "And again go in peace" (καὶ πάλιν πορεύεσθε ἐν εἰρήνῃ, *kai palin poreuesthe en eirēnē*), is found in the standard Euchologion of ʿAbd al-Masīḥ Ṣalīb despite its having fallen out of use in actual practice. See Ṣalīb, ⲡⲓϫⲱⲙ ⲛ̀ⲧⲉ ⲡⲓⲉⲩⲭⲟⲗⲟⲅⲓⲟⲛ, 435; Brightman, *Liturgies Eastern and Western*, 193; Burmester, "The Greek Kīrugmata," 384.

And after the priest has taken off the priestly vestment, the sacristan (*al-qayyim*) brings to him what has remained [of the bread] after elevating the lamb to distribute it to the people piece by piece. And anyone who receives a portion of the blessing, before consuming it he is to turn his face to the east and say, "O God, forgive the sins of the one who brought forth this oblation bread," so that there would be for that person both the entreaty of the priest individually and that of all the congregation generally.

Then the archdeacon is to command one of the servants of that day to close and lock the door of the sanctuary, so that no one may find a way to enter into it except at the time of the service. He is also to close the veil and close the doors of the temple (*iskīnā*), and they go in the peace of the Lord, amen. And the archdeacon is to command one of the servants to fold the priestly vestment and to remove the books and [he commands] the sacristans of the church to guard them, and they depart in peace.

After this, the head of the priests, the bishops, and the presbyters chant before the father the patriarch, while they follow him until he ascends to his cell.

CHAPTER

3

The Ritual Order

(AL-TARTĪB AL-ṬAQṢĪ)

By Pope Gabriel V (AD 1409–1427)

The Order of the Liturgy of Saint Basil In the name of God, the one in essence, the triune in persons and attributes

[Rites of Preparation and the Prothesis]

The order of the service of the liturgy of Saint Basil. The priest ought first to examine his thoughts and his condition, internally and externally, as was explained first in the service of prayer.[1] [He ought] not to be angry at or resentful of anyone. He is to search and inspect himself, lest someone might have something against him. For if the priest's heart and mind are not well disposed toward his people, and the people's minds [are not] well disposed toward him, God will not accept his entreaty for his people, nor their entreaties for him, and may God save us from this![2]

Then the priest begins to purify his body and wash his hands and feet. God said to the honorable prophet Moses, "Say to Aaron your brother to make a basin in the tabernacle and a copper vessel and fill it with water. Whoever desires to serve from among the sons of Levi, let him wash his hands and his feet before crossing to the tabernacle. And whoever does not

1. That is, in the previous chapter of the *Ritual Order* on the morning and evening prayers.

2. The same appears as the initial instructions at the beginning of the Liturgy of Saint Basil in ʿAbd al-Masīḥ Ṣalīb, ⲡⲓϫⲱⲙ ⲛ̀ⲧⲉ ⲡⲓⲉⲩⲭⲟⲗⲟⲅⲓⲟⲛ, 193–194.

do this, may this soul perish from among its people."[3] For this reason, our Lord—to him be the glory—established [this] for us, when he instituted for us the mystery of the service and gave us the bread and the wine. Thus, the fathers the apostles came forward and established this for us, and they placed a basin in the church for the washing of the hands and feet before ascending to the sanctuary.[4]

And afterward the priest begins. If he desires the pure service,[5] he proceeds first to inspect the oblation that he is about to offer, [to determine] whether it is of good quality. Likewise, the wine, as was said, is to be precious without blemish. And when the priest has chosen it, he is to place it on the left side of the altar where he stands. Then he proceeds to put on the garments of the priesthood and the vestment, as our good Savior—to him be the glory—has said. Its description is known; it is the silk robe, the white silken *ṭaylasān*, the stole (*baṭrashīn*), the girdle, the sleeves, and the white silken robe (*burnus*).[6]

[Excursus: On the Urgent Need for this Work]

You have previously informed me,[7] O my beloved brother—may God assist you with the spirit of his holiness—that when you go to certain parishes

3. Exodus 30:17–20.

4. On the tank or basin as an architectural feature of medieval Coptic churches and its use on the feast of the Theophany, see Alfred J. Butler, *The Ancient Coptic Churches of Egypt*, 2:346–349. According to the fifteenth-century Muslim historian al-Maqrīzī, the Copts used to celebrate the annual blessing of the water for the feast of the Theophany at the banks of the Nile. This custom was prohibited—most famously—by the Fatimid Caliph al-Ḥākim (AD 996–1021) during the Patriarchate of Zacharias (AD 1004–1032). This prohibition presumably gave rise to the use of the basin as an architectural feature in Coptic churches to be used also for the annual blessing of the water on Theophany. See Ayman Fu'ād Sayyid, *Al-mawāʿiẓ*, 4:1008; S. C. Malan, *A Short History of the Copts*, 89.

5. That is, if he is intent upon performing the service correctly and according to the appropriate rites.

6. For a discussion of the history of the vestments of the presbyter, see Ramez Mikhail, "Towards a History of Liturgical Vestments I," 55–70. For descriptions of these vestments, see the glossary in this volume.

7. Gabriel V digresses from following the unfolding of the eucharistic liturgy to give an account and explanation to his reader(s) concerning the pressing need for this *Ritual Order*. Briefly stated, the pope has been made aware of the chaotic nature of liturgical events in some places and the ignorance of many clergy of what he considers the basics of liturgical knowledge. Gabriel's *Tartīb* is given here as a remedy in the form of a standardized

you find new presbyters who do not know the rules of the order of the liturgy, nor the number of crosses that are signed upon the oblation and the wine. They know neither the order of baptism, nor the [service of] absolution of women. The majority of the presbyters, who have not served the liturgy, approach [communion] as though they have served.[8] They know neither the order of betrothal, nor the prayer of the lamp,[9] nor many other matters too lengthy to explain.

The majority of the laity do not know what is to be eaten in the fore-feasts[10] and the fasts, then they enter the bathhouses at inappropriate times, because they are not instructed in the known precepts that were handed down since the days of the patriarchs of the past.[11] The presbyters who are secure in position are negligent in their affairs and do not instruct

description of the most important liturgical services and how presbyters, deacons, and chanters can perform their roles correctly. It is curious that this excursus on the pressing need for this work appears only here in the chapter on the eucharistic liturgy and not—as one would expect—at the very beginning of the *Ritual Order*. In fact, this digression from the description of services is an expansion of the introduction to *The Guide to the Beginners and the Correction for the Laity*. For more information on this work, see the Introduction to this volume. This particular passage on the urgent need for liturgical guides appears only in the second oldest manuscript of *The Guide to the Beginners*, *Baramūs 9 Canons* (AD 1353), fol. 3r–39r. For the text of this later recension together with an inventory of all known manuscripts of this work (13th–19th c.), see Mīṣā'īl al-Baramūsī, "Dallāl al-mubtadi'īn," 117–169.

8. That is, they come forward to commune as though they have been in attendance and serving in that liturgy. The author implies that members of the clergy who were not present from the beginning in a given service are not to receive communion.

9. That is, the order of the sacrament of anointing the sick. For a brief description of the Coptic rite, see O. H. E. Burmester, *The Egyptian or Coptic Church*, 144–151. The early history and subsequent development of this ritual in the Byzantine tradition can be consulted in Paul Meyendorff, *The Anointing of the Sick*.

10. *Barūmānāt*, from the Greek παραμονή (*paramonē*) the day of preparation or eve before a feast. See Georg Graf, *Verzeichnis*, 19; G. W. H. Lampe, *A Patristic Greek Lexicon*, 1022.

11. Going to a public bath was a luxurious activity in late antique and medieval society. As such, certain canonical texts forbid going to the bath during fasts. Here, the author is echoing Canon 77 of the Arabic *Canons of Pseudo-Basil*, which forbids going to the bath and drinking wine during the forty-day fast and Wednesdays and Fridays. See Wilhelm Riedel, *Die Kirchenrechtsquellen*, 268. The canon was cited also—albeit erroneously as Canon 79—in the canonical collection of Ibn al-'Assāl. See Jirjis Fīlūthā'us 'Awaḍ, *Al-majmū' al-ṣafawī*, 1:176.

the newly consecrated so that they may follow the rules.[12] In the majority of parishes, fighting ensues on the part of deacons and priests because of rituals. I am thus in great distress because of this, for you judge a servant who does not belong to you and you lose yourself.[13]

I have been to the majority of churches and have found most of them in this condition, so I became sorely grieved. There are some priests whom one finds negligent in God's ministry during the service of the liturgy on account of their idle talk with people, in which there is no benefit. They incur judgment upon themselves because of this. If one were to see someone standing before an earthly king from among the kings of the earth, one would find them standing, pulling together their hands and feet, trembling, afraid, distinguished in their speech, lest they be reproved if they were negligent in this matter, though the king is not able [to do anything] more than to harm this dying body. How then can you not be afraid or tremble before the dignity of the King of kings and the Lord of lords, in whose hand is the authority of life and death and who is able to destroy both soul and body?[14] Thus, it is incumbent upon the priest or the deacon—when they are in the service of God—not to be negligent therein, lest the same happen to him as that which happened to Judas, who was negligent in the service of God such that the devil attacked him. Thus, the priest, when he is in God's service, ought not to turn to anyone even if he were to be stabbed by a knife. May God deliver us from this!

[The Rites of Preparation and the Prothesis—Continued]

Thus, the celebrant priest should examine himself and inspect his affairs, and after this he is to prepare himself and put on the priestly vestment. Then he greets his brothers the priests and asks them to assist him in entreating [the Lord]. He bows to the Lord before his holy sanctuary, and to his brothers the priests and the rest of the clergy. The manner of his ascending to and descending from the sanctuary is according to what was

12. That is, according to the author, elderly priests with many years of service, who feel too comfortable in their position, are negligent in instructing the newly ordained clergy in the proper performance of the rites.

13. That is, when members of the clergy criticize each other, they engage in judgment of the servants of God. Cf. the similar injunction in Romans, "Who are you to pass judgment on the servant of another?" (Mt 14:4).

14. Matthew 10:28.

explained in the order of prayer.[15] When he ascends to the altar, he kisses it with his mouth. The eastern lamp should be lit, and the two candles are to be lit.[16] Then he uncovers the table from the veil and places the vessels in front of him, untied from their band.[17] The deacon should ascend and stand across from him, and the priest is to begin with the prayer of the preparation, which is *O Lord who knows the hearts*, while they chant *Alleluia this is the day*, or another chant, whatever is appropriate for each season.[18] For all non-fasts, Sundays, and the fifty days, [they should chant] *This is the day*, but during the fast of the Nativity, on Sundays of the Great Fast, the fast of the disciples, and the fast of the Virgin [they should chant], *Alleluia for the thought of man*, and likewise on Wednesday and Friday throughout the year.[19] But during the days of the fast of the holy forty days and the three days of Jonah, they say, *Alleluia I enter into* [*the sanctuary of God*][20] and *Alleluia Remember.*[21]

And when he [the priest] has finished reading the prayer of preparation, and it is *O Lord who knows the hearts*, he reads until "so that I begin," and

15. In reference to the customary manner of ascending to the altar with the right foot first and descending from the altar with the left foot first.

16. See the identical instructions in Ṣalīb, ⲡⲓϫⲱⲙ ⲛ̀ⲧⲉ ⲡⲓⲉⲩⲭⲟⲗⲟⲅⲓⲟⲛ, 196–197. For the tradition of and requirement for the eastern lamp to be lit at all times, see chapter 1, note 14.

17. When not in use, the eucharistic vessels and associated cloths are gathered together in a large white sheet. The four corners of the sheet are tied together to form a sort of sack to carry all the necessary equipment. This sack is usually placed in the cavity of the altar or on top of it until the next liturgy.

18. For the *Prayer of the Preparation of the Altar*, see F. E. Brightman, *Liturgies Eastern and Western*, 144. For the text of this chant from Psalm 117 (118):24–26, identified in P98, fol. 47r as alleluia ⲫⲁⲓⲡⲉ (*phaipe*), see ibid., 216, and the appendix in this volume.

19. The chant identified in P98, fol. 47r as alleluia ⲫⲙⲉⲓ (*phmei*) refers to a chant from Psalm 75 (76):11. For the text, see ibid, 216–217, and the appendix.

20. The chant identified in P98, fol. 47v as alleluia ⲉⲓⲉ̀ⲓ ⲉ̀ϧⲟⲩⲛ (*eiei ekhoun*) refers to a chant from Psalms 42 (43):4 and 131 (132):1. For the text see ibid., 217, and the appendix.

21. The chant identified in P98, fol. 47v as alleluia ⲁⲣⲓⲫⲙⲉⲩⲓ (*ariphmeui*) refers to a chant from Psalm 131 (132):1–3, 7. For the text, see the appendix. This particular chant is no longer performed in current practice, but is attested in a number of medieval chant manuscripts, such as *Cairo, Coptic Patriarchate Lit. 73* (AD 1444), *Baramūs 6/278* (AD 1514), *Cairo, Coptic Patriarchate Lit. 117* (AD 1910), and other manuscripts of the *Tartīb al-bīʿah* genre published by Bishop Samuel of Shibīn al-Qanāṭir. See Samuel, *Tartīb al-bīʿah*, 1:17, 20, 22.

here the priest begins to wipe the vessels placed before him, and he places the paten in its place and the chalice in its place, after examining the chalice throne.[22] Then he places the spoon on top of the chalice throne and puts the veils in their places. All this is while he is reading the remainder of the *Prayer of Preparation*. When he has finished all this, he reads the prayer that is after the preparation, and it is *You O Lord have taught us* to its end.[23]

He kisses the altar and turns to the west to choose the lamb, which is the bread of the offering. He inspects this well to be a lamb of one year without blemish.[24] Then he takes the lamb after he has inspected it well and wipes its reverse side with a clean cloth, kisses it, and places it on the right side of the altar in a silk veil. He inspects the condition of the wine thoroughly by smelling it or lets one of those who are not fasting taste from it in their palm. For the wine, if it changes, becomes vinegar, but the oblation bread does not change from the nature of bread if, out of necessity, he does not find any other [bread].[25]

Then the priest washes his hands three times, while he says the first time, "Purge me with hyssop and I shall be clean."[26] The second time, [he says], "Wash me and I shall be whiter than snow, make me to hear joy and gladness,

22. This altar object is a box for housing the chalice during the eucharistic service. For a detailed description, please see the glossary. Not mentioned in the other medieval commentaries in this volume, one of the earliest textual witnesses to its existence is the thirteenth-century *Order of the Priesthood* or *Tartīb al-kahanūt* of Pseudo-Sāwīrus ibn al-Muqaffaʿ, where it receives no particular consecration, unlike other altar equipment. See Julius Assfalg, *Die Ordnung des Priestertums*, 15 (Arabic), 24 (German). It is also mentioned in the heading of a prayer of consecration in the manuscript *Cairo, Coptic Museum Lit. 253* (AD 1364), fol. 149r. This, and other evidence, has led Youhanna Youssef to suggest a very recent origin for this object. See Youssef, "The Ark/Tabernacle/Throne/Chalice-Stand," 251–259. However, iconographical evidence may in fact demonstrate the existence of chalice thrones much earlier. An eighth-century wall painting in the Red Monastery near Suhāj depicts an angel carrying a communion spoon and a chalice throne. See Dominique Bénazeth, "De l'autel au musée," 35, pl. 3.

23. For the *Prayer After the Preparation*, "You, O Lord, have taught us," see Brightman, *Liturgies Eastern and Western*, 144–145.

24. Exodus 12:15.

25. That is, the priest may offer a bread offering that is less than ideal in quality or condition if no other bread is available. On the other hand, a stricter attitude is necessary with respect to the wine, since it cannot be offered at all if it has soured.

26. Psalm 50 (51):7.

the bones of the humble shall rejoice."[27] The third time he says, "I wash my hands in the holies, and go about your altar O Lord, to hear the voice of your praise."[28] And if he has mastered reciting the psalm to its end, he shall say it. Then he dries his hands in a clean white linen veil only a little and takes the bread of offering and wipes it with his hands above and below, while saying, "Grant, O Lord, that our sacrifice may be acceptable before you, for my own sins and for the acts of ignorance of your people, and that it may be purified by the gift of your Holy Spirit, in Christ Jesus our Lord. This is he . . ."[29]

And if the offering is on behalf of someone living, dead, weak, traveling, or in tribulation, the priest is to remember their name also after this. If it were a living person, he says "Remember O Lord your servant so-and-so. Preserve him by the angel of peace and forgive him his sins." And if it were a reposed person, he says this Coptic [saying], as follows: "[Grant] repose and refreshment to the soul of your servant so-and-so. Repose him in the bosom [of Abraham, Isaac, and Jacob],"[30] and he completes it as usual. And if it is a weak person, he says, "Remember, O Lord your servant so-and-so. Preserve him by the angel of peace and heal him of all his sicknesses." And if it is a group, he says, "Preserve them with the angel of peace and heal them of all their sicknesses." And if it is a traveler by land or sea, he says, "Remember, O Lord, and return him to his own dwelling in peace and safety." And if it is a group, he says, "Remember, O Lord, and return them to their own dwelling in peace and safety." And if it is a group in tribulation, prison, or necessity, he says, "Remember, O Lord, and deliver them from all their tribulations." And if it is someone in tribulation, prison, or necessity, he says, "Remember, O Lord, and deliver him from all his tribula-

27. Psalm 50 (51):8.

28. Psalm 25 (26):6–7. The original text alternates between the Arabic and Coptic texts of the psalm verses in a way that presented exceptional translation challenges. The text provided here represents the most likely intended arrangement of these psalm verses.

29. Given in the text on fol. 48v–r in Coptic. For the text of this prayer in Coptic and Arabic, see Ṣalīb, ⲡⲓϫⲱⲙ ⲛ̀ⲧⲉ ⲡⲓⲉⲩⲭⲟⲗⲟⲅⲓⲟⲛ, 202–203. The full text of this concluding doxology of the prayer reads: "This is he through whom the glory, the honor, the dominion, and the worship are due unto you, with him and the Holy Spirit, the giver of life, who is of one essence with you, now and at all times, and unto the ages of all ages, amen."

30. The section in square brackets appears only in the Arabic translation of this line.

tions." If it is a man, he says, your male servant. If it is a woman, your female servant, and if it is a group, your servants.[31]

And when all of this has been accomplished, he wraps the lamb in a silk veil and lifts it above his head. And a deacon should stand in front of him carrying a candle. Likewise, the deacon lifts the vessel of wine above his head wrapped in a silk veil and in front of him a deacon should stand carrying a candle. And they go around the altar one time, while the priest says the following, "Glory and honor, honor and glory to the all-holy Trinity, the Father, the Son, and the Holy Spirit. Peace and edification of the one and only, holy, catholic, and apostolic Church of God, amen. Remember, O Lord, those who have offered to you these gifts, those on whose behalf they have been offered, and those through whom they have been offered. Give them all recompense from the heavens. Remember, O Lord, everyone who has asked us to remember them in our entreaties and prayers. May the Lord remember them in his heavenly kingdom."[32]

And when he has completed the circuit according to everything that has been explained, he stands in his place with his face to the east, while the deacon stands in his place with his face to the west.[33] The priest places the oblation on his left hand and signs it and the vessel of wine with a total of three crosses, while the deacon carries the vessel of wine with a silk cloth as explained. First, the priest, after bowing to his brethren the priests and saying to them "Bless," and after they respond to him [saying], "You bless," says, "In the name of the Father," in its entirety.[34] Then he makes the first sign saying, "Blessed be God the Father the Pantocrator, amen."

31. The text of all these commemorative formulas is provided in Coptic and Arabic. The meticulousness in providing exact formulas for each situation, even as far as providing alternate gender and number forms, is a function of the declining level of Coptic fluency, which by then in the early fifteenth century was certainly restricted to the liturgical context. The recitation of short prayers for various categories of people during the prothesis rite is a remnant of the ancient practice, in which the people provided donations including bread and wine upon entering the church. As these gifts were received by deacons, they recorded the names of the departed family members of the donors (see note 19 in the text of the *Lamp of Darkness*). Naturally, these commemorations came also to include other types, such as those who are sick, traveling, or in adversity.

32. Given in the text on fol. 50v–51r in Coptic and Arabic. For the text of this prayer, see Brightman, *Liturgies Eastern and Western*, 145.

33. On the position of the deacon in medieval Coptic sources, see chapter 1, note 68.

34. That is, in the name of the Father and the Son and the Holy Spirit, one God, amen. See Brightman, *Liturgies Eastern and Western*, 146.

[While making] the second sign, he says, "Blessed be his only begotten Son, Jesus Christ our Lord, amen." Then he makes the third sign and says, "Blessed be the Holy Spirit, the Paraclete, amen."[35]

Then he places the oblation bread in the paten with a silk cloth under it, while he says in full, "Glory and honor."[36] And the deacon pours the wine in the chalice, while he says, "Amen, one is the holy Father" until the end of "All nations."[37] He mixes the wine with a little water in a known ratio and completely empties the vessel of wine.[38] Then he wipes the tip of the vessel with a white cloth and removes it from the altar. After the chanting of *Glory to the Father*,[39] the priest says, "Peace to all" before [praying] the *Prayer of Thanksgiving*.[40] He turns to his brethren the priests and bows his head to them in submission; then he turns to the west and signs the people once. He recites the *Prayer of Thanksgiving* until "cast them away from us and from all your people," [at which point] he turns west and signs the people and turns to his brethren the priests while signing himself. [When he says] "and from this holy place that is yours," he turns east and signs the holy altar.[41]

When the reading of the *Prayer of Thanksgiving* has been completed, they chant, "May you be saved," in its melody.[42] Then he begins reading the

35. The wording of the blessings is given in both Coptic and Arabic in P98, fol. 51v–52r.

36. It would appear that the priest here is to repeat the same *Glory and honor* prayer that he already proclaimed at the procession around the altar. Manuscripts and printed editions however have the slightly shorter, "Glory and honor, honor and glory to the all-holy Trinity, the Father, the Son, and the Holy Spirit, both now and ever and unto the ages of the ages, amen." See Brightman, *Liturgies Eastern and Western*, 146.

37. Psalm 116 (117). For the diaconal role of pouring the wine in the chalice, widespread in late-antique and medieval sources, see chapter 1, note 38. On the accompanying Trinitarian response, see chapter 2, note 29.

38. On the ratio of water to wine, see chapter 1, note 39.

39. I.e. the congregation's chanting of "Glory to the Father and to the Son and to the Holy Spirit, both now and forever and unto the ages of the ages, amen." See Brightman, *Liturgies Eastern and Western*, 146.

40. Identified on fol. 52r by the Arabized Coptic term *al-shibihmūt*, from the first word of the prayer in Coptic (ⲙⲁⲣⲉⲛϣⲉⲡϩ̀ⲙⲟⲧ, *marenshep*^e*hmot*) "Let us give thanks." For the full text, see Brightman, *Liturgies Eastern and Western*, 147–148. For more on this prayer, see chapter 1, note 41.

41. Here, the author is describing in detail the number of crosses to be made while reciting the *Prayer of Thanksgiving*.

42. "May you be saved" is rendered on fol. 52r as ⲥⲱⲑⲓⲥ (*sōthis*). For more on this acclamation, see chapter 1, note 44.

Prayer of the Offering and it is, "O Master, Lord, Jesus Christ, the coeternal."[43] When he says, "Shine your face upon this bread," he points with his hands to the bread placed before him in the paten. [When he says] "and upon this chalice," he points with his hands to the chalice that is filled with wine. And when he says, "Bless them," he signs here upon the body and the blood with one sign [of the cross]. [When he says] "sanctify them," he signs a second time, and at "purify them and change them," he blesses them also a third time.[44] Thus, the signings upon the bread and the wine have been completed, six signings, three at first and three at this point.[45] Likewise, when he says the conclusion of this prayer, "So that this bread may become your holy body," he points to the bread, and then says, "and the mixture in this cup [may become] your honored blood," and points to the chalice.

Afterward, he completes the remainder of the prayer to its end. He covers the oblation bread in the paten with a cloth and likewise the chalice with a cloth. This is in the likeness of the shrouding of the body of the Savior when they brought him down from the cross and placed him in a tomb.[46] Afterward, he covers it with the *prospherin* veil, and it is in the likeness of the stone that they placed on the life-giving tomb, which overflows with life.[47]

The standing of the deacon opposite the priest, [is] in the likeness of the two angels, one of whom was at the head and the other at the feet, as are also the two lighted candles. When the priest has carefully covered [the altar] with the *prospherin* veil, he kisses it and goes to the southern side of the sanctuary. He makes a prostration to the east thanking God, who has

43. Identified on fol. 52r by the title *Prayer of the Offering* (*awshīyat al-taqdimah*), this is the *Prothesis Prayer* that concludes the preparation of the gifts. For more on this prayer, see chapter 1, note 42.

44. Here, the author is describing in detail the number of crosses to be made while reciting the *Prothesis Prayer.*

45. That is, the priest blesses the gifts three times in the beginning of the prothesis after going around the altar and three times at this point during the *Prothesis Prayer.* Descriptions of the number of crosses to be performed during the liturgy became a sort of common liturgical genre in medieval sources. For more information, see chapter 1, note 121.

46. See the similar remarks by Ibn Kabar in chapter 1, as well as the interplay between the altar as both tomb and manger discussed in chapter 2, note 28.

47. On the *prospherin* veil, a large veil that covers the eucharistic gifts on the altar, see chapter 1, note 43, as well as the glossary.

made him worthy of this pure service. Then he rises and kisses the altar and goes toward the northern side of the sanctuary. There, the celebrant deacon (*al-shammās al-khadīm*) makes a prostration to him, so the priest extends his hands, raises the deacon's head, and blesses him.[48] Both of them kiss the altar and descend from the sanctuary, each of them facing east and turning their backs to the west. Their descent is to be with the left foot and their ascent with the right.

The deacon then sits before the altar and likewise the rest of the servants, while the priest stands behind them and recites the absolution prayer. If there is with him an assisting priest (*kāhin sharīk*), the celebrant priest is to also sit, while the assistant is to recite the absolution. If it is the liturgy of Basil, they say the *Absolution to the Son*, "O Master Lord Jesus Christ, the only begotten Son and Word of God." But if it is the liturgies of Gregory and Cyril, they say the *Absolution to the Father*, and it is, "O Master Lord God the Pantocrator, the healer," until the end of the reading of the absolution prayer.[49] Then he says after it, "Your servants the servants of this day."[50] If a priest is seated before him, he is to say, "my father the presbyter." He says it after turning to his brethren the priests signing in the likeness of the cross over the one who is seated before him. But if more than one person is seated before him, he is to say, "my fathers the presbyters," signing over all the seated priests once. While signing over the celebrant deacon once, he says, "And the deacon." Then he says, "and the clergy," and he turns and signs the remaining servants and those standing in the choir once. After this, he says, "and all the people," and turns to the west, signing the entire people once. Then he says, "and my weakness," and signs himself once.[51] The total here is five signings, as well as one in the beginning and three in the middle of the *Prayer of Thanksgiving*, as was explained previously. Thus, the total [signings] on himself, on the people, on the servants, and on the place is nine signings. Then he completes the

48. The reference to a single deacon identified as the celebrant or serving deacon (*al-shammās al-khadīm*) is significant in highlighting the importance of the diaconate at that time. For a discussion of the deacon as a concelebrant in medieval Coptic witnesses, see Maged S. A. Mikhail, "The Deacon as Concelebrant," 101–123, esp. 109.

49. For the text of these absolution prayers, see Brightman, *Liturgies Eastern and Western*, 148–149, 183–184, respectively.

50. For the *Absolution of the Servants*, see ibid., 149.

51. Here the author is describing in detail the number of crosses to be made while reciting the *Absolution of the Servants*.

remainder of the prayer to its end. He is to kiss the head of the priest seated before him, and they all rise.

[The Liturgy of the Word]

Then the celebrant priest kisses the threshold of the entrance to the sanctuary and ascends to the altar to kiss it. If an assisting priest is with him, he takes the censer and hands it to him. But if no assisting priest is with him, the celebrant deacon hands it to him and he turns to the east.

Now, the celebrant is to raise the incense of the Pauline [epistle, using] five spoons [of incense] just like the order of the evening raising of incense, no more and no less. But he is to say the *Prayer of the Pauline Incense*, "O God the eternal and without beginning," in its entirety.[52] Likewise, when he has finished the prayer of incense just like the order of vespers, he follows the same order explained previously in his way of descending, giving incense to the priests and to others, covering the entire church, men and women, with incense, as well as in his return to the altar.

After "May you be saved," they chant either "You are the censer" or—if there is time—they sing *This censer* to the Virgin.[53] After it, [they chant] *We worship*, or they sing *We worship* [only].[54] One of the deacons intones the Pauline epistle in Coptic. After it, during its Arabic translation, the assisting priest prays *O Lord of knowledge*, but if there be no assisting priest, the celebrant is to say it himself.[55]

After the reading of the catholic epistle in Coptic and during its Arabic translation, the celebrant priest in particular says the silent prayer of the catholic epistle, "O Lord our God, who through your apostles."[56] After

52. See Brightman, *Liturgies Eastern and Western*, 150

53. On the chants accompanying the initial incensing, see chapter 1, note 50. For the texts of these chants, see the appendix.

54. The title on fol. 55r, in Coptic (ⲧⲉⲛⲟⲩⲱϣⲧ, *tenouōsht*) corresponds to the familiar formula, "We worship you, O Christ, with your good Father and the Holy Spirit, for you came and saved us." The author here allows for this short formula alone to be chanted in lieu of any of the hymns referenced previously for the censer.

55. The title on fol. 55r, is given in Coptic as ⲡⲟ̅ⲥ̅ ⲛ̀ⲧⲉ ϯⲅⲛⲱⲥⲓⲥ, (*pchois ᵉnte tignōsis*) and corresponds to the so-called *Mystery of the Pauline Incense*. See Brightman, *Liturgies Eastern and Western*, 153.

56. The title on fol. 55r, is given in Coptic as ⲡⲟ̅ⲥ̅ ⲡⲉⲛⲛⲟⲩϯ ⲫⲏⲉⲧⲉ ⲉⲃⲟⲗϩⲓⲧⲉⲛ ⲛⲉⲕⲁⲡⲟⲥⲧⲟⲗⲟⲥ (*pchois pennouti phēete ebolhiten nekapostolos*) and corresponds to the so-called *Mystery of the Catholic Reading*. See ibid., 154.

the conclusion of the silent prayer of the catholic epistle, they chant *There God lifts up* and after it, *Truly you are blessed*, or they say the latter alone.[57] Now, the celebrant priest ascends to the altar and raises one spoon of incense and says, "Glory and honor," entirely followed by "O God who accepted to himself the sacrifice of Abraham."[58]

The order followed in the three incense rounds is like the order of vespers, and likewise also in the offering of incense, but the priest is not to go around the entire church but only around the choir. When he has finished offering incense in the choir and has returned, he is not to ascend to the altar as in the evening and the Pauline incense, but he is to stand before the door of the sanctuary offering incense three times and saying, "O God who has accepted to himself the confession of the thief."[59] Just as he says it in the evening and morning prayers, likewise here also.

When he has finished this, he hangs the censer and makes a prostration to the altar, to the priests, and to the deacons. When they have finished reading the Acts in Coptic and Arabic, they chant the three *Holies*.[60] and the priest says the *Prayer of the Gospel* to its end.[61] Then the psalm of the liturgy is chanted and responded to. The priest ascends to the altar and raises incense one time, while saying *Glory and honor* in its entirety. The rite of the incense here, the psalm, the procession of the Gospel, the offering of incense before and after, what the priest says in doing so, the veneration of the Gospel by the priests, all of this was written in the [section]

57. The title on fol. 55r is given in Coptic as ⲭⲉⲣⲉ [*sic*] ⲫϯ ⲱⲗⲓ ⲙ̀ⲙⲁⲩ (*chere phnouti ōli ᵉmmau*) and corresponds to a chant performed today only on weekday liturgies during the Lenten fast. For the text, see Albair Jamāl Mīkhā'īl, *Al-asās fī khidmat al-shammās*, 405, and the appendix for a translation. All chants at this point—before the reading from the Acts—are concluded with the familiar formula, "Truly you are blessed with your good Father and the Holy Spirit for you came and saved us," indicated here by the title ⲕⲥⲙⲁⲣⲱⲟⲩⲧ ⲁⲗⲓⲑⲟⲥ (*ksmarōout alithos*).

58. The title of the prayer on fol. 55r ⲫϯ ⲫⲏⲉⲧⲁϥϣⲟⲡ ⲉⲣⲟϥ ⲙ̀ⲡⲓϭⲗⲓⲗ ⲛ̀ⲧⲉ ⲁⲃⲣⲁⲁⲙ (*phnouti phēetafshop erof ᵉmpichlil ᵉnte abraam*) corresponds to the *Prayer of the Incense of the Acts* (*Awshīyat bakhūr al-ibraksīs*). See Brightman, *Liturgies Eastern and Western*, 154.

59. On the practice of confessing over the censer during the Liturgy of the Word, see chapter 1, note 112.

60. That is, the Trisagion, referenced here as *ajyūs al-talatah*. On the Trisagion chant and related bibliography, see chapter 1, note 56.

61. On the *Litany of the Gospel*, see Brightman, *Liturgies Eastern and Western*, 219, and chapter 1, note 59.

on the recitation of the psalm and the Gospel in the evening prayer.[62] But during the Arabic translation of the Gospel, the consecrating [priest], that is, the celebrant priest, says, *O compassionate one.*[63] If however he has an assisting priest (*sharīk*), [this prayer] is entirely given to him. When it has been finished, the celebrant priest in particular is to recite the *Prayer of the Veil* to its end, which he says while standing before the veil, namely, *O God, who because of your love for mankind.* When he has finished it, he makes a prostration before the sanctuary.[64]

[The Liturgy of the Word: Commentary]

But as for the seven rounds of incense that the priest makes at the time of the liturgy, they are the sign of the seven processions, which the people of Israel performed around Jericho, when God caused its walls to fall at the hands of Joshua the Son of Nun, the disciple of Moses the prophet.[65] These are the three rounds of incense: When he ascends to the altar at the time

62. The author eschews a detailed explanation of the rites surrounding the reading of the Gospel during the Liturgy of the Word, since he has already done so in the previous chapter on the rites of the morning and evening prayers. There, he describes the rites of the Gospel reading thus: The priest takes the censer and prays the *Prayer of the Gospel*, after which a chanter—or more—chant the psalm verse(s) appointed in the lectionary. At the third line of the psalm, the priest censes the Gospel saying, "Worship the Gospel of Jesus Christ. Through the prayers of the chanter David the prophet, O Lord grant us the forgiveness of our sins." At the fourth line of the psalm, the priest ascends to the altar, followed by the deacon carrying the Gospel book. Together with other deacons carrying candles, they all perform a procession around the altar with the Gospel book, during which the chanters intone other psalm verses appointed for the procession, termed *al-ṭawwāf* (from *yaṭūf*, to go around; see chapter 2, note 76). After the procession, the priest descends from the sanctuary and censes the Gospel once again, saying, "Worship the Gospel of Jesus Christ the Son of the living God, glory be to him forever." Then the priest takes the Gospel book and all the present clergy come forward to venerate it. This is followed by the reading of the Gospel by the deacon either from the lectern or the ambo, preceded still by the priest continuing to give incense and introducing the Gospel saying, "Blessed is he who comes in the name of the Lord." The reading of the Gospel in Coptic is then followed by its translation in Arabic. See ʿAbdallah, *L'ordinamento*, 164–165 (Arabic), 356–357 (Italian).

63. The incipit on fol. 56r ⲡⲓⲣⲉϥϣⲟⲩⲛ̀ϩⲏⲧ (*pirefōouᵉnhēt*) corresponds to the *Mystery of the Gospel* (*Sirr al-injīl*). See Brightman, *Liturgies Eastern and Western*, 157–158.

64. For *The Prayer of the Veil*, see chapter 1, note 64.

65. Joshua 6:1–5.

of the Pauline epistle when the incense is placed, and when he descends and goes around with the incense to the people. Afterward, he ascends to the altar and goes around the altar once on account of the confession of the people. At the time of the reading from Acts, he ascends to the sanctuary and places the incense according to the established pattern, and he circles three times. This then is the completion of the seven circuits.[66] The fathers have established them in this manner to tear down the power of the enemy and the wall of sin.

He no longer ascends to the sanctuary with the incense, for he has accomplished the seven rounds. But as for the incense procession with the Gospel, it is for the chanters who have prepared themselves for service in order to alert the people to listen to the reading of the pure Gospel and in honor of it. For Moses the prophet commanded the sons of Levi to alert the people to prepare themselves for the hearing of the law.[67] So, this [procession] is in addition to the seven circuits, and whoever adds to this shall become like the sons of Korah, who entered the altar with foreign fire.[68]

As for the chanting of the Trisagion, it is to be after the reading of the narratives of the fathers on account of completing their preaching and perfecting what they have established. Thus, the fathers have arranged for the reading of the holy Gospel to follow them[69] [as a symbol] of the completion of their preaching and the perfection of the faith, for they wrote it after they came to believe and began preaching. But regarding the incense at the time of reading the holy Gospel, it is reserved only for the [reading of] the New Testament and not the Old, for the former is the perfection. It is adhered to—just as they used to adhere to the Torah—and in it is found the injunctions and the interdictions (*al-amr wa-l-nahy*).[70] As for

66. The common manner of counting these seven circuits takes into account only the incensing at the Pauline epistle as follows: three times around the altar, three around the nave, and one final time around the altar. Here, Gabriel V seems to be including both rounds of incense (during the Pauline and the Acts respectively) for this total of seven in the following division: three rounds during the Pauline incense, once after around the altar, and another three times during the Acts incense.

67. Deuteronomy 31:9–10.

68. Numbers 16:1–20.

69. That is, to follow the reading of the epistles and Acts.

70. The verbal expression *al-amr wa-l-nahy* is reminiscent of the Islamic expression "commanding right and forbidding wrong (*al-amr bi-l-ma'rūf wa-l-nahy 'an al-munkar*)." The expression refers to the duty to enforce the moral code, appearing in the Qur'ān as a

his going around the altar, it is like when the fathers the apostles went out with it [the Gospel] to the four corners of the inhabited world.

As for his saying, "Stand up with the fear of God and listen to the Gospel of God,"[71] it is incumbent upon everyone to stand, and not to walk or speak, or occupy their minds with anything, for the sake of listening to the words of God. They are to listen carefully, bowing, submitting, bending their heads toward the ground in fear and trembling, in awe and reverence to the recitation of the words of the Gospel. No one from the congregation ought to speak, nor occupy himself with a prayer,[72] nor walk from place to place. If anyone walks through the doors of the church [during] the reading of the Gospel, he is to stop and not walk in until the one who is reading it has finished. For the reader has enjoined standing, remaining silent, and listening to what is said.

It was the same for the people of Israel when [the Scripture] was read to them. They would bow their heads so as not to look at it or at the light on the face of Moses.[73] For at the time of reading the law, he used to remove the veil that was on his face and they all would bow with their heads so as not to gaze upon his face. For anyone who would behold his face would die on account of the light of the Lord that was upon him. No one would read the law except the priest or the prophet. Thus, our fathers have appointed that no one would read the Gospel except the priest. This is so even now among all the sects: It is not to be read except by the priest.[74] So, when it has been appointed now that the deacon is to read it, the priest

collective duty of the community in Sūrah 3. See M. Cook, "Al-Nahy ʿan al-Munkar," *EI²*, 12:644–646.

71. See O. H. E. Burmester, "The Greek Kīrugmata," 372.

72. Interestingly, at least one manuscript preserves a series of individual prayers in Coptic and Arabic for private use *during* key moments in the service. A book of prayers now preserved as *Monastery of the Syrians Lit. 383* (AD 1255) copied in Cairo by the future pope Gabriel III (AD 1268–1271) contains a series of such prayers for private devotional use during the reading of the Gospel, the Creed, the kiss, the anaphoral prayer, the epiclesis, the commemoration of the departed, and the recitation of the Our Father. The series of prayers is not part of the received tradition but may witness to a pious tradition among the laity. The text of these prayers remains unpublished and in need of further investigation.

73. Exodus 34:29–35.

74. This is clearly in contradiction to the information provided by Ibn Kabar on the variety of traditions concerning who had the privilege of reading the Gospel in different regions of Egypt.

began to observe the custom of standing with his face to the west, differing from all the people, so that everyone might bow their heads so as not to look at the priest at this time, and [so that they might] submit to the Gospel. For this reason, the priest ought to stand and not walk or speak or seek [anything]. For whoever speaks will become like Dathan and Abiram when they resisted Moses, sought after the work of the priesthood, and resisted Aaron and his sons. They distracted the minds of the people from listening to the words of God [spoken] to Moses and Aaron. They used to talk among the people and cause their hearts to be hardened toward Moses and Aaron. They were ashamed from Moses or from God or from the law which they used to read. So, God commanded the earth and it opened its mouth and swallowed them up, they and their children and cattle, and God requited them thereby.[75] For this reason, our fathers commanded us that no one ought to speak during the liturgy nor during prayer. But we are to bow our heads to the earth and listen attentively to the Gospel. When the reader says, "Stand and listen," the priest ought not to speak or move, and likewise the people.

[The Liturgy of the Eucharist]

Afterward, they kiss the Gospel on account of their acceptance of God's words. After the Arabic translation of the Gospel, they respond to it according to the custom until [they say] *For blessed*,[76] and they say, "May you be saved, amen, and with your spirit."[77]

Then the priest begins praying the *Three Great Prayers*.[78] As soon as he says, "Peace to all," he turns to his brethren the priests and bows his head to them. Then he turns west and signs the people once in the likeness of the cross. Thus far, there have been ten blessings. When he says in the *Prayer*

75. Numbers 16:32.

76. This is a reference to the *Gospel Response* (*maradd al-injīl*), a hymn that follows the reading of the Gospel in the services of evening, morning, and the liturgy. See chapter 1, note 63. The concluding verse referenced here is "Blessed is the Father and the Son and the Holy Spirit, the perfect Trinity. We worship him and glorify him." See Mīkhā'īl, *Al-asās fī khidmat al-shammās*, 100.

77. The title on fol. 58v is ⲥⲱⲑⲓⲥ ⲁⲙⲏⲛ ⲕⲉ ⲧⲟ ⲡ̅ⲛ̅ⲁ̅ⲧⲓ ⲥⲱⲟⲩ (*sōthis amēn ke to pneumati sōou*) corresponding to the acclamation σωθείης ἀμήν (*sōtheiēs amen*). See chapter 1, notes 44 and 65.

78. See Brightman, *Liturgies Eastern and Western*, 160–161.

for the Patriarch, "Accept them to yourself upon your altar," he raises here one spoon of incense. This shall be sufficient until the end of the liturgy, and if there is an assisting priest (*sharīk*) with him, it shall be for him [to do so]. When he says the *Prayer for the Assembly*, and it begins with, "Our assemblies," he also signs the people once after bowing to his brethren the priests. Thus, the total blessings have reached eleven. After this, he takes the censer in his hand and gives incense to the altar three times. When he says, "Arise O Lord God," and when he says, "As for your people," he turns west and gives incense three times to the priests, the deacons, and the people.[79] Then he turns again to the east and gives incense three times until the end of "This is he,"[80] when he gives incense to his brother the priest and hands him the censer. But if initially the assisting priest had given him the censer, the celebrant is to give him incense then.[81]

And when they recite the Creed, the priest is to wash his hands in the northern side of the altar three times.[82] Then he turns west and shakes his hands before all the people, meaning that he is warning them to take heed to themselves before receiving communion. That is, he is not to be held accountable on behalf of anyone who dares to receive the body and blood of Christ unworthily, for this person will befall him what befell Judas Iscariot when he received the body and blood of Christ unworthily. The devil attacked him and dwelled in him until he sold out his teacher

79. The Coptic titles given for these prayers on fol. 59r read ⲧⲱⲛⲕ ⲡⲟ̅ⲥ̅ ⲫ︦ⲧ︦ (*tōnk pchois phnouti*) and ⲡⲉⲕⲗⲁⲟⲥ ⲇⲉ ⲙⲁⲣⲉϥ (*peklaos de maref*) respectively, corresponding to the following lines in the *Three Great Litanies*, "Arise, O Lord God. May all your enemies be scattered. May everyone who hates your holy name flee from your face. As for your people, may they become with the blessing thousands of thousands and myriads of myriads doing your will [Ps 67 (68):1]." See ibid., 288–289.

80. That is, when he pronounces the concluding doxology of the litany, "This is he through whom the glory, the honor, the dominion, and the worship are due unto you, with him and the Holy Spirit, the giver of life, who is of one essence with you, now and at all times, and unto the age of all ages, amen."

81. That is, the celebrant who is praying the litanies is to swing the censer in the direction of the assisting priest, honoring him. He is to do so at the conclusion of the litanies, or, if he initially received the censer from the assisting priest to begin with, he should have performed this honorific swinging of the censer at that point.

82. The handwashing is a standard ritual action in preparation for the eucharistic liturgy. On the Creed and the washing of hands in the pre-anaphoral rites, see the references in chapter 1, notes 72 and 74.

and turned him over to the cursed Jews who crucified him. May God protect us from temptations. Then the priest dries [his hands] in a clean cloth.

When they have finished reciting the Creed, the priest says, "Peace to all," and he turns west, blessing the people once after bowing to the priests. Thus far, the total blessings have reached twelve. Then he prays the *Prayer of Reconciliation* to its end.[83] When the deacon says, "Greet," the priests kiss one another and the deacons one another.[84] This is a likeness of the reconciliation that God brought about between the heavenly and the earthly. For the apostle says, "He came to reconcile the heavenly and the earthly."[85] Thus, whoever might have something against his brother, whether major or minor, should forgive him at this time and kiss him. And his act of kissing him is not to be with deceit, corruption, or malice, thus [causing him to] become like Judas, who kissed the Master with deceit, corruption, and malice. When they have forgiven and kissed each other with love and a clear conscience, they become partakers with the angels in [offering] the sanctification, which is, "Holy, Holy, Holy, Lord of Sabaoth. Heaven and earth are full of your holy glory."[86]

Once the chanting has finished at the time of the reconciliation, the deacon says "Offer!"[87] When the priest says, "Lift up your hearts," he turns east and blesses the servants once, and when he says, "Let us thank the Lord," he blesses himself once. Then he turns to the east and says, "Worthy and right," three times.[88] When they say, "Holy, Holy, Holy," he

83. The *Prayer of Reconciliation* is a priestly prayer recited before the ritual exchange of the kiss. On this prayer, see chapter 1, note 75.

84. The title of the deacon's command on fol. 59v reads ⲁⲣⲓⲏⲁⲥⲡⲁⲍⲉⲥⲑⲉ (*ariēaspazesthe*) likely corresponding to the Greek diaconal command "Greet one another with a holy kiss," the first word of which is more accurately rendered ἀσπάσασθε (*aspasasthe*). See Burmester, "The Greek Kīrugmata," 374. The Coptic prefix ⲁⲣⲓ is likely due to confusion with an optional congregational chant said at this time and similarly titled ⲁⲣⲓⲁⲥⲡⲁⲍⲉⲥⲑⲉ (*ariaspazesthe*). See Ṣalīb, ⲡⲓϫⲱⲙ ⲛ̀ⲧⲉ ⲡⲓⲉⲩⲭⲟⲗⲟⲅⲓⲟⲛ, 305–306 as well as chapter 1, notes 75 and 77.

85. Colossians 1:20.

86. Isaiah 6:3. The author seems to be paraphrasing from the optional *asbasmus* chant "O Christ our Savior," which similarly integrates the theme of the kiss with the *Sanctus*. For the text of this chant, see the appendix.

87. For a discussion of this diaconal response and related literature, see chapter 1, note 5.

88. The dialogue before the anaphora is given on fol. 60r in Greek. For the corrected Greek text, see Burmester, "The Greek Kīrugmata," 375. See also the literature cited in chapter 2, note 92.

also makes the sign of the cross three times, the first upon himself, the second over the serving deacons, and the third over the people. Thus, they amount to six blessings on himself, the servants, and the people, for a total of eighteen.

Henceforth, the priest recites the liturgy until he says, "According to your mercy, O Lord."[89] The celebrant deacon (*al-shammās al-khadīm*) presents the censer to the celebrant priest,[90] who places his hands three times over the censer that contains the incense to prepare himself to handle that which is placed before him and to carry it in his hands.

When he says, "And he established for us this great mystery of godliness," he points with his hands to the bread and the wine placed before him.[91] And when he says, "He took bread," he takes the oblation bread on his hands, lifts the silk cloth that is in the paten, kisses it, places it on his eyes, then leaves it on the altar. When he says, "He looked up to heaven," he raises his gaze upward. When he says, "When he has given thanks," he signs the oblation bread once. Then he says, "He blessed it," and signs the oblation bread once, and when he says, "He sanctified it," he signs the oblation bread once. So far, there have been a total of three blessings.

And when he says, "He broke it," he gently divides the oblation bread into two thirds and another third without separating them from one another and without touching the *despotikon*, being extremely cautious lest it break or lest something should fall from it.[92] And when he says, "Which is broken for you," he gently breaks the top of the oblation bread only a little without separation and places the oblation in the paten. Then he cleans his hands inside the paten for fear that something might have clung to them from the oblation.

89. The Coptic phrase on fol. 60v reads ⲕⲁⲧⲁ ⲧⲟ ⲉⲗⲉⲟⲥ ⲥⲟⲩ ⲕ̅ⲉ̅ (*kata to eleos sou kyrie*), which corresponds to the congregational response "According to your mercy, O Lord, and not according to our sins," said immediately before the words of institution in the liturgies of Basil and Gregory. The corrected Greek text is κατὰ τὸ ἔλεός σου Κύριε, καὶ μὴ κατὰ τὰς ἁμαρτίας ἡμῶν (*kata to eleos sou kyrie, kai mē kata tas hamartias hēmōn*). See Burmester, "The Greek Kīrugmata," 377. For more information on this response, see Achim Budde, *Die ägyptische Basilios-Anaphora*, 307–309.

90. See note 48.

91. Here begins the commentary on the words of institution, with a particular focus on the hand gestures and blessings performed by the celebrant.

92. The *despotikon* is the central square portion of the eucharistic bread. For more information, refer to chapter 1, note 101.

When he has said, "Likewise also the chalice," he holds it in his fingers until he has said also [the same words] as before.[93] He blesses the chalice three times: [Once, when he says] "When he has given thanks," once [when he says], "He blessed it," once [when he says], "He sanctified it." The priest blesses a total of three blessings. After the blessings, he holds it in his hand until he says, "Take, drink of it all of you." He gently tilts the chalice in the likeness of the cross without shaking [the chalice]. When he says, "For this is my blood," he also points with his hands to the chalice. After this, when he says, "For every time you eat of this bread," he points with his hands to the oblation. When he says, "And drink of this chalice," he points with his hands to the chalice.

When the deacon says, "Worship God," the people prostrate themselves. Then the priest says the prayer of the mystery of the descent of the Holy Spirit to transform the bread that is placed [on the altar] to become the body of Christ and the wine the blood of Christ.[94] This [prayer] is, "And we ask you, O Lord our God," and it ends with, "of your saints," [when] the priest points to himself, to the bread, and to the wine.[95] For when the priest utters this great mystery, the Holy Spirit descends to purify the priest and all the people in the church of all their sins, if they persevere henceforth in purity and pure repentance. The bread that is placed [on the altar] also changes and becomes the body of Christ, and the wine the blood of Christ.

And when the priest cries out after this great mystery and says, "And this bread," he signs at this word in particular three blessings upon the oblation before he says, "becomes your holy body." For as soon as he has said, "becomes," the body of Christ is perfected, [the body] which he has taken from the Virgin Mary, which is given to his pure disciples, through which he accepted the life-giving sufferings, was shrouded, buried, rose from the dead, and with which he ascended to the heights of the heavens. With it he also comes to judge the living and the dead.

93. That is, when he has repeated the same verbs pronounced earlier over the bread, "When he had given thanks, he blessed, and he sanctified it." See Brightman, *Liturgies Eastern and Western*, 177.

94. That is, the *epiclesis prayer*. For more information, see the references in chapter 2, note 140.

95. For the text of the *epiclesis prayer* of the Liturgy of Basil, see Ṣalīb, ⲡⲓϫⲱⲙ ⲛ̀ⲧⲉ ⲡⲓⲉⲩⲭⲟⲗⲟⲅⲓⲟⲛ, 339–340, and the discussion in Budde, *Die ägyptische Basilios-Anaphora*, 378–430.

And when he says, "Our Lord, our God, our Savior" to its end, his hands are to be lifted up before the pure body, bowing with his head to Christ, along with the people. When he says, "This chalice also," he signs also over the chalice at this word three times, before saying, "the honored blood of your new covenant." For as soon as he has said "the honored blood," the wine placed before him becomes the blood of Christ that is shed on the wood of the Cross, [the blood] which he gave to his pure disciples and said, "This is my blood that is shed on the wood of the Cross for the salvation of Adam and his children. Take it for the forgiveness of your sins."[96]

[On the Proper Posture of the Priests]

Also, when he says after this, "Our Lord, our God, our Savior Jesus Christ" to its end, his hands are to be lifted up, while he bows to the Lord along with the people as well. From this moment, the priest no longer has authority to bless even once, and he is to turn neither to a superior nor to a subordinate. For Christ lies before him slain. Thus, it is for [Christ] to command and to him belongs the entreaty first and last. Therefore, from this moment, blessings are to be from him and to him. With these six blessings that are mentioned, the total over the bread and the wine reaches eighteen, and likewise upon the people and the servants. The priest also, as mentioned before, [has] eighteen, for a total of thirty-six signings. Follow this [pattern] in this way without adding or subtracting. Whoever departs from this is without rule, and he who does so has become ignorant.

When the priest says, "This, which you have acquired through the honored blood of your Christ," he points with his hand first to the blood and then to the body.[97]

From the beginning of the liturgy until the mystery of the descent of the Holy Spirit, and when the deacon says, "Worship God," the priest's hands are to be lifted up, directing his gaze upward, asking and entreating for the descent of the Holy Spirit. Thus, when the Holy Spirit has descended, and has purified and changed [the oblation],[98] [the priest's act of] entreating

96. Matthew 26:28.

97. This phrase appears in the prayer for the peace of the Church, one of many post-epiclesis entreaties in the Liturgy of Basil. See Ṣalīb, ⲡⲓϫⲱⲙ ⲛ̀ⲧⲉ ⲡⲓⲉⲩⲭⲟⲗⲟⲅⲓⲟⲛ, 344–345 and the discussion in Budde, *Die ägyptische Basilios-Anaphora*, 434–441.

98. In reference to the actions mentioned in the *epiclesis prayer* of the Liturgy of Basil.

becomes directed to the one who is before him as explained previously. Christ has become slain in the hands of the priest. Thus, from this point, there is no authority for the priest to bless. For if the superior is present, it is not permitted for anyone else to bless. Just as, if the patriarch or bishop were present, it would not be permitted for anyone else to bless. When the priest has reached this point, the bread becomes the body and the wine becomes the blood. So, it becomes forbidden for anyone else to bless.

[This is] like the children of Israel, when they said to Moses the prophet, "Why does God speak to you, but not to us. Just as you are from the sons of Israel, we also are his children, but he does not speak to us." So, the prophet ascended to the mountain and prayed, and the Creator (glory be to him)[99] commanded him to tell them to cleanse their clothes, to wash, and after three days to ascend the mountain, where he would speak to them. So, he commanded them thus, and they ascended the mountain. The glory of God appeared on the mountain, the stone smoked, and there was thunder, lightning, and earthquakes. And the prophet was standing, so he could point them with his right hand toward God (may he be exalted). He said to them, come forward to listen. But when they saw the glory of God, they were all terror-stricken and afraid. They stood on the ground [below the mountain] and cried out saying to Moses, the prophet of God, "From henceforth, we shall listen to you. Thus, whatever God says to you, we shall hear it. Henceforth, we repent of what we have said."[100] Thus, the cloud and darkness were lifted up, and likewise the fire. For this reason, our fathers appointed this matter. The priest makes the sign of the cross with his hands indicating that God is present among us, and that they [the people] are not to disobey the commands of the priests, but to be under their obedience.

[The Liturgy of the Eucharist—Continued]

The fractioning of the body in the paten is in the likeness of what our Savior did the night of his sufferings, when he broke the bread, gave to them,

99. The author here in P98, fol. 64r uses an expression (*subḥānuhu*) stemming from Qur'ānic vocabulary and referring to God's transcendence above any description or image falling short of his glory, though the term is difficult to translate accurately. See the explanation of this term in D. Gimaret, "Subḥān," *EI*^{2}, 9:742–743.

100. Exodus 20:18–21.

and said to them, "This is my body."[101] He broke a third and placed it over the two thirds in the sign of the cross.[102] He also took from the two thirds the top and the bottom and placed one in the east, another in the west, another left, and another right, and likewise the remainder of the third in its entirety. For all this is a likeness of his descent to the earth and our transfer from the left to the right and the fulfillment of the prophecy. For the prophet said that he was to come from the tribe of Judah.[103] [That is the meaning of] the top and the bottom.[104] And he points from left to right.[105] The third means the incarnate Son, while the other two thirds are the Father and the Holy Spirit.

When the priest says, "Remember those who have brought to you [these gifts]," he points with his hands to that which is placed before him of oblations and burnt offerings (*al-muḥraqāt*).[106] When the deacon says, "The readers,"[107] the priest says the mystery, "Remember also, O Lord."[108] Afterward, the priest takes a silk veil on his hand.

For when the priest touches the oblations with his hands, from the time he says, "He took bread," until the end of the liturgy, he cannot point to the

101. Matthew 26:26; Mark 14:22; Luke 22:19. Here the author begins to comment on the act of dividing the oblation bread during the precommunion rites. However, he quickly returns to discuss ritual actions performed during the post-epiclesis prayers. Thus, this section seems to not follow a strict chronological order.

102. Curiously, the author here consistently uses past-tense verbs. This seems to suggest that he attributes these intricate acts of breaking the bread not just to Coptic ritual but also to the actions of Christ himself at the Last Supper.

103. Matthew 2:6.

104. That is, the top and bottom pieces are to be understood as a visual representation of the descent of Christ from heaven and his taking flesh on earth.

105. Here, the author reverts again to describing events in the present, indicating actions performed by the celebrant today in performing the rites of the liturgy.

106. In reference to the litany of the oblations, part of the post-epiclesis set of litanies, for which see Ṣalīb, ⲡⲓϫⲱⲙ ⲛ̀ⲧⲉ ⲡⲓⲉⲩⲭⲟⲗⲟⲅⲓⲟⲛ, 351, and the discussion in Budde, *Die ägyptische Basilios-Anaphora*, 474–478. The author does not always strictly follow the unfolding of the service.

107. The incipit on fol. 65r ⲛⲓⲉⲧⲱϣ (*nietōsh*) corresponds to the diaconal response, "Let the readers recite the names of our holy fathers the departed patriarchs. May the Lord repose all their souls and forgive us our sins." The response introduces the reading of the names of the departed patriarchs, no longer read aloud in its entirety. See Ṣalīb, ⲡⲓϫⲱⲙ ⲛ̀ⲧⲉ ⲡⲓⲉⲩⲭⲟⲗⲟⲅⲓⲟⲛ, 361, and Budde, *Die ägyptische Basilios-Anaphora*, 504–507.

108. That is, the prayer for the departed. See Ṣalīb, ⲡⲓϫⲱⲙ ⲛ̀ⲧⲉ ⲡⲓⲉⲩⲭⲟⲗⲟⲅⲓⲟⲛ, 362–363, and Budde, *Die ägyptische Basilios-Anaphora*, 507–513.

people with uncovered hands, but [they are to be] wrapped with a silk veil in honor and exaltation of the one he has touched. Thus, when he has finished reading this mystery, he wraps his right hand with a silk veil and points with it westward to the people, while standing to the side with his left hand extended over the paten, entreating Christ. And he recites the blessing to its end.

Meanwhile, the deacons say the commemoration (*tarḥīm*) of the fathers the patriarchs [whose names are] written to its end [entitled], *Through the prayers and intercessions.*[109] The priest turns to the altar and raises his hands. Likewise, the celebrant deacon raises the cross and cries out [the hymn] *Abba Macarius* to its end.[110] Meanwhile, the priest is to ask silently for the forgiveness of his sins and the sins of the people, for the repose of the souls of our fathers and brothers whose names are written down.[111] After this, the priest says [the prayer] *Those O Lord*, and he says this with hands lifted up.[112]

[The Precommunion Rites]

When he has said, "The holy body," he takes the pure body, places it on his left hand and puts his finger on it.[113] When he says, "And the honored

109. On the diaconal diptychs, see chapter 1, note 88. For the full text of this commemoration, see the appendix.

110. This chant by the deacon is a list of the most prominent Egyptian monastic saints. The *textus receptus* begins with the name of Saint Antony, while some sources as the present text transmit a different order of saints beginning with Macarius the Great. This alternate beginning, "Abba Macarius, Abba Antony," is seen also in the Greek/Arabic Euchologion *Paris, BnF Gr. 325* (14th c.), fol. 50r. The incipit is omitted in the edition of this manuscript text by Eusèbe Renaudot, *Liturgiarum Orientalium Collectio*, 1:71. See also the edition of the Liturgy of Saint Basil by John M. Rodwell based on *Manchester, Rylands Copt. 426* (13th c.), *The Liturgies of S. Basil, S. Gregory, and S. Cyril*, 37.

111. A common practice is for congregants to present the names of their reposed family members to the deacons, written on paper, or alternately for the deacons to write down these names themselves. At the commemoration of the departed, the priest reads the names from this list.

112. The Coptic on fol. 65v is ⲛⲉⲙⲉⲛ ⲡⲟ̅ⲥ̅ (*nemen pchois*) and corresponds to the following prayer in the Liturgy of Basil: "But those, O Lord, whose souls you have received, repose them in the paradise of joy in the land of the living forever in the Jerusalem of heaven in that place. And we too the strangers in this place, keep us in your faith, grant us your peace to the end, lead us into your kingdom." See Ṣalīb, ⲡⲓϫⲱⲙ ⲛ̀ⲧⲉ ⲡⲓⲉⲩⲭⲟⲗⲟⲅⲓⲟⲛ, 380–381, and the discussion in Budde, *Die ägyptische Basilios-Anaphora*, 522–525.

113. On the ritual of consignation before the fraction, see Burmester, *The Egyptian or Coptic Church*, 71–72; Brightman, *Liturgies Eastern and Western*, 180–181.

blood," he lifts his finger from the body and extends it to the chalice. He dips his index finger in the precious blood without wetting his fingernail. When he has done so, he lifts it from the blood, then makes the sign of the cross with [his finger] over the chalice. Then he raises his hand from the chalice after drying it lest something drops from it. He is to be careful in doing so. Then he signs with the blood that is in his finger on the pure body over the [part] that he divided before. He also signs the back of the body from the bottom. For according to what was explained before, the blessings are to be from him [Christ] and to him. The number of blessings here has reached three, and these three blessings are at the end of [the priest's saying], "the body," until he says, "Peace to all."

At this point, the priest begins reciting the *Fraction Prayer*, while he divides the pure body into two thirds and a third as he did before when he said, "He broke it."[114] He takes the third and puts it over the two thirds in the likeness of the holy cross. He takes a particle from the top of the two thirds and places it in the midst of the paten toward the east, then takes a particle from the bottom of the two thirds and places it in the paten toward the west. From the right side of the third, he takes a particle and places it in the paten to the right and takes the third and places it in the side of the paten to the left. This is to be in the likeness of the cross. Then he takes [a part] from the two thirds that has the *despotikon* and puts it from top to bottom in the middle of the paten, then begins to divide the third that is in his hand. When he has finished, he takes the third that was put down at first and divides that. When that is finished, he takes the third that he had placed in the center and removes from it the *despotikon* specifically from the top. He is to be careful lest it break or crumble. Then he puts it in its place and puts the third in the center and gathers to it the entire pure body that he has divided. And if he is a meticulous priest, well instructed by elders, he is to divide the oblation bread in an orderly way until it is divided but complete. And he is to raise it with his hands, divided and complete, for this is the correct manner. When this is finished, the priest wipes his hands inside the paten so that nothing clings to it, not even a small particle.[115]

114. Regarding the fractioning of the body and the so-called *Fraction Prayer*, see chapter 2, note 111.

115. The manner by which the body is fractioned in the Coptic Rite is extremely intricate and follows a variety of patterns, all of which have an equal claim of authority and oral tradition. For one such description, see O. H. E. Burmester, *The Egyptian or Coptic Church*, 72–74. Cf. the fractioning patterns in the West Syrian rite discussed in Bryan D.

When he has finished reading the *Prayer of the Fraction*, he says *Our Father*. Then the priest says, "We ask you O Holy Father," and after it, "[The graces] are fulfilled."[116] After this, the priest says the *Absolution to the Father* until [the phrase] "And all your people absolved."[117] He covers his right hand with a silk veil, turns slightly to the west, and points with his hand to the people. His left hand is to be extended, while he maintains his gaze at the pure body, asking of Christ and entreating for the people. Here, he remembers the parish (*al-bīʿah*), and the people both alive and dead, until the end of the absolution prayer.

Then he turns east, and the deacon cries out with a loud voice, while the heads of the people are to be uncovered and their hands raised. The deacon says, "May you be saved, amen. And with your spirit. Attend in the fear of God."[118] The people respond to him with a loud voice, "Lord have mercy, Lord have mercy." Then the priest takes the *despotikon* in his hands and raises it up high with arms fully extended, bowing the head, while he cries out with a loud voice saying, "The holy [gifts] for the saints." So, all the people bow their heads, prostrating to the Lord in fear and trembling, entreating with tears and supplication while beating their breasts for the forgiveness of their sins and their confirmation in the orthodox faith to the last breath.[119]

Spinks, "From Functional to Artistic," 89–114. The manner described here by Gabriel V is the same as that described by Burmester and is copied verbatim in the Euchologion of 1902 by Hegumen ʿAbd al-Masīḥ Ṣalīb. See Ṣalīb, ⲡⲓϫⲱⲙ ⲛ̀ⲧⲉ ⲡⲓⲉⲩⲭⲟⲗⲟⲅⲓⲟⲛ, 386–388.

116. The incipits on fol. 67r, ⲥⲉⲧⲉⲛϯϩⲟ ⲉ̀ⲣⲟⲕ (*setentiho erok*) and ⲁⲩⲙⲟϩ ⲉⲃⲟⲗ (*aumoh ebol*), correspond to the so-called *Prayer after Our Father* and the *Prayer of Inclination*, respectively. For the text of these prayers in the Liturgy of Saint Basil, see Ṣalīb, ⲡⲓϫⲱⲙ ⲛ̀ⲧⲉ ⲡⲓⲉⲩⲭⲟⲗⲟⲅⲓⲟⲛ, 392–396. On the analogous prayer in the Byzantine liturgy, see Robert F. Taft, "The Inclination Prayer," 29–60.

117. For the text of the *Absolution to the Father*, see Brightman, *Liturgies Eastern and Western*, 183–184.

118. The incipit on fol. 67v is ⲥⲱⲑⲓⲥ ⲁⲙⲏⲛ ⲕⲁ ⲧⲟ ⲡⲛ̅ⲁ̅ⲧⲓ ⲥⲱⲟⲩ ⲙⲁⲧ ⲫⲱⲃⲟⲩ ⲑ̅ⲩ̅ ⲡ̀ⲣⲟⲥⲭⲱⲙⲉⲛ (*sōthis amēn ka to pneumati sōou. Mat phōbou theou*ᵉ*proschōmen*) corresponding to the diaconal response σωθείης ἀμήν καὶ τῷ πνεῦματί σου. Μετά φόβου θεοῦ πρόσχωμεν (*sōtheiēs amēn kai tō pneumati sou. Meta phobou theou proschōmen*). See Burmester, "The Greek Kīrugmata," 382. The response consists in fact of three separate units, syntactically unrelated: 1. May you be saved, amen, 2. And with your spirit, 3. Let us attend with the fear of God.

119. For the call to communion and its response, see Robert F. Taft, *The Precommunion Rites*, 230–248.

Then the priest takes the *despotikon* with his right hand and with the sign of the cross he blesses it along with the precious blood in the chalice. He raises it, dipped in blood, watching lest something drop from it, and with it he signs also the entire pure body in the paten with the sign of the cross. Then he returns with it to the blood, signs with it the blood with the sign of the cross, and places it in the blood that is in the chalice. All this while he says, "Blessed is the Lord Jesus Christ, the Son of God. Sanctification is the Holy Spirit, amen."[120]

The people rise from their prostrated state and respond to him with a loud voice saying, "One is the Holy Father, one is the Holy Son, one is the Holy Spirit, amen." The priest says, "Peace to all," and the people respond to him, "And to your spirit." Then the priest says the confession. First, he says, "A holy body." After he says this, he takes the third that was placed in the center of the paten, from which he had removed the *despotikon*, and he divides it into three parts. But if it is large [still], he takes from it three parts in his hands. And he does this fraction in the paten. When he has finished reciting the confession until he has said, "He took it from our lady, the holy Theotokos Saint Mary," he takes a particle from his hand and places it in the paten. Then he takes another in its place from the paten and places it in his hand.[121]

When the recitation of the confession is finished, he places the three particles that are in his hand on the body that is in the paten and guards them, for these are the ones of which he and his partners will partake, or he and the celebrant deacon. Then he covers the paten and the chalice, each with a silk cloth, and the deacon says, "Pray for the Christians."[122]

After this, the priest says, "This is the one to whom glory," to its end, while bowing his head with his two hands wrapped in a silk cloth.[123] When this has concluded, they all respond to him with loud voices saying, "A

120. Given in P98, fol. 68r thus: ⲉⲩⲗⲟⲅⲓⲧⲟⲥ ⲕ̅ⲥ̅ ⲓ̅ⲥ̅ ⲭ̅ⲥ̅ ⲩ̅ⲥ̅ ⲑ̅ⲩ̅ ⲁ̀ⲅⲓⲁⲥⲙⲟⲥ ⲡ̅ⲛ̅ⲁ̅ ⲁ̀ⲅⲓⲟⲛ ⲁ̀ⲙⲏⲛ, which is resolved as such (*eulogitos kyrios iēsous christos huios theou agiasmos pneuma hagion amen*). On the precommunion ritual of consignation and commixture following it, see chapter 2, note 119.

121. On the precommunion confession and its historical development, see Engberding, "Ein Problem in der Homologia," 145–154.

122. The incipit on fol. 68v, ⲧⲱⲃϩ ⲉϫⲉⲛ ⲛⲓⲭⲣⲏⲥⲧⲓⲁⲛⲟⲥ ⲛⲓⲃⲉⲛ (*tōbh ejen nichrēstianos niben*) corresponds to the diaconal response before communion, "Pray for all the Christians, who have said to us concerning them, remember us in the house of the Lord." See Brightman, *Liturgies Eastern and Western*, 185.

123. I.e., he is to recite the concluding doxology of the confession.

hundred years!"[124] He turns and bows his head to his brothers the priests and his brothers the deacons on the left and right. And they chant *Alleluia Praise God* and whatever is appropriate to that season.[125] As for him, he turns to the table, uncovers the side of the paten in front of him, and asks Christ to make him and all the communicants worthy of this and deserving of the forgiveness of their sins through their partaking of the body of Christ and his pure blood.

Then, before he communes, the priest says, "Make us all worthy, O our Master, to receive of your holy body and honored blood, unto purity for our souls, our bodies, and our spirits; unto the forgiveness of our sins and transgressions. So that we may become one body and one spirit with you. Glory to you and to your good Father and the Holy Spirit, forever, amen."[126]

Its Arabic translation is, "Make us all worthy, O our king, to receive of your pure body and honored blood, purity for our souls, our bodies, and our spirits, and forgiveness for our sins and transgressions. So that we may become one body and one spirit with you, for you are blessed, and to you belongs the glory with your good Father and the Holy Spirit forever, amen."[127]

But some priests say, "O our Lord Jesus Christ make us worthy to receive of your pure body and honored blood. May it not be for us unto condemnation. But as you have said to your pure disciples, 'Take of my body and my blood for the forgiveness of your sins,' may it be for us communion with your pure disciples, so that by partaking of your life-giving mysteries, we may receive forgiveness of our sins, remission of our transgressions, purity for our souls, bodies, and spirits, and steadfastness of faith in your holy name to the last breath, through the entreaties of the pure Saint Mary and all the saints, amen."[128]

124. See Ṣalīb, ⲡⲓϫⲱⲙ ⲛ̀ⲧⲉ ⲡⲓⲉⲩⲭⲟⲗⲟⲅⲓⲟⲛ, 410. Although printed in the influential Euchologion of 1902, this response is not utilized in actual practice. For such acclamatory responses, descending from the late-antique origins of Christian worship, see Robert F. Taft, "The Dialogue before the Anaphora III," 69–73 and the extended references in Taft, *The Diptychs*, 2–3.

125. On the chanting of Psalm 150 as a communion chant, see chapter 2, note 152.

126. The text of the prayer is given in Coptic in the manuscript, followed by the Arabic translation below.

127. Given on fol. 69r–v in Coptic followed by an Arabic translation, this prayer was included in the 1902 Euchologion as the third of four alternative private prayers for the celebrant before communion. See Ṣalīb, ⲡⲓϫⲱⲙ ⲛ̀ⲧⲉ ⲡⲓⲉⲩⲭⲟⲗⲟⲅⲓⲟⲛ, 413.

128. Given as the final alternative prayer in the 1902 Euchologion, characteristically without a Coptic text. See ibid., 414.

[Communion]

After this, he kisses the pure body with his mouth and partakes of it, then covers the paten. He then extends his hand to uncover the chalice and takes a cloth in his left hand. He raises the chalice from the throne and partakes of the honored blood of Christ in it. He wipes his mouth with the cloth and likewise the rim of the chalice from which he partook.

Then, if the celebrant deacon is an adult, he offers him communion with him from the chalice and he hands him the spoon by the tip. The deacon takes the chalice and circles with it from the southern side with another deacon in front of him carrying a lighted candle. All the servants ought to prostrate to him with their heads bowed until he stands at the northern side. Then the priest begins to offer communion to the young servants. He is to dip [his finger] for them, while someone stands with a cloth to wipe their mouths for them after communion.[129] [But to] the adults he gives the body, while the deacon gives them the blood with the spoon.

If the priest gives the servants and all the people the body dipped [in the blood], he says, "The body and the blood of Emmanuel our God. This is true, amen." But if he gives the pure body without the blood he says, "The body of Emmanuel our God. This is true, amen." So, the communicants say amen.[130]

If an assisting priest is with him, the celebrant is to offer him communion after he himself has partaken. The celebrant is to place the piece in the hand of the priest or in the spoon, while the assisting priest is to receive it from him. Then the assisting priest takes the cloth from the chalice and places it on the hand of the celebrant priest and administers to him also the chalice. The celebrant receives from him and gives to him. He receives from him and completes [the act of communion] with him.[131] But

129. That is, rather than administer the blood to infants using the communion spoon, he is to dip his finger into the chalice and then into their mouths. This alternative method is common today for the communion of infants.

130. Gabriel V clearly assumes that administering communion in both kinds *together* is a valid practice, something copied also in the 1902 Euchologion. See Ṣalīb, ⲡⲓϫⲱⲙ ⲛ̀ⲧⲉ ⲡⲓⲉⲩⲭⲟⲗⲟⲅⲓⲟⲛ, 416. Today, this is only practiced in case of bringing communion to those absent from the liturgical service, i.e., communion for the sick or those in prison.

131. On the order of communion of the clergy and other related matters, see Robert F. Taft, *The Communion, Thanksgiving, and Concluding Rites*, 94–96.

if the deacon is young in age, he ought not to dare or venture upon any of what we have said.

Then each one of the servants receives communion. When they have received, they wipe their mouths with the cloth that is in the hand of the deacon who shines a light over the paten. When the priest has finished communing the servants, he carries the paten on his left hand with a silk cloth, with its edges gathered inside the paten. This is to be done carefully, lest he should let one of its edges outside the paten. God forbid that some of the precious pearls (*durr*) cling to it and fall to the ground.[132] Likewise, the deacon is to watch lest he leave the spoon from his hand in the chalice and turn his hand toward something else. God forbid that he pushes it with his sleeve, his *pallium* (*ballīnahu*), or that someone else [does so], and it falls to the ground, or that it falls by itself to the ground. Thereby [the deacons] would receive condemnation from God and from the people for their negligence and lack of care.

Then the deacon descends with the chalice of the blood of Christ, with an older deacon before him paying close attention, carrying a candle. His descent is to be prior to the priest. After him, the priest carrying the paten turns with the body of Christ to the west and descends outside the altar. He blesses the people with the paten in the likeness of the cross, so they all prostrate to the ground, from the oldest among them to the youngest. Then they begin to receive communion one after the other as explained. Whoever receives communion among the people ought to make a prostration before the altar of God and receive communion with his head uncovered.[133] When he has received communion, he is not to turn his back, but he is to retreat backward little by little. For Judas, when he received the bread from the Master, turned his back [and went] outside filled with the deceit of the devil. May God protect us from this!

When the communion of the men has concluded, the priest signs the people with the paten again in the likeness of the cross. And they proceed to the women's area (*bayt al-nisā*), the celebrant priest and a deacon before

132. It is common to refer to small pieces of the body as pearls or jewels (*jawharah*). See Graf, *Verzeichnis*, 36.

133. Clearly, Gabriel V is speaking specifically about the communion of men, who are to remove any head covering before approaching. The author then turns his attention to the communion of women, who customarily cover their heads throughout the services.

him with a lighted candle, in order to offer communion to the women.[134] It is proper for all the people, when the priests walk through with the body of Christ heading to the women's area, and likewise also when the priest returns, that they all uncover their heads and bow to the Lord, thanking him and glorifying him, who has made them worthy of this great gift, which the angels cannot behold.

The communion of the women ought to be done with extreme caution and scrutiny. For the woman is veiled and no one knows who she is. Thus, it is right that she be meticulously scrutinized by you, O priests, lest you give the body and blood of Christ unworthily, and you be condemned for that.

Also, when the priest enters the women's area, he is to make the sign of the cross upon them with the paten. Likewise, when he has finished giving them communion, he is to make the sign of the cross upon them before proceeding back to the altar. During their communion, he is to say the same as previously explained for the communion of men. When he has returned to the altar and has ascended up to it, he also turns west and signs upon the people as he did before, while they bow down to the earth saying, "Remember us, O Lord, when you come in your kingdom. Holy is the Father, Holy is the Son, Holy is the Holy Spirit, the Holy Trinity."

[On the Eucharist]

What we have explained about the body and the blood means that the body and the blood are one divinity, that his divinity never departed from his

134. The term likely refers to the area in the nave designated for women and isolated behind a screen. Basilicas in late antiquity were constructed with galleries for women over the lateral isles and the narthex. However, according to Butler based on the construction of the Church of Abū Sayfayn, the practice of admitting women into the nave while continuing to keep them apart from the men had already become normative by the tenth century. This is likely the sense of the text, unless it was providing an idealized archaic description hearkening back to a time when women occupied the galleries. According to Coquin, the patriarchal residence and cathedral at the time of Gabriel V was likely the Church of the Virgin Mary in Ḥārit Zuwaylah. See Alfred J. Butler, *The Ancient Coptic Churches of Egypt*, 2:19–22; René-Georges Coquin, "Patriarchal Residences," *CE*, 6:1912a–1913b. The term "house of women" (*bayt al-nisā*) referring to this special area is analogous to the Greek term *gynaceum*, used rarely in Byzantine sources precisely for the galleries. On the location assigned to women in Byzantine churches, see Robert F. Taft, "Women at Church in Byzantium," 27–87.

humanity, and that the three persons are one will and one volition. [His divinity] did not depart from him at the time of the crucifixion, nor after the crucifixion. These crosses proceed from him and are by him,[135] which the Master performed when he broke the bread and gave it to his disciples in the upper room and his name filled all the earth. As for covering it with the veils, it indicates that John came to the tomb but did not enter, and that Peter came and entered first, but they did not find the body of the Lord.[136] Uncovering it points to his appearance to Mary Magdalene in the garden.[137] As for the priest's turning his face to the people, it is a likeness of our Master appearing to his disciples with the doors closed.[138] As for the priest not giving the body to the people in their hands as is done in certain sects,[139] it is for the sake of his saying to Mary, "Do not touch me, for I have not yet ascended to my father. But go to my brethren and say to them that I am ascending to my Father and your Father, and to my God and your God."[140] This indicates that they have partaken of his body and have become one with him.

[Concluding Rites]

He places the paten on the altar, while he who has the chalice is to go around with it until he stands at the northern side of the altar. Then the celebrant, if there remains anything with him, begins to distribute it to the older servants. As for children who are unable to eat, or who are upset or crying, their communion of it should not take place unless the priest dips his index finger in the precious blood, places it on the body, and places this in the roof of their mouth. Then he is to command them [the adults] to give water to the children.

When all this has concluded, the priest is to wipe the paten and the chalice and inspect them visually, together with whoever is beside him from

135. This refers to the priest's blessing the people with the paten and the chalice in the sign of the cross.

136. John 20:3–6.

137. John 20:11–18.

138. John 20:19.

139. For the ancient custom of receiving the body in the hand—including Egyptian sources—and its later extinction, see Taft, *The Communion, Thanksgiving, and Concluding Rites*, 230–242.

140. John 20:17.

among the priests and deacons who shine a light for him. For they are guarantors and witnesses for him regarding what has been assigned to him. When he has done this, and they have given witness to the truthfulness of his affair (*ḥaqīqati amrihi*),[141] he is to be free of blame. Afterward, the priest begins to wash the chalice, first once, then twice, and the third time he gives it to the celebrant deacon in order to drink from it. Then he washes the spoon inside the paten, and likewise his hands after washing outside the paten with water. The second time [he also washes] his hands and then he finishes washing his hands a third time and drinks [the water].

Then he wipes the paten with a clean cloth and pours water inside his [cupped] hands and pours some of it over the table. He wipes his face with his hands and turns to his brothers the priests and shares the water with them with his hands [on their faces] above and below.[142] Whoever shares with him, he is to wipe that person's face with his hands, and likewise they are to do the same. Then he places his hand on the heads of the people and blesses them, giving them the dismissal. He concludes this by reciting the blessing.[143] When all this has been completed, he turns and kisses the altar, going around it once and saying, "Clap your hands all you nations."[144] If he happens not to have memorized it in Coptic, he is to read it in Arabic. Then he descends from the altar, takes off the vestments of the priesthood, and distributes the blessing.[145] He is to watch lest something should fall from him to the ground and the people tread upon it with their feet. Then he dismisses the people in the peace of the Lord.

Finished and completed by the help of God.

141. That is, that the priest has thoroughly cleaned the paten from any remains of the body of Christ.

142. That is, the celebrant is to wipe his wet hands on his own face and beard, then turns to the other assisting priests and likewise touches their hair and beards with his wet hands as a sign of sharing the blessing with them. On the entire ritual of cleaning the vessels, see Burmester, *The Egyptian or Coptic Church*, 87.

143. For the text of the dismissal blessing, see Ṣalīb, ⲡⲓϫⲱⲙ ⲛ̀ⲧⲉ ⲡⲓⲉⲩⲭⲟⲗⲟⲅⲓⲟⲛ, 428–433 and continued in matins on 140–148.

144. Psalm 46 (47).

145. That is, the blessed bread that has not been chosen for the consecration, commonly called in Arabic by the Greek-derived word, *al-ūlūjiyyah*. See the references in chapter 1, note 106.

APPENDIX

Coptic Liturgical Chants

Absolve and forgive (*bōl ebol*):
Absolve, forgive, and remit unto us our transgressions, O God. Those that we have done willingly and those we have done unwillingly, those that we have done knowingly, and those that we have done out of ignorance, O Lord forgive them unto us.

All the wise men of Israel (*nisabeu tērou*):
All you wise men of Israel, who weave golden threads, make an Aaronic garment[1] according to the honor of the priesthood of our honored father, the high priest, Pope Abba so-and-so and our father the bishop Abba so-and-so, the beloved of Christ.

Alleluia for the thought of man (*allēlouia je phmeui*):
The thought of man shall confess to you, O Lord, and the remainder of thought shall keep a feast to you.[2] Accept unto you the sacrifices and the offerings, alleluia.

Alleluia, I will go (*allēlouia eiei ekhoun*):
I will go to the altar of God, before the face of God, who gives joy to my youth. I will praise you, O God my God, with a harp, alleluia.[3] Remember, O Lord, David and all his meekness.[4]

1. Exodus 28:1–5.
2. Psalm 75 (76):11.
3. Psalm 42 (43):4.
4. Psalm 131 (132):1.

Alleluia, remember O Lord (*allēlouia ariphmeui pchois*):
Remember, O Lord, David and all his meekness, how he swore to the Lord and vowed to the God of Jacob, will I enter into the dwelling of my house? We will enter into his dwelling place to worship at the place wherein your feet have stood.[5]

Alleluia, this is the day (*allēlouia phai pe piehoou*):
This is the day the Lord has made. Let us rejoice and be glad in it. O Lord save us, O Lord straighten our ways. Blessed is he who comes in the name of the Lord, alleluia.[6]

The cherubim worship you (*nicheroubim seouōsht*):
The cherubim worship you and the seraphim glorify you, crying out saying, "Holy, Holy, Holy, Lord Sabaoth. Heaven and earth are full of your holy glory."[7]

Christ is risen (*christos anestē*):
Christ is risen from the dead, having trampled down death by death and having granted life to those in the tombs.

Come to the table (*deute eis tēn trapezan*):
Come to the table to bless God with angels and archangels, crying out and saying, "Holy, Holy, Holy are you, O Lord, alleluia. Glory to the Father and to the Son and to the Holy Spirit." We send up the hymn with the cherubim. Holy, Holy, Holy are you, O Lord, alleluia. Both now and ever, and unto the ages of the ages, amen.

He was looking with the eyes (*nafnau khen nibal*):
Isaiah the great prophet was looking with prophetic eyes at the mystery of Emmanuel, wherefore he cried out, saying, "Unto us a child has been born and to us a son has been given, whose leadership is upon his shoulders, the mighty God who has authority and the angel of great council."[8]

Holy God (Trisagion, *hagios ho theos*):
Holy God, Holy mighty, Holy immortal, who was born of the Virgin. Have mercy on us. Holy God, Holy mighty, Holy immortal, who was crucified for us. Have mercy on us. Holy God, Holy mighty, Holy

5. Psalm 131 (132):1–3, 7.
6. Psalm 117 (118): 24–26.
7. Isaiah 6:3.
8. Isaiah 9:6.

immortal, who arose from the dead and ascended to the heavens. Have mercy on us. Glory to the Father and the Son and the Holy Spirit, both now and ever and unto the ages of ages, amen. O Holy Trinity have mercy on us.

Just as it was (*hōsper ēn*):
Just as it was, it is and will be from generation to generation, and unto all the ages of the ages, amen.

Kiss with a holy kiss (*ariaspazesthe*):
Kiss with a holy kiss. Purify your hearts from every evil. Be prepared for the gift of God, so that you may partake of these mysteries. By these we will obtain mercy and forgiveness of our sins according to his great mercy.

O Christ our Savior (*pichristos pensōtēr*):
O Christ our Savior, make us worthy of your holy kiss in the heavens, so that we may praise you with the cherubim and the seraphim, crying out saying, "Holy, Holy, Holy, O Lord the Pantocrator. Heaven and earth are full of your glory and your honor."[9]

One is the Holy Father (*heis patēr hagios*):
One is the Holy Father, one is the Holy Son, one is the Holy Spirit, amen. Blessed be the Lord God unto the ages, amen.

Rejoice and be glad (*rashi ouoh thelēl*):
Rejoice and be glad, O human race, for God so loved the world that he gave his beloved Son for those who believe in him in order for them to live thereby.[10]

Therefore truly (*tote alēthōs*):
Therefore, truly I do not err when I call you the golden censer.

There, God will lift up (*share phnouti ōli ᵉmmau*):
There, God will lift up the sins of the people through the burnt offerings and the fragrance of incense.

This golden censer (*tai shourē*):
This pure golden censer that is carrying the fragrances, which is in the hands of Aaron the priest as he raises incense upon the altar.

9. Isaiah 6:3.
10. John 3:16.

This is the time of praise (*phnau ᵉmpismou pe phai*):

This is the time of praise, the time of the chosen incense, the time to praise our Savior, the good lover of humankind. Mary is incense; incense is in her womb. It is incense to whom she gave birth, and He forgave us our sins. Jesus is incense; come let us worship him. If we keep his commandments, he will forgive us our sins. He established the tabernacle of witness for the Word of the Lord. Aaron the priest is in the tabernacle raising incense. Mercy was given to Michael, the annunciation to Gabriel. The gift of the heavenly ones was given to the Virgin Mary. The law was given to Moses, the priesthood to Aaron. The chosen incense was given to Zachariah the priest. Understanding was given to David, wisdom to Solomon. The horn was given to Samuel, for he anointed the kings. The keys were given to our father Peter, virginity to John. Preaching was given to our father Paul; he is the splendor of the Church. Incense emanates from the Virgin Mary, for all the incense came and took flesh from her. God the Father has adorned the holy Virgin Mary; he decorated her as a tabernacle of Jesus, his only begotten Son.[11]

Through the prayers (*euchais*):

Through the prayers and intercessions of the all-holy, exceedingly glorious, immaculate, most blessed, our lady the Theotokos and ever-Virgin Mary, and the holy prophet and forerunner, Baptist and martyr John, and Saint Stephen the archdeacon and first martyr, and the holy apostles, glorious prophets, and victorious martyrs, and all the choir of your saints, [and] of the thank-offerings of the lord Abba so-and-so the archbishop of the great city of Alexandria and of our orthodox bishops, and also for the falling asleep and repose of our holy fathers, Mark the holy apostle, evangelist, archbishop, and martyr, [list of the reposed patriarchs of Alexandria], and of all those who have correctly taught the word of truth, the orthodox bishops, presbyters, deacons, clergy, laity, these and all the orthodox.

11. Since this chant does not survive in the current repertoire, it is given here from the text published in Zanetti, "Voici le temps de la bénédiction," 27–30. Zanetti gives the Coptic text mainly from the fourteenth-century manuscript *Cairo, Coptic Patriarchate Lit. 106*, which describes the making of the chrism by Pope Gabriel IV in AD 1374.

Truly You are blessed (*ksmarōout alēthōs*):
Truly you are blessed with your good Father and the Holy Spirit, for you came and saved us.

We worship you (*tenouōsht ᵉmmok*):
We worship you, O Christ, with your good Father and the Holy Spirit, for you came and saved us.

You are the censer (*ᵉntho te tishourē*):
You are the pure golden censer that carries the blessed burning coal.

GLOSSARY

Absolution of the Servants: A prayer of absolution by the bishop or priest pronounced after the preparation of the gifts over all the liturgical ministers in a given celebration (priests, deacons, and minor orders). It asks for the servants to be absolved from their sins before beginning the Liturgy of the Word by the Holy Trinity and by the mouths of a number of saints, such as the Virgin Mary, Saint Mark, notable patriarchs, and the current patriarch and bishop.

Absolution to the Son: A prayer of absolution addressed to Christ by the bishop or priest at the conclusion of the morning and evening services, the preparation of the gifts, and—if celebrating the Liturgy of Saint Gregory—before communion.

Aghnusṭus (Gr. *anagnōstēs*, reader): A member of the minor orders of the church assigned to read the scriptural readings in liturgical ceremonies.

Ajbiyyah (Copt. *ȧjp*, hour): The *Book of Hours* of the Coptic tradition, containing the psalms and prayers for each set of prayers (termed hour) of the daily cycle. The term is an Arabized adjective of the Coptic word for hour. It is equivalent in usage to the term Horologion in the Byzantine tradition.

al-ʿarḍī: A wide white shawl traditionally worn in different styles by priests or bishops wrapped around the head. It is possibly a descendant of the Eastern *omophorion*, a wide shoulder shawl worn by bishops in churches of the Byzantine rite.

al-Būlus (Pauline): The reading from one of the fourteen epistles attributed to Paul the Apostle. It comes as the first in a sequence of four scriptural readings in the Liturgy of the Word.

al-Kāthūlīkūn (also *al-Qatālīqūn*, Gr. *katholikon*): The reading from one of the catholic epistles attributed to Peter, James, John, or Jude. It comes as the second in a sequence of four scriptural readings in the Liturgy of the Word.

Ambo (also *Anbal*, *Anbun*, Gr. *ambōn*): A raised platform or pulpit from which, traditionally, the Gospel was proclaimed. Most frequently, it is located in the nave on the northern side.

Anaphora: The central prayer of the eucharistic service. Many such prayers are attested in sources, while only three remain in Coptic usage. With some variation, the anaphora includes an introductory dialogue, the angelic praise from Isaiah 3:6, the words of institution from the Last Supper, a recalling of key events of Christ's life, and a commemoration of departed saints and faithful.

Archdeacon (Gr. *archidiakonos*): A rank traditionally bestowed only on the most senior deacon in a diocese or parish.

Asbasmus (Gr. *aspasmos*, greeting): 1. The priestly prayer preceding the exchange of the kiss of peace among the clergy and congregation during the eucharistic liturgy. 2. A variable chant accompanying the exchange of the kiss.

Awshīyah (Gr. *euchē*, prayer): Any one of the prayers contained in the Euchologion, especially but not exclusively those of an intercessory character (e.g., for the Church, the hierarchs, those who have departed, and those who are sick).

Ballīn (Gr. *pallion*, pallium): A long band of cloth worn as a liturgical garment. In medieval sources, it seems to have been a versatile term for any garment of such shape for the deacon, priest, or bishop. Today, it is used to refer to a particular long rectangular cloth worn over the head by bishops, somewhat analogous to the Latin pallium or the Greek *omophorion*.

Baramūn (Gr. *paramonē*, vigil): The day(s) of preparation preceding a feast in the liturgical calendar, such as the eves of the Nativity or the Theophany, though the *baramūn* of a feast could be more than just one day before. Such days are usually days of strict fasting and special liturgical services. Unlike the term "vigil," which may indicate only the nighttime services prior to a feast, the *baramūn* is the entire day preceding the feast.

Baṭrashīl (also *Baṭrashīn*, Gr. *epitrachēlion*): 1. A long band of cloth worn by subdeacons and deacons, usually in red and embroidered with crosses (equivalent to the less common term *orarion*). 2. A vestment for presbyters and bishops worn over the neck.

Burnus: A robe worn by presbyters and bishops similar to the Western cope or the Byzantine *phelonion*.

Catechumens (Gr. *katēchoumenoi*): Those preparing for baptism and admission to eucharistic communion. In late antiquity, members of this group were allowed to attend the Liturgy of the Word and other catechetical assemblies. In the context of the eucharistic service, they were formally dismissed after the homily and a blessing.

Commixture: A ritual before communion performed by the celebrant, who places the central part of the oblation bread (see *despotikon*) in the chalice, meant to highlight the unity between the body and the blood.

Compline (Ar. *Ṣalāt al-nawm*, the prayer of sleep): One of the prayers of the hours of the daily cycle, corresponding to the twelfth hour of the day or 6 p.m. in modern usage.

Despotikon (Ar. *Isbādīqūn*): The central portion of the eucharistic bread bearing a cross seal and accorded special honor in the precommunion rites.

Diaconicon (Ar. *Khidmat al-shammās*, the service of the deacon): A liturgical book containing the responses and acclamations pronounced by the deacon during the morning/evening services and the three liturgies. It also contains the congregational responses and a selection of variable chants, functioning also as a hymnal.

Dismissal: The final rites of a liturgical service, in which the celebrant pronounces a final blessing for the people that concludes with the collective recitation of the Our Father marking the end of the service.

Epiclesis Prayer: A priestly prayer in the course of the anaphora. Through it, the Holy Spirit is called upon (Gr. *epikaleō*) to descend on the bread and wine and complete their consecration into the body and blood of Christ. Each anaphora possesses its own version of the Epiclesis Prayer.

Euchologion (Ar. *Khūlājī*, Gr. *euchologion*): A liturgical book containing the texts of the three eucharistic liturgies (Basil, Gregory, and Mark/Cyril) and other related material (e.g., Fraction Prayers and the morning and evening services). It is the primary liturgical book used by the celebrant to perform the eucharistic service and the evening and morning prayers. It is traditionally for the priest's use, though modern printed editions also include diaconal responses and congregational chants.

Fraction Prayer (Ar. *Ṣalāt al-qismah*): A priestly prayer functioning as a prelude to the recitation of Our Father and communion in the eucharistic liturgy. It accompanies the breaking of the bread by the priest, hence its name. A large number of such prayers survive in Coptic books thematically tied to seasons of the liturgical year.

Gospel Response (Ar. *Maradd al-injīl*): A short chant composed of approximately one to four stanzas of four lines each. Chanted after the Gospel reading, it functions as a summary of and reflection on the passage at hand.

Hegumen (Ar. *Qummuṣ*, Gr. *hēgoumenos*): In Coptic usage, an honorary ecclesiastical rank bestowed on presbyters, equivalent to protopresbyter.

Ibraksīs (Gr. *praxis*): A scriptural reading from the Acts of the Apostles. It comes as the third in a sequence of four scriptural readings in the Liturgy of the Word.

Iklīrus (Gr. *klēros*, inheritance): The clergy as a group.

Khamsīniyyah: Literally, belonging to the fifty, in reference to the Pentecost period, or fifty days after the feast of the Resurrection. The adjective is applied to musical style or liturgical practices unique to this period.

Kiyahk (Copt. *choiak*): The fourth month of the Coptic year, corresponding to the Advent season and known for its particular liturgical services and vigils in preparation for the Nativity.

Kursī al-ka's (Chalice throne): A box of four or more sides, approximately the height of the chalice, with a round hole at the top. The sides are decorated with various iconographic scenes. During the preparation of the altar, the chalice is placed inside this box and remains there until communion.

Lectionary (Ar. *Qāṭamārus*, Gr. *kata meros*): A liturgical book containing the scriptural readings appointed for each day or celebration. The following types of lectionaries exist in the modern period for the following uses: Sundays, other days of the week, Great Lent, Holy Week, and the Pentecost period.

Lifāfah: A small cloth or veil used either as one of the altar coverings or to cover the mouth of the communicant after receiving the body.

Liturgy of the Word: The second part of the eucharistic liturgy in the Coptic tradition following the preparation of the gifts. It includes the readings of Scripture, accompanying chants and prayers, and traditionally includes a homily on the readings.

Feast of the Lord (Ar. *ʿīdun sayyidī*): One of the feasts related to the life of Christ. Their exact number varied throughout history, with a more recent categorization of major and minor feasts. Currently, the official list consists of seven major feasts (Annunciation, Nativity, Theophany, Palm Sunday, Easter, Ascension, and Pentecost) and seven minor feasts (Circumcision, the Wedding at Cana, the Presentation in the Temple, Great Thursday, Thomas Sunday, the Flight into Egypt, and the Transfiguration).

Māʾ al-ṭaghṭiyyah (The water of covering): A term referring to the practice of drinking water immediately after communion, obligatory in the Coptic tradition to remove any particles of the body remaining in the mouth.

Mystery of the Catholic (Ar. *Sirr al-kāthūlīkūn*): A prayer recited by the priest inaudibly during the reading of the catholic epistle in Arabic (or other vernaculars understood by the congregation).

Mystery of the Gospel (Ar. *Sirr al-injīl*): A prayer recited by the priest inaudibly during the Gospel reading in Arabic (or other vernaculars understood by the congregation).

Mystery of the Pauline Incense (Ar. *Sirr bakhūr al-būlus*): A prayer recited by the priest inaudibly during the reading of the Pauline epistle in Arabic (or other vernaculars understood by the congregation).

Mystery of the Praxis (Ar. *Sirr al-ibraksīs*): A prayer of incense, recited by the priest inaudibly during the reading from the Acts in Arabic (or other vernaculars understood by the congregation).

Offering of Incense (Ar. *Raf' al-bakhūr*): A term referring to the morning and evening prayer services, in which the offering of incense is an integral part.

Pastophorion: One of many rooms common in Syrian, Coptic, and Ethiopian ancient churches, located to the east on either side of the apse. Some pastophoria were used for the reception and preparation of the eucharistic gifts and for storing eucharistic vessels, vestments, and books.

Prayer After Our Father: An inaudible prayer by the priest prayed after the common recitation of the Our Father in the precommunion rites and taking inspiration from its words.

Prayer of Incense (Ar. *Awshīyat al-bakhūr*): A class of prayers accompanying the offering of incense in various services. Particular such prayers are known for the morning and evening services, as well as during the Liturgy of the Word.

Prayer of Inclination (Ar. *Ṣalāt al-khuḍū'*): A class of prayers by the celebrant, found often near the end of liturgical services. They are usually prayed while the people bow their heads or prostrate to the ground.

Prayer of Reconciliation (Ar. *Ṣalāt al-ṣulḥ*): See *asbasmus*.

Prayer of Thanksgiving (Ar. *al-Shibihmūt*, *Ṣalāt al-shukr*): A prayer of thanksgiving at the beginning of most liturgical services in the Coptic tradition.

Prayer of the Gospel (Ar. *Awshīyat al-injīl*): A prayer by the priest preceding the reading of the Gospel passage in the morning, evening, and eucharistic services.

Prayer of the Kiss (Ar. *Ṣalāt al-qublah*): See *asbasmus*.

Prayer of the Oblation (Ar. *Awshīyat al-taqdimah*): See *Prothesis Prayer*.

Prayer of the Pauline Incense (Ar. *Awshīyat bakhūr al-būlus*): A prayer of incense by the priest at the beginning of the Liturgy of the Word, not to be confused with *The Mystery of the Pauline Incense*, said inaudibly during the translation of the Pauline reading.

Prayer of the Table (Ar. *Awshīyat al-mā'idah*): See *Prothesis Prayer*.

Prayer of the Veil (Ar. *Ṣalāt al-ḥijāb*): A prayer that occurs in the pre-anaphora of the Coptic liturgy and constitutes a priest's *apologia* of his unworthiness to perform his priestly duty of celebrating the Eucharist. Prayers of this type are common through the Eastern traditions, though prayers by this particular title are found mainly appended to Syrian anaphoras.

Pre-anaphoral rites: Rituals situated between the Liturgy of the Word and the Liturgy of the Eucharist and consisting of a prelude and preparation to the latter. They include the three great prayers for peace, the hierarchs, and the assemblies, the washing of hands by the priests, the recitation of the Creed, and the exchange of the kiss.

Prospherin (Gr. *prospherein*): A large white veil that covers the eucharistic gifts on the altar from the conclusion of the prothesis until its removal prior to the anaphora.

Prothesis: A ritual to choose and prepare the bread and wine for the Eucharist in the beginning of the liturgy. In the Coptic liturgy, this rite is performed publicly on the altar as the first stage of the eucharistic service. It includes the selection of eucharistic bread and the mixing of the chalice with wine and water accompanied with priestly blessings, prayers, and congregational chants.

Prothesis Prayer: A consecratory prayer for the bread and wine at the conclusion of the prothesis rite. It calls upon Christ to shine his face upon the gifts in order to change the bread and the wine into the body and blood of Christ. Although pronounced silently in current Coptic practice, it is thematically the central priestly prayer of the prothesis rite.

Psalmodia (Gr. *psalmōdia*): A liturgical book containing the chants and praises. Modern editions include the texts serving the offices of morning, evening, and midnight praise, as well as variable chants for saints and feasts known as doxologies.

Qaṣlah (Lat. *casula*): A hood attached to and distinguishing the *burnus* worn by bishops from that worn by presbyters.

Qiṭaʿ: Literally, selections or pieces. A term used to refer to nonversical chants or scriptural readings.

Responses (Ar. *Ibrūsāt*, Gr. *proseuxasthe*): Responses and proclamations of the deacon, known by their most common incipit in the Coptic tradition, from the Greek command "pray."

Sanctus: A liturgical chant based on the vision of the prophet in Isaiah 6:3, also appearing in Revelation 4:8. Its origin as a liturgical chant is unclear, but today forms an integral part of the anaphoral prayer in most traditions, often, though not in Egypt, appended with the so-called *benedictus* or the praise of the children of Jerusalem, "Hosanna in the highest," in Matthew 21:9.

Subdeacon (Ar. *Ibūdyāqūn*, Gr. *hypodiakonos*): One of the ranks of the minor orders assigned to assist the deacon, to perform other supportive functions in the sanctuary, and to guard the doors of the church.

Synaxarion (Ar. *Sinaksār*): A liturgical book containing narratives of the daily commemorations of saints' lives as well as major biblical and ecclesiastical events. It is arranged by day and is currently read in the Liturgy of the Word after the reading from the Acts of the Apostles.

Taḥlīl: A term applied to any prayer of absolution, from the Arabic root *ḥalla*, to untie or to make free.

Ṭawwāf: Verses from the psalms chanted during the procession of the Gospel around the altar in Coptic liturgical usage, from the Arabic *yaṭūf*, to encircle or go around.

Ṭaylasān: A crown-like stiff hat worn by presbyters usually with a band of cloth extending from the bottom and draped over the back of the wearer.

Theotokia (Ar. *Thā'ūtūkiyyah*, Gr. *theotokion*): Poetic pieces composed in Bohairic Coptic in praise of the Theotokos Virgin Mary and expounding the orthodox miaphysite theology of the incarnation. There are seven Theotokias in the Coptic repertoire, one for each day of the week. Unlike the Greek neuter plural *theotokia*, the term is used in Arabic as a feminine singular adjective.

Trisagion (Gr. *trishagion*, thrice-holy): A chant inspired by the vision in Isaiah 6:3 beginning with the words "Holy God, Holy mighty, Holy immortal." In the Coptic tradition, it is directed to Christ and contains phrases expressing key events in Christ's life, among them "who was born of the Virgin, who was crucified for us, and who rose from the dead." It is chanted in the Liturgy of the Word before the reading of the Gospel.

Tūniyah (Gr. *othonion*, tunic): A white robe worn by all clergy and minor orders beginning from chanters, equivalent to the Western *alb* or the Byzantine *sticharion.*

Ūlūjiyyah (Gr. *eulogia*, blessing): Pieces of the bread baked for the Eucharist but not chosen for the consecration. It is distributed to the attendees after the dismissal of the liturgy as a blessing.

Wahman (Copt. *bōhem*, hymn): A generic term for a hymn or chanted composition.

WORKS CITED

'Abdallah, Alfonso. *L'ordinamento liturgico di Gabriele V, 88° Patriarca Copto (1409–1427)*. Cairo: Edizioni del Centro Francescano di Studi Orientali Cristiani, 1962.

Abdelsayed, John Paul [Bishop Kyrillos]. "Liturgy: Heaven on Earth." In *The Coptic Christian Heritage: History, Faith, and Culture*, edited by Lois M. Farag, 143–159. New York: Routledge, 2014.

Alexopoulos, Stefanos. *The Presanctified Liturgy in the Byzantine Rite: A Comparative Analysis of Its Origins, Evolution, and Structural Components*. Leuven: Peeters, 2009.

Armanios, Febe. *Coptic Christianity in Ottoman Egypt*. Oxford: Oxford University Press, 2011.

Assfalg, Julius. "Arabisch qaṣla = Kapuze, verzierter Rand am Meßgewand des Bischofs." *Oriens Christianus* 2 (1954): 133–139.

———. *Die Ordnung des Priestertums: Ein altes liturgisches Handbuch der koptischen Kirche*. Cairo: [Centre d'Études Orientales de la Custodie Franciscaine de Terre-Sainte], 1955.

Atanassova, Diliana. "The Primary Sources of Southern Egyptian Liturgy: Retrospect and Prospect." In *Rites and Rituals of the Christian East: Proceedings of the Fourth International Congress of the Society of Oriental Liturgy, Lebanon, 10–15 July 2012*, edited by Bert Groen et al., 47–96. Leuven: Peeters, 2014.

'Awaḍ, Jirjis Fīlūthā'us. *Al-Majmū' al-ṣafawī: Yataḍamman al-qawānīn allatī jama'ahā al-'allāmah al-shaykh al-Ṣafī Abū al-Faḍā'il ibn Al-'assāl* [The Ṣafī collection: Contains the canons, which the scholarly elder Al-Ṣafī Abū al-Faḍā'il ibn al-'Assāl has collected]. Vol. 1. Cairo, 1908.

———. *Ibn Kabar: Akbar faylasūf qibṭī qadīr fī al-qarn al-rābiʿ ʿashar* [Ibn Kabar: The greatest capable Coptic philosopher in the 14th century]. Cairo: Al-maṭbaʿah al-miṣriyyah al-ahliyyah, 1930.
ʿAwaḍ, Wadīʿ. "al-Shams ibn Kabar." *Christian-Muslim Relations: A Bibliographical History*, edited by David Thomas et al., 4:762–766. Leiden: Brill, 2009–16.
———. "Testo della traduzione araba della Messa Copta di San Basilio secondo un manoscritto del 1288." *SOC Collectanea* 41 (2008): 129–149.
Baramūsī, Mīnā al-. *Kitāb al-ibṣalmūdiyyah al-muqaddasah al-sanawiyyah ḥasab ṭaqs wa-tartīb al-kanīsah al-qibṭiyyah al-urthūḍksiyyah* [The book of the year-round holy Psalmodia according to the rite and arrangement of the Coptic Orthodox Church]. Alexandria: Al-Kamāl ʿAbd al-Masīḥ Tadrus, 1908.
Baramūsī, Mīṣāʾīl al-. "Dallāl al-mubtadiʾīn wa-tahdhīb al-ʿalmāniyyīn. Aqdam dallāl ṭaqsī lil-kanīsah al-qibṭiyyah [The guide to the beginners and the disciplining of the laity, the oldest ritual guide of the Coptic Church]." *Majallat Madrasat al-Iskandariyyah* 24 (2018): 117–169.
Bärsch, Jürgen, and Benedikt Kranemann, eds. *Geschichte der Liturgie in den Kirchen des Westens: Rituelle Entwicklungen, theologische Konzepte und kulturelle Kontexte.* 2 vols. Münster: Aschendorff, 2018.
Bénazeth, Dominique. "De l'autel au musée: Quelques objets liturgiques conserves au Musée Copte du Caire." In *Egypt 1350 BC–AD 1800: Art Historical and Archeological Studies for Gawdat Gabra*, edited by Marianne Eaton-Krauss, Cäcilia Fluck, and Gertrud J. M. van Loon, 35–52. Wiesbaden: Ludwig Reichert Verlag, 2011.
Bornert, René. *Les commentaires byzantins de la Divine Liturgie du VIIe au XVe siècle.* Paris: Institut Français d'Études Byzantines, 1966.
Bouras, Laskarina, and Robert Taft. "Ambo." *The Oxford Dictionary of Byzantium*, edited by Alexander P. Kazhdan et al., 1:75–76. New York: Oxford University Press, 1991.
Bradshaw, Paul F. *Eucharistic Origins.* Eugene, OR: Wipf & Stock, 2012.
———. *The Search for the Origins of Christian Worship: Sources and Methods for the Study of Early Liturgy.* 2nd ed. Oxford: Oxford University Press, 2002.
Brakmann, Heinzgerd. "Die altkirchlichen Ordinationsgebete Jerusalems." *Jahrbuch für Antike und Christentum* 47 (2006): 108–127.
———. "Le déroulement de la Messe copte: Structure et histoire." In *L'Eucharistie: Célébrations, rites, piétés: Conférences Saint-Serge, XLIe semaine d'études liturgiques, Paris, 28 Juin–1 Juillet 1994*, edited by Achille M. Triacca and Alessandro Pistoia, 107–132. Rome: Edizioni Liturgiche, 1995.
———. "Neue Funde und Forschungen zur Liturgie der Kopten (1988–1992)." In *Acts of the Fifth International Congress of Coptic Studies, Washington, 12–15 August 1992*, edited by Tito Orlandi, 1:9–32. Rome: CIM, 1993.

———. "New Discoveries and Studies in the Liturgy of the Copts (2004–2012)." In *Coptic Society, Literature and Religion from Late Antiquity to Modern Times: Proceedings of the Tenth International Congress of Coptic Studies, Rome, September 17th–22nd, 2012 and Plenary Reports of the Ninth International Congress of Coptic Studies, Cairo, September 15th–19th, 2008*, edited by Paola Buzi, Alberto Camplani, and Federico Contardi, 1:457–481. Leuven: Peeters, 2016.

Brightman, F. E., ed. *Liturgies Eastern and Western Being the Texts Original or Translated of the Principal Liturgies of the Church.* Vol. 1, *Eastern Liturgies.* Oxford, 1896.

Browning, Robert. "Dionysius the Areopagite, Pseudo-." *The Oxford Dictionary of Byzantium*, edited by Alexander P. Kazhdan et al., 1:629–630. New York: Oxford University Press, 1991.

Budde, Achim. *Die ägyptische Basilios-Anaphora: Text—Kommentar—Geschichte.* Münster: Aschendorff, 2004.

Budge, E. A. Wallis, ed. *Coptic Martyrdoms etc. in the Dialect of Upper Egypt.* Vol. 1. Oxford, 1914.

Burmester, O. H. E. "The Canonical Hours of the Coptic Church." *Orientalia Christiana Periodica* 2, nos. 1–2 (1936): 78–100.

———. "The Canons of Christodulos, Patriarch of Alexandria (1047–1077)." *Le Muséon* 45 (1932): 71–84.

———. "The Canons of Cyril II, LXVII Patriarch of Alexandria." *Le Muséon* 49 (1936): 245–288.

———. "The Canons of Cyril III Ibn Laḳlaḳ, 75th Patriarch of Alexandria (Part II)." *Bulletin de la Société d'Archéologie Copte* 14 (1950): 113–150.

———. "The Canons of Gabriel Ibn Turaik, LXX Patriarch of Alexandria." *Le Muséon* 36 (1933): 43–54.

———. "The Canons of Gabriel Ibn Turaik, LXX Patriarch of Alexandria." *Orientalia Christiana Periodica* 1 (1935): 5–45.

———. *The Egyptian or Coptic Church: A Detailed Description of Her Liturgical Services and the Rites and Ceremonies Observed in the Administration of Her Sacraments.* Cairo: [Société d'Archéologie Copte], 1967.

———. "The Greek Kīrugmata Versicles & Responses and Hymns in the Coptic Liturgy." *Orientalia Christiana Periodica* 2, no. 3–4 (1936): 363–394.

———. *The Horologion of the Egyptian Church: Coptic and Arabic Text from a Mediaeval Manuscript.* Cairo: Edizioni del Centro Francescano di Studi Orientali Cristiani, 1973.

———. "The Liturgy *Coram Patriarcha aut Episcopo* in the Coptic Church." *Le Muséon* 49 (1936): 79–84.

———. *Ordination Rites of the Coptic Church: Text According to MS. 253 Lit., Coptic Museum.* Cairo: [Société d'Archéologie Copte], 1985.

———. "The Sayings of Michael, Metropolitan of Damietta." *Orientalia Christiana Periodica* 2, no. 1–2 (1936): 101–128.
———. "Vesting Prayers and Ceremonies of the Coptic Church." *Orientalia Christiana Periodica* 1, nos. 1–2 (1935): 305–314.
Butler, Alfred J. *The Ancient Coptic Churches of Egypt*. Vol. 2. Oxford: Clarendon Press, 1884.
Carr, Ephrem. "Liturgical Families in the East." In *Handbook for Liturgical Studies*. Vol. 1, *Introduction to the Liturgy*, edited by Anscar J. Chupungco, 11–24. Collegeville, MN: Liturgical Press, 1997.
Chéhab, Mamdouh. "Traduction de la version arabe de la messe copte de s. Basile. Vatican copte 17 (1288 A.D.)." *SOC Collectanea* 44 (2011): 49–68.
Codey, Aelred. "Calendar, Coptic." *The Coptic Encyclopedia*, edited by Aziz S. Atiya, 2:433a–436a. New York: Macmillan, 1991.
Connolly, R. H., and H. W. Codrington. *Two Commentaries on the Jacobite Liturgy by George Bishop of the Arab Tribes and Moses Bār Kēpha: Together with the Syriac Anaphora of St. James and a Document Entitled the Book of Life*. Oxford: Williams & Norgate, 1913.
Cook, M. "Al-Nahy ʿan al-Munkar." *Encyclopaedia of Islam*, 2nd ed., edited by P. Bearman et al., 12:644–646. Leiden: Brill, 1986–2004.
Coquin, René-Georges. *Les canons d'Hippolyte: Édition critique de la version arabe, introduction et traduction française*. Paris: Firmin-Didot, 1966.
———. "Nicaea, Arabic Canons of." *The Coptic Encyclopedia*, edited by Aziz S. Atiya, 6:1789a–1790a. New York: Macmillan, 1991.
———. "Patriarchal Residences." *The Coptic Encyclopedia*, edited by Aziz S. Atiya, 6:1912a–1913b.
Crum, W. E. *Catalogue of the Coptic Manuscripts in the British Museum*. London: British Museum, 1906.
Cuming, Geoffrey J. *The Liturgy of St Mark: Edited from the Manuscripts with a Commentary*. Rome: Pontificium Institutum Studiorum Orientalium, 1990.
Cunningham, Mary B., and Pauline Allen, eds. *Preacher and Audience: Studies in Early Christian and Byzantine Homiletics*. Leiden: Brill, 1998.
Dā'ūd, Marqus. *Al-Disqūliyyah aw taʿālīm al-rusul*. 5th ed. Cairo: Maktabat al-maḥabbah, 1979.
Davis, Stephen J. *Coptic Christology in Practice: Incarnation and Divine Participation in Late Antique and Medieval Egypt*. Oxford: Oxford University Press, 2008.
———. "Review of *De la Trinité à la Trinité: La christologie liturgique d'Ibn Sabbāʿ, auteur copte du XIIIe siècle*. By Milad Sidky Zakhary." *The Journal of Theological Studies* 60, no. 2 (2009): 733–737.
Davis, Stephen J., Bilal Orfali, and Samuel Noble. *A Disputation over a Fragment of the Cross: A Medieval Arabic Text from the History of Christian-Jewish-Muslim Relations in Egypt*. Beirut: Dar El-Machreq, 2012.

den Heijer, Johannes. "Les patriarches coptes d'origine syrienne." In *Studies of the Christian Arabic Heritage in Honour of Father Prof. Dr. Samir Khalil Samir S.I. at the Occasion of His Sixty-Fifth Birthday*, edited by R. Y. Ebied and H. G. B. Teule, 45–63. Leuven: Peeters, 2005.

Dous, Roshdi Wassef Behman. "'Ο Αγιασμός των υδάτων του Νείλου Ποταμού στην Αλεξανδρινή Λειτουργική Παράδοση." Doctoral dissertation, Aristotle University of Thessaloniki, 2011.

Dujarier, Michel. *A History of the Catechumenate: The First Six Centuries.* Translated by Edward J. Haasl. New York: Sadlier, 1979.

Engberding, Hieronymus. "Der Nil in der liturgischen Frömmigkeit des christlichen Ostens." *Oriens Christianus* 37 (1953): 56–88.

———. "Ein Problem in der Homologia vor der hl. Kommunion in der ägyptischen Liturgie." *Orientalia Christiana Periodica* 2 (1936): 145–154.

Evetts, B. T. A. *The Churches & Monasteries of Egypt and Some Neighbouring Countries Attributed to Abū Ṣāliḥ the Armenian.* Oxford, 1895.

Feltoe, Charles Lett, ed. *Διονυσίου λείψανα: The Letters and Other Remains of Dionysius of Alexandria.* Cambridge: Cambridge University Press, 1904.

Fiey, Jean Maurice. "Coptes et syriaques: Contacts et échanges." *SOC Collectanea* 15 (1972–73): 295–365.

Fransiskānī, Wadī' al-. "Aqdam al-tarjamāt al-'arabiyyah (Qurūn 12–14) li-quddāsāt al-kanīsah al-qibṭiyyah [The oldest Arabic translations (12th–14th centuries) of the liturgies of the Coptic Church]." *Majallat madrasat al-Iskandarīyah* 7 (2011): 217–235.

Fritsch, Emmanuel. "The Order of the Mystery: An Ancient Catechesis Preserved in BnF Ethiopic Ms d'Abbadie 66–66bis (Fifteenth Century) with a Liturgical Commentary." In *Studies in Oriental Liturgy: Proceedings of the Fifth International Congress of the Society of Oriental Liturgy, New York, 10–15 June 2014*, edited by Bert Groen et al., 195–263. Leuven: Peeters, 2019.

———. "The Preparation of the Gifts and the Pre-Anaphora in the Ethiopian Eucharistic Liturgy in Around A.D. 1100." In *Rites and Rituals of the Christian East: Proceedings of the Fourth International Congress of the Society of Oriental Liturgy, Lebanon, 10–15 July 2012*, edited by Bert Groen et al., 97–152. Leuven: Peeters, 2014.

Gabra, Gawdat. *Coptic Monasteries: Egypt's Monastic Art and Architecture.* Cairo: American University in Cairo Press, 2002.

Galadza, Daniel. *Liturgy and Byzantinization in Jerusalem.* Oxford: Oxford University Press, 2018.

Gimaret, D. "Subḥān." *Encyclopaedia of Islam*, 2nd ed., edited by P. Bearman et al., 9:742–743. Leiden: Brill, 1986–2004.

Graf, Georg. *Catalogue de manuscrits arabes chrétiens conservés au Caire.* Vatican: Biblioteca Apostolica Vaticana, 1934.

———. *Ein Reformversuch innerhalb der koptischen Kirche im zwölften Jahrhundert*. Paderborn: Ferdinand Schöningh, 1923.
———. "Liturgische Anweisungen des koptischen Patriarchen Kyrillos ibn Laklak." *Jahrbuch für Liturgiewissenschaft* 4 (1924): 119–134.
———. *Verzeichnis arabischer kirchlicher Termini*. 2nd ed. Louvain: Secrétariat du Corpus, 1954.
Graf, Georg, ed. *Geschichte der christlichen arabischen Literatur*. 5 vols. Vatican City: Biblioteca Apostolica Vaticana, 1944–1953.
Grillmeier, Aloys, and Theresia Hainthaler. *Christ in Christian Tradition*. Vol. 2, *From the Council of Chalcedon (451) to Gregory the Great (590–604)*, Part 2, *The Church of Alexandria with Nubia and Ethiopia after 451*. Translated by O. C. Dean Jr. Louisville, KY: Westminster John Knox Press, 1996.
Grossmann, Peter. *Christliche Architektur in Ägypten*. Leiden: Brill, 2002.
Hammerschmidt, Ernst. *Die koptische Gregoriosanaphora: Syrische und griechische Einflüsse auf eine ägyptische Liturgie*. Berlin: Akademie Verlag, 1957.
Hammerstaedt, Jürgen. *Griechische Anaphorenfragmente aus Ägypten und Nubien*. Opladen: Westdeutscher Verlag, 1999.
Haq, S. Nomanul. "Rukn." *Encyclopaedia of Islam*, 2nd ed., edited by P. Bearman et al., 8:596b. Leiden: Brill, 1986–2004.
Hebbelynck, Adolph, and Arnold van Lantschoot. *Codices Coptici Vaticani Barberiniani Borgiani Rossiani*. Vol. 1, *Codices Coptici Vaticani*. Vatican City: Biblioteca Vaticana, 1937.
Hellholm, David, and Dieter Sänger, eds. *The Eucharist: Its Origins and Contexts—Sacred Meal, Communal Meal, Table Fellowship in Late Antiquity, Early Judaism, and Early Christianity*. 3 vols. Tübingen: Mohr Siebeck, 2017.
Hussey, J. M., and P. A. McNulty, trans. *A Commentary on the Divine Liturgy: Nicholas Cabasilas*. Crestwood, NY: St Vladimir's Seminary Press, 2002.
Innemée, Karel C. *Ecclesiastical Dress in the Medieval Near East*. Leiden: Brill, 1992.
Ishaq, Emile Maher. "Trisagion." *The Coptic Encyclopedia*, edited by Aziz S. Atiya, 7:2278a–2279a. New York: Macmillan, 1991.
Janeras, Sebastià. "Le Trisagion: Une formule brève en liturgie compare." In *Acts of the International Congress: Comparative Liturgy Fifty Years after Anton Baumstark (1872–1948), Rome, 25–29 September 1998*, edited by Robert F. Taft and Gabriele Winkler, 495–562. Rome: Pontificio Istituto Orientale, 2001.
Jasper, R. C. D., and G. J. Cuming. *Prayers of the Eucharist: Early and Reformed. Texts Translated and Edited with Commentary*. 3rd ed. Collegeville, MN: Liturgical Press, 1990.
Jirjis, Ḥabīb. *al-Jawharah al-nafīsah fī khuṭab al-kanīsah* [The precious jewel in the orations of the church]. Cairo: Maṭba'at al-karmah, 1914.
Jirjis, Marqus. *al-Durr al-thamīn fī īḍāḥ al-dīn* [The precious pearl in elucidating the faith]. 2nd ed. Cairo, 1992.

Johnson, Maxwell E. *Liturgy in Early Christian Egypt*. Cambridge: Grove Books, 1995.

———. *The Prayers of Sarapion of Thmuis: A Literary, Liturgical, and Theological Analysis*. Rome: Pontificio Istituto Orientale, 1995.

Jungmann, Josef A. *The Mass of the Roman Rite: Its Origins and Development (Missarum Sollemnia)*. Translated by Francis A. Brunner. 2nd ed. 2 vols. Notre Dame, IN: Ave Maria, 2012.

Jyunboll, T. W. "Farḍ." *Encyclopaedia of Islam*, 2nd ed., edited by P. Bearman et al., 2:790. Leiden: Brill, 1986–2004.

Khater, Antoine, and O. H. E. Burmester, trans. *History of the Patriarchs of the Egyptian Church Known as the History of the Holy Church by Saîrwus Ibn al-Muḳaffaʿ Bishop of al-Ašmûnîn*, vol. 3.3, *Cyril II–Cyril V (A.D. 1235–1894)*. Cairo: La Société d'Archéologie Copte, 1970.

Kircher, Athanasius. *Lingua aegyptiaca restitute*. Rome, 1648.

Krause, Martin. "The Importance of Wadi al-Natrun for Coptology." In *Christianity and Monasticism in Wadi al-Natrun: Essays from the 2002 International Symposium of the Saint Mark Foundation and the Saint Shenouda the Archimandrite Coptic Society*, edited by Maged S. A. Mikhail and Mark Moussa, 1–11. Cairo: American University in Cairo Press, 2009.

Łajtar, Adam, and Grzegorz Ochała. "Two Wall Inscriptions from the Faras Cathedral with Lists of People and Goods." In *Nubian Voices II: New Texts and Studies of Christian Nubian Culture*, edited by Adam Łajtar, Grzegorz Ochała, and Jacques van der Vliet, 73–102. Warsaw: Warsaw University, Faculty of Law and Administration, Institute of Archaeology, Department of Papyrology, 2015.

Lampe, G. W. H. *A Patristic Greek Lexicon*. Oxford: Clarendon Press, 1961.

Lanne, Emmanuel. *Le grand euchologe du Monastère Blanc: Texte copte édité avec traduction française*. Turnhout: Brepols, 2003.

Leithy, Tamer el-. "Coptic Culture and Conversion in Medieval Cairo, 1293–1524 A.D." Doctoral dissertation, Princeton University, 2005.

Liddell, Henry George, and Robert Scott. *A Greek-English Lexicon*. Revised by Sir Henry Stuart Jones. Oxford: Clarendon Press, 1996.

Little, Donald P. "Coptic Conversion to Islam under the Baḥrī Mamlūks, 692–755/1293–1354." *Bulletin of the School of Oriental and African Studies* 39, no. 3 (1976): 552–569.

Luibheid, Colm, trans. *Pseudo-Dionysius: The Complete Works*. New York: Paulist Press, 1987.

Lutfi, Huda. "Coptic Festivals of the Nile: Aberrations of the Past?" In *The Mamluks in Egyptian Politics and Society*, edited by Thomas Philipp and Ulrich Haarmann, 254–282. Cambridge: Cambridge University Press, 1998.

MacCoull, Leslie S. B. "'A Dwelling Place of Christ, a Healing Place of Knowledge': The Non-Chalcedonian Eucharist in Late Antique Egypt and its Setting." In *Documenting Christianity in Egypt, Sixth to Fourteenth Centuries*, 1–16. Burlington, VT: Ashgate, 2011.

Macomber, William F. *Final Inventory of the Microfilmed Manuscripts of the Coptic Museum, Old Cairo, Egypt: Rolls A1–20, Manuscripts in Arabic, Coptic, (Bohairic, Oxyrhynchite [1], Sahidic), Greek*. Provo, UT: Harold B. Lee Library, Brigham Young University, 1995.

———. "The Greek Text of the Coptic Mass and of the Anaphoras of Basil and Gregory According to the Kacmarcik Codex." *Orientalia Christiana Periodica* 43 (1977): 308–334.

———. "The Nicene Creed in a Liturgical Fragment of the 5th or 6th Century from Upper Egypt." *Oriens Christianus* 77 (1993): 98–103.

Malan, S. C. *A Short History of the Copts and of Their Church, Translated from the Arabic of Tāqi-ed-Dīn El-Maqrīzī*. London: D. Nutt, 1873.

Maqārī, Athanasius al-. *al-Quddās al-ilāhī: Sirr malakūt allāh* [The Divine Liturgy: The mystery of the kingdom of God]. 2nd ed. 2 vols. Cairo: Dār nūbār, 2011.

Maṣrī, Īrīs Ḥabīb al-. "The Rite of the Filling of the Chalice." *Bulletin de la Société d'Archéologie Copte* 6 (1940): 77–90.

Mateos, Juan. *La célébration de la Parole dans la liturgie byzantine: Étude historique*. Rome: Pontificium Institutum Studiorum Orientalium, 1971.

Mathews, Thomas F. *The Early Churches of Constantinople: Architecture and Liturgy*. University Park: Pennsylvania State University Press, 1971.

McGowan, Andrew B. *Ancient Christian Worship: Early Church Practices in Social, Historical, and Anthropological Perspective*. Grand Rapids, MI: Baker Academic, 2014.

McGuckin, John A. *St. Cyril of Alexandria: The Christological Controversy: Its History, Theology, and Texts*. Crestwood, NY: St. Vladimir's Seminary Press, 2004.

McKenna, John H. *The Eucharistic Epiclesis: A Detailed History from the Patristic to the Modern Era*. 2nd ed. Chicago: Hillenbrand Books, 2009.

Mercier, B. Charles. *La liturgie de Saint Jacques: Édition critique du texte grec avec traduction latine*. Turnhout: Brepols, 1997.

Metzger, Marcel. *Les constitutions apostoliques*. Vol. 3, *Livres 7–8: Introduction, texte critique, traduction et notes*. Paris: Cerf, 2008.

Metzger, Marcel, Wolfram Drews, and Heinzgerd Brakmann. "Katechumenat." In *Reallexikon für Antike und Christentum: Sachwörterbuch zur Auseinandersetzung des Christentums mit der Antiken Welt*, edited by Georg Schöllgen et al., 20:498–574. Stuttgart: Anton Hiersmann, 2004.

Meyendorff, Paul. *The Anointing of the Sick*. Crestwood, NY: St Vladimir's Seminary Press, 2009.

———. *St Germanus of Constantinople on the Divine Liturgy: The Greek Text with Translation, Introduction, and Commentary*. Crestwood, NY: St Vladimir's Seminary Press, 1984.

Mīkhā'īl, Albair Jamāl. *Al-Asās fī khidmat al-shammās: Kitāb al-ṭuqūs wa-al-alḥān wa-ṣalawāt ṭaqs al-laqqān wa-dallāl usbū' al-ālām* [The foundation in the service of the deacon: The book of rites and hymns and the prayers of the rite of the basin and the guide of holy week]. Cairo: Maktabat Marijirjis Shīkūlānī, 2013.

Mikhail, Maged S. A. "The Deacon as Concelebrant and Liturgical Witness in the Coptic Rite." *Greek Orthodox Theological Review* 61, nos. 3–4 (2016): 101–123.

———. *From Byzantine to Islamic Egypt: Religion, Identity and Politics after the Arab Conquest*. New York: I. B. Tauris, 2016.

Mikhail, Ramez. "'And They Shall Stand Bareheaded': On the Historical Development of Liturgical Head-Covering in the Coptic Rite." Forthcoming in Proceedings of the Eleventh International Congress of Coptic Studies, Claremont, California, July 25th–30th, 2016.

———. "The Coptic Church and the Presanctified Liturgy: The Story of a Rejected Tradition." *Alexandria School Journal* 3 (2016): 2–30.

———. "The Liturgy *Coram Patriarcha* Revisited: The Prothesis of the Coptic Patriarchal Liturgy in Sources of the 15th–16th Centuries." *Le Muséon* 131, no. 3–4 (2018): 279–312.

———. "A Magical Cure for Rabies: The Coptic Liturgical Service in Honor of Abū Tarbū." In *Ritualia Orientalia Mixta: Reflexionen über Rituale in der Religionsgeschichte des Orients und angrenzender Gebiete*, edited by Predrag Bukovec and Vedrana Tadić, 267–289. Hamburg: Verlag Dr. Kovac, 2017.

———. *The Presentation of the Lamb: The Prothesis and Preparatory Rites of the Coptic Liturgy*. Münster: Aschendorff, 2020.

———. "Towards a History of Liturgical Vestments in the Coptic Rite: I—Minor Orders, Deacons, and Presbyters." *Coptica* 15 (2016): 55–70.

Mistrīḥ, Vincentio. *Yūḥannā ibn Abī Zakarīā ibn Sibā', Pretiosa margarita de scientiis ecclesiasticis*. Cairo: Centrum Franciscanum Studiorum Orientalium Christianorum, 1966.

Moawad, Samuel. "Liturgische Hinweise in koptischen literarischen Werken." In *From Old Cairo to the New World: Coptic Studies Presented to Gawdat Gabra on the Occasion of His Sixty-Fifth Birthday*, edited by Youhanna Nessim Youssef and Samuel Moawad, 125–145. Leuven: Peeters, 2013.

Nasrallah, Joseph. *Histoire du movement littéraire dans l'Église Melchite du Ve au XXe siècle: Contribution à l'étude de la littérature arabe chrétienne*, vol. 3.1 (969–1250). Louvain: Peeters, 1983.

———. "La liturgie des Patriarcats melchites de 969 à 1300." *Oriens Christianus* 71 (1987): 156–181.

Nau, François. "Opuscules maronites." *Revue de l'orient chrétien* 4, no. 3 (1899): 318–353.
Nicolotti, Andrea. "Forme di partecipazione alla liturgia eucaristica nel rito copto." In *Liturgia e partecipazione: Forme del coinvolgimento rituale*, edited by Luigi Girardi, 223–267. Padua: Messaggero, 2013.
O'Leary, De Lacy Evans. *The Daily Office and Theotokia of the Coptic Church*. London: Simpkin, Marshall, Hamilton, Kent, 1911.
———. *The Saints of Egypt*. New York: Macmillan, 1937.
Olivar, Alexandre. *La predicación cristiana antigua*. Barcelona: Herder, 1991.
Parenti, Stefano. "Towards a Regional History of the Byzantine Euchology." *Ecclesia Orans* 37 (2010): 109–121.
Périchon, Pierre, and Pierre Maraval, trans. *Socrate de Constantinople: Histoire ecclésiastique, livres IV–VI—Texte grec de l'édition G. C. Hansen (GCS)*. Paris: Cerf, 2006.
Price, Richard. "The Council of Chalcedon (451): A Narrative." In *Chalcedon in Context: Church Councils 400–700*, edited by Richard Price and Mary Whitby, 70–91. Liverpool: Liverpool University Press, 2009.
Qilādah, William Sulaymān. *Ta'ālīm al-rusul al-Disqūliyyah*. 2nd ed. Cairo: Dār al-thaqāfah, 1989.
Quecke, Hans. *Untersuchungen zum koptischen Stundengebet*. Louvain: Université Catholique de Louvain, Institut Orientaliste, 1970.
———. "Zum 'Gebet der Lossprechung des Vaters' in der ägyptischen Basilius-Liturgie. Ein bisher unbeachteter Textzeuge: Brit. Libr., Ms. Or. 4718(1) 3." *Orientalia* 48 (1979): 68–81.
Radle, Gabriel. "Embodied Eschatology: The Council of Nicaea's Regulation of Kneeling and Its Reception across Liturgical Traditions, Part 1." *Worship* 90 (July 2016): 345–371.
———. "Embodied Eschatology: The Council of Nicaea's Regulation of Kneeling and Its Reception across Liturgical Traditions, Part 2." *Worship* 90 (September 2016): 433–461.
———. "Uncovering the Alexandrian Greek Rite of Marriage: The Liturgical Evidence of Sinai NF/MG 67 (9th/10th c.)." *Ecclesia Orans* 28 (2011): 49–73.
Ramis, Gabriel. "Liturgical Families in the West." in *Introduction to the Liturgy*, edited by Anscar J. Chupungco, 25–32. Collegeville, MN: Liturgical Press, 1997.
Ramzī, Fādī Ra'fat. "Tartīb al-quddās wa-al-qurbān (1): Naṣṣ al-bāb al-sābi' 'ashar min miṣbāḥ al-ẓulmah fī īḍāḥ al-khidmah ḥasab makhṭūṭ bārīs [The order of the liturgy and the oblation (1): The text of the seventeenth chapter of the lamp of darkness in the elucidation of the service according to the Paris manuscript]." *Majallat madrasat al-Iskandariyyah* 17 (2014): 193–214.

Reinhart, A. Kevin. "'Like the Difference between Heaven and Earth': Ḥanafī and Shāfiʿī Discussions of *farḍ* and *wājib*." In *Studies in Islamic Legal Theory*, edited by Bernard G. Weiss, 205–234. Leiden: Brill, 2002.

Renaudot, Eusèbe. *Liturgiarum Orientalium Collectio*. 2nd ed. Vol. 1. Frankfurt, 1847.

Riedel, Wilhelm. "Der Katalog der christlichen Schriften in arabischer Sprache von Abū 'l-Barakāt'." *Nachrichten von der königlichen Gesellschaft der Wissenschaften zu Göttingen* 5 (1902): 635–706.

———. *Die Kirchenrechtsquellen des Patriarchats Alexandrien*. Leipzig: A. Deichert'sche Verlagsbuchhandlung, 1900.

Riedel, Wilhelm, and W. E. Crum. *The Canons of Athanasius of Alexandria: The Arabic and Coptic Versions*. Oxford: Williams & Norgate, 1904.

Roberts, Alexander, and James Donaldson, eds. *The Ante-Nicene Fathers: Translations of the Writings of the Fathers down to A.D. 325*. Vol. 6. Peabody, MA: Hendrickson, 1994.

Rodwell, John M. *The Liturgies of S. Basil, S. Gregory, and S. Cyril, Translated from a Coptic Manuscript of the Thirteenth Century*. London, 1870.

Rubenson, Samuel. "Translating the Tradition: Some Remarks on the Arabization of the Patristic Heritage in Egypt." *Medieval Encounters* 2, no. 1 (1996): 4–14.

Ṣalīb, ʿAbd al-Masīḥ. ⲡⲓϫⲱⲙ ⲛ̀ⲧⲉ ⲡⲓⲉⲩⲭⲟⲗⲟⲅⲓⲟⲛ ⲉⲑⲟⲩⲁⲃ ⲉ̀ⲧⲉ ⲫⲁⲓ ⲡⲉ ⲡⲓϫⲱⲙ ⲛ̀ⲧⲉ ϯϣⲟⲙϯ ⲛ̀ⲁⲛⲁⲫⲟⲣⲁ ⲛ̀ⲧⲉ ⲡⲓⲁⲅⲓⲟⲥ ⲃⲁⲥⲓⲗⲓⲟⲥ ⲛⲉⲙ ⲡⲓⲁⲅⲓⲟⲥ ⲅⲣⲏⲅⲟⲣⲓⲟⲥ ⲛⲉⲙ ⲡⲓⲁⲅⲓⲟⲥ ⲕⲩⲣⲓⲗⲗⲟⲥ ⲛⲉⲙ ϩⲁⲛⲕⲉⲉⲩⲭⲏ ⲉⲩⲟⲩⲁⲃ [The book of the Holy Euchologion, which is the book of the three Anaphoras of Saint Basil and Saint Gregory and Saint Cyril, and other holy prayers]. Cairo: ʿAyn shams, 1902.

Samir, Kussaim. "Contribution à l'étude du Moyen Arabe des Coptes." *Le Muséon* 80 (1967): 153–209.

Samir, Samir Khalil. "Book of Epact." In *The Coptic Encyclopedia*, edited by Aziz S. Atiya, 2:490a–411b. New York: Macmillan, 1991.

———. "Gabriel V." *The Coptic Encyclopedia*, edited by Aziz S. Atiya, 4:1130a–1133a.

———. "L'encyclopédie liturgique d'Ibn Kabar († 1324) et son apologie d'usages coptes." In *Crossroad of Cultures: Studies in Liturgy and Patristics in Honor of Gabriele Winkler*, edited by Hans-Jürgen Feulner, Elena Velkovska, and Robert F. Taft, 619–655. Rome: Pontificio Istituto Orientale, 2000.

Samuel, ed. *Tartīb al-biʿah: ʿan makhṭūṭāt al-baṭriyarkiyyah bi-miṣr wa-al-iskandariyyah wa-makhṭūṭāt al-adyirah wa-al-kanāʾis* [The church order: From the manuscripts of the Patriarchate in Cairo and Alexandria, and the manuscripts of the monasteries and churches]. Vol. 3. Cairo: Al-naʿām lil-ṭibāʿah wa-al-tawrīdāt, 2000.

Sayyid, Ayman Fuʾād. *Al-mawāʿiẓ wa-al-iʿtibār fī dhikr al-khiṭaṭ wa-al-āthār li-Ṭaqī al-Dīn Aḥmad ibn ʿAlī ibn ʿAbd al-Qāḍir al-Maqrīzī* [Admonitions and reflections on the quarters and monuments by Taqī al-Dīn Aḥmad ibn 'Alī ibn 'Abd al-Qādir al-Maqrīzī]. Vol. 4. London: Mu'assasat al-furqān lil-turāth al-islāmī, 2004.

Schermann, Theodor. *Ägyptische Abendmahlsliturgien des ersten Jahrtausends.* Paderborn: Ferdinand Schöningh, 1912.

Schmelz, Georg. *Kirchliche Amtsträger im spätantiken Ägypten nach den Aussagen der griechischen und koptischen Papyri und Ostraka.* Munich: K. G. Saur, 2002.

Schulz, Hans-Joachim. *The Byzantine Liturgy: Symbolic Structure and Faith Expression.* Translated by Matthew J. O'Connell. New York: Pueblo Publishing, 1986.

Shoshan, Boaz. *Popular Culture in Medieval Cairo.* Cambridge: Cambridge University Press, 1993.

Sidarus, Adel Y. "The Copto-Arabic Renaissance in the Middle Ages: Characteristics and Socio-Political Context." *Coptica* 1 (2002): 141–160.

———. "La renaissance copte arabe du Moyen Âge." In *The Syriac Renaissance*, edited by H. G. B. Teule et al., 311–340. Leuven: Peeters, 2010.

Simaika, Marcus, and Yassa 'abd al-Masiḥ. *Catalogue of the Coptic and Arabic Manuscripts in the Coptic Museum, the Patriarchate, the Principal Churches of Cairo and Alexandria and the Monasteries of Egypt.* 3 vols. Cairo: Government Press, 1939.

Soliman, Sameh Farouk. "Re-Translating the Byzantine Paschal Troparion 'ΧΡΙΣΤΟΣ ΑΝΕΣΤΗ' into English on the Basis of the Two Participles: (ΠΑΤΗΣΑΣ & ΧΑΡΙΣΑΜΕΝΟΣ)." *Ephemerides Liturgicae* 130 (2016): 232–235.

Spinks, Bryan D. "From Functional to Artistic? The Development of the Fraction in the Syrian Orthodox Tradition." *Anaphora* 10, no. 2 (2016): 89–114.

———. *The Sanctus in the Eucharistic Prayer.* Cambridge: Cambridge University Press, 1991.

Stewart-Sykes, Alistair. *The Didascalia Apostolorum: An English Version with Introduction and Annotation.* Turnhout: Brepols, 2009.

Suryānī, Samuel al-. *Miṣbāḥ al-ẓulmah fī īḍāḥ al-khidmah li-ibn kabar (al-qarn 14)* [The lamp of darkness in the elucidation of the service by Ibn Kabar (14th century)]. Vol. 2, *Risāmat al-shamāmisah wa-al-ruhbān wa-al-rahibāt wa-al-ma'mūdiyyah wa-al-ṣalawāt wa-al-aṣwām wa-al-a'yād wa-al-zījah wa-al-tajnīz wa-ḥisāb al-abaqṭī* [The ordination of deacons, monks, nuns, baptism, the prayers, fasts, feasts, marriage, funerals, and the epact calculation]. (N.p. 1992).

Swanson, Mark N. *The Coptic Papacy in Islamic Egypt (641–1517).* Cairo: American University in Cairo Press, 2010.

———. "A Copto-Arabic Catechism of the Later Fatimid Period: "Ten Questions that One of the Disciples Asked of His Master." *Parole de l'Orient* 22 (1997): 473–501.

———. "Ibn Sabbāʿ." *Christian-Muslim Relations: A Bibliographical History*, edited by David Thomas et al., 4:918–923. Leiden: Brill, 2009–16.

———. "*Kitāb al-īḍāḥ*." *Christian-Muslim Relations: A Bibliographical History*, edited by David Thomas et al., 3:265–269.

———. "Marqus ibn al-Qunbar." *Christian-Muslim Relations: A Bibliographical History*, edited by David Thomas et al., 4:98–108.

———. "Michael of Damietta." *Christian-Muslim Relations: A Bibliographical History*, edited by David Thomas et al., 4:109–114.

———. "The Specifically Egyptian Context of a Coptic Arabic Text: Chapter Nine of the *Kitāb al-Īḍāḥ of Sawīrus ibn al-Muqaffaʿ*." *Medieval Encounters* 2, no. 3 (1996): 214–227.

Synodal Committee for Rituals. *Kitāb al-Sinaksār: Alladhi yaḥwī akhbār al-anbiyā' wa-al-rusul wa-al-shuhadā' wa-al-qiddīsīn al-mustaʿmal fī kanā'is al-kirāzah al-marqusiyyah* [The book of the Syanxarion: Which contains the accounts of the prophets and apostles and martyrs and saints used in the churches of the see of Mark]. 2nd ed. Vol. 2. Cairo: Dayr al-Sayyidah al-ʿAdhrā' al-Suryān, 2012.

Taft, Robert F. "The Dialogue before the Anaphora in the Byzantine Eucharistic Liturgy. I: The Opening Greeting." *Orientalia Christiana Periodica* 52 (1986): 299–324.

———. "The Dialogue before the Anaphora in the Byzantine Eucharistic Liturgy, II: The Sursum corda." *Orientalia Christiana Periodica* 54 (1988): 47–77.

———. "The Dialogue before the Anaphora in the Byzantine Eucharistic Liturgy, III: 'Let us give thanks to the Lord—It is fitting and right.'" *Orientalia Christiana Periodica* 55 (1989): 63–74.

———. "From Logos to Spirit: On the Early History of the Epiclesis." In *Gratias Agamus: Studien zum eucharistischen Hochgebet: Für Balthasar Fischer*, edited by Andreas Heinz and Heinrich Rennings, 489–502. Freiburg: Herder, 1992.

———. *A History of the Liturgy of St. John Chrysostom*. Vol. 2, *The Great Entrance: A History of the Transfer of Gifts and Other Pre-anaphoral Rites*. 2nd ed. Rome: Pontificium Institutum Studiorum Orientalium, 1978.

———. *A History of the Liturgy of St. John Chrysostom*. Vol. 4, *The Diptychs*. Rome: Pontificium Institutum Studiorum Orientalium, 1991.

———. *A History of the Liturgy of St. John Chrysostom*. Vol. 5, *The Precommunion Rites*. Rome: Pontificio Istituto Orientale, 2000.

———. *A History of the Liturgy of St. John Chrysostom*. Vol. 6, *The Communion, Thanksgiving, and Concluding Rites*. Rome: Pontificio Istituto Orientale, 2008.

———. "The Inclination Prayer before Communion in the Byzantine Liturgy of St. John Chrysostom: A Study in Comparative Liturgy." *Ecclesia Orans* 3 (1986): 29–60.

———. "The Liturgy of the Great Church: An Initial Synthesis of Structure and Interpretation on the Eve of Iconoclasm." *Dumbarton Oaks Papers* 34–35 (1980–81): 45–75.

———. *The Liturgy of the Hours in East and West: The Origins of the Divine Office and Its Meaning for Today*. 2nd ed. Collegeville, MN: Liturgical Press, 1993.

———. "*Quaestiones disputatae:* The Skeuophylakion of Hagia Sophia and the Entrances of the Liturgy Revisited." *Oriens Christianus* 81 (1997): 1–35.

———. "Textual Problems in the Diaconal Admonition before the Anaphora in the Byzantine Tradition." *Orientalia Christiana Periodica* 49 (1983): 340–365.

———. "Trisagion." *The Oxford Dictionary of Byzantium*, edited by Alexander P. Kazhdan et al, 3:2121. New York: Oxford University Press, 1991.

———. "When Did the Catechumenate Die Out in Constantinople?" in *ΑΝΑΘΗΜΑΤΑ ΕΟΡΤΙΚΑ: Studies in Honor of Thomas F. Mathews*, edited by Joseph D. Alchermes, Helen C. Evans, and Thelma K. Thomas. 288–295. Mainz am Rhein: Philipp von Zabern, 2009.

———. "Women at Church in Byzantium: Where, When—and Why?" *Dumbarton Oaks Papers* 52 (1998): 27–87.

Taft, Robert F., and Stefano Parenti. *Il grande ingresso: Edizione italiana rivista, ampliata e aggiornata*. Grottaferrata: Monastero Esarchico, 2014.

Teule, H. G. B. "Ya'ḳūbiyyūn." *Encyclopaedia of Islam*, 2nd ed., edited by P. Bearman et al., 11:258–262. Leiden: Brill, 1986–2004.

Tornberg, Carl Johan. *Codices Arabici, Persici et Turcici Bibliothecae Regiae Universitatis Upsaliensis*. Uppsala, 1849.

Troupeau, Gérard. *Catalogue des manuscrits arabes*. Part 1, *Manuscrits chrétiens*, vol. 1, *No. 1–323*. Paris: Bibliothèque Nationale, 1972.

Ṭūkhī, Raphael al-. ⲡⲓϫⲱⲙ ⲛ̀ⲧⲉ ⲡⲓϣⲟⲙⲧ ⲛ̀ⲁⲛⲁⲫⲟⲣⲁ ⲉ̀ⲧⲉ ⲛⲁⲓ ⲛⲉ ⲙ̀ⲡⲓⲁⲅⲓⲟⲥ ⲃⲁⲥⲓⲗⲓⲟⲥ ⲛⲉⲙ ⲡⲓⲁⲅⲓⲟⲥ ⲅⲣⲏⲅⲟⲣⲓⲟⲥ ⲡⲓⲑⲉⲟⲗⲟⲅⲟⲥ ⲛⲉⲙ ⲡⲓⲁⲅⲓⲟⲥ ⲕⲩⲣⲓⲗⲗⲟⲥ ⲛⲉⲙ ⲛⲓⲕⲉ ⲉⲩⲭⲏ ⲉⲑⲟⲩⲁⲃ [The book of the three anaphoras, which are of Saint Basil and Saint Gregory the Theologian and Saint Cyril, and other holy prayers]. Rome, 1736.

Verrone, Kerry E. *Mighty Deeds and Miracles by Saint Apa Phoebammon: Edition and Translation of Coptic Manuscript M582 ff. 21r–30r in the Pierpont Morgan Library*. Providence, RI: Brown University, 2002.

Villecourt, Louis. "La lettre de Macaire, évêque de Memphis, sur la liturgie antique du chrême et du baptême à Alexandrie." *Le Muséon* 36 (1923): 33–46.

———. "Les observances liturgiques et la discipline du jeûne dans l'Église copte." *Le Muséon* 37 (1924): 201–280.

———. "Les observances liturgiques et la discipline du jeûne dans l'Église copte (Ch. XVI–XIX de la Lampe des ténèbres)." *Le Muséon* 36 (1923): 249–292.

Vööbus, Arthur. *The Synodicon in the West Syrian Tradition I*. Louvain: Secrétariat du Corpus SCO, 1975.

Wegman, H. A. J. "Une anaphore incomplète? Les fragments sur Papyrus Strasbourg Gr. 254." In *Studies in Gnosticism and Hellenistic Religions Presented to Gilles Quispel on the Occasion of His 65th Birthday*, edited by M. J. Vermaseren and Roel B. van den Broek. 432–450. Leiden: Brill, 1981.

Wehr, Hans. *A Dictionary of Modern Written Arabic (Arabic-English)*. Edited by J. Milton Cowan. 4th ed. Wiesbaden: Otto Harrassowitz, 1979.

Wipszycka, Ewa. "Les ordres mineurs dans l'Église d'Égypte du IVe au VIIIe siècle." In *Études sur le christianisme dans l'Égypte de l'antiquité tardive*, edited by Ewa Wipszycka, 225–255. Roma: Institutum Patristicum Augustinianum, 1996.

Youssef, Youhanna Nessim. "The Ark/Tabernacle/Throne/Chalice-Stand in the Coptic Church (Revisited)." *Ancient Near Eastern Studies* 48 (2011): 251–259.

Youssef, Youhanna Nessim, and Ugo Zanetti. *La consécration du Myron par Gabriel IV 86e Patriarche d'Alexandrie en 1374 A.D.* Münster: Aschendorff, 2014.

Zakhary, Milad Sidky. *De la Trinité à la Trinité: La christologie liturgique d'Ibn Sabbāʿ, auteur copte du XIIIe siècle*. Rome: Edizioni Liturgiche, 2007.

Zanetti, Ugo. "Bohairic Liturgical Manuscripts." *Orientalia Christiana Periodica* 61 (1995): 65–94.

———. "Inventaire des prières de la fraction de la liturgie copte." In ⲥⲩⲛⲁⲝⲓⲥ ⲕⲁⲑⲟⲗⲓⲕⲏ: *Beiträge zu Gottesdienst und Geschichte der fünf altkirchlichen Patriarchate für Heinzgerd Brakmann zum 70. Geburtstag*, edited by Diliana Atanassova and Tinatin Chronz, 767–800. Vienna: Lit Verlag, 2014.

———. *Les lectionnaires coptes annuels: Basse-Égypte*. Louvain-la-Neuve: Université Catholique de Louvain, Institut Orientaliste, 1985.

———. "Liturgy at Wadi al-Natrun." In *Christianity and Monasticism in Wadi al-Natrun: Essays from the 2002 International Symposium of the Saint Mark Foundation and the Saint Shenouda the Archimandrite Coptic Society*, edited by Maged S. A. Mikhail and Mark Moussa, 122–141. Cairo: American University in Cairo Press, 2009.

———. "'Voici le temps de la bénédiction . . .': Origine copte d'une hymne liturgique éthiopienne." *Orientalia Christiana Periodica* 75 (2009): 25–50.

Zheltov, Michael. "The Anaphora and the Thanksgiving Prayer from the Barcelona Papyrus: An Underestimated Testimony to the Anaphoral History in the Fourth Century." *Vigiliae Christianae* 62 (2008): 467–504.

———. "The Moment of Eucharistic Consecration in Byzantine Thought." In *Issues in Eucharistic Praying in East and West: Essays in Liturgical and Theological Analysis*, edited by Maxwell E. Johnson, 263–306. Collegeville, MN: Liturgical Press, 2010.

BIBLICAL INDEX

Exodus
12:5, *67*
12:15, *113*
20:18–21, *130*
27:20–21, *34*
30:17–20, *109*
34:29–35, *123*
Leviticus
4:12, *55*
Numbers
16:1–20, *122*
16:32, *124*
17:7, *64*
Deuteronomy
31:9–10, *122*
Joshua
6:1–5, *121*
Psalms
1:3, *103*
18 (19):13–14, *38*
25 (26):6–7, *114*
27 (28):4, *66*
33 (34):9, *100*
42 (43):4, *112, 143*
46 (47), *141*
48 (49):3, *99*
50 (51):7, *38, 113*
50 (51): 8, *114*
67 (68):1, *125*
67 (68): 32–33, *45*
75 (76): 11, *112, 143*
116 (117):1–2, *69, 99, 100, 116*
117 (118): 24–26, *112, 144*
131 (132): 1, *112, 143*
131 (132): 1–3, 7, *112, 144*
140 (141): 1–2, *83*
142 (143): 8, *83*
142 (143): 10, *83*
Isaiah
6:3, *28, 43, 126, 144, 145, 156*
9:6, *144*
Ezekiel
3:17–21, *100*
Matthew
2:6, *131*
2:11, *54*
5:7, *100*
10:27, *84*
10:28, *111*
14:4, *111*
26:26, *90, 131*
26:28, *91, 129*
27:24, *102*
Mark
12:41–44, *79*
14:22, *90, 131*
14:24, *91*
Luke
19:23, *102*
21:1–4, *79*
22:19, *131*
24:35, *67*
John
1:29, *103*
6:51, *100*
6:55, *69, 100*
6:57, *100*
13:10, *65*

John (cont.)
20:3–6, *140*
20:11–18, *140*
20:12, *45*
20:17, *140*
20:19, *140*
Acts
20:28, *99*
1 Corinthians
8:4, *55*
6:9–10, *102*
11:25–26, *35, 91*
11:27, 30, *101*
14:28, *42, 77*
Colossians
1:20, *126*
Hebrews
13:11, *55*

MANUSCRIPTS INDEX

Alexandria
Greek Orthodox Patriarchate 173/36 (1586), *98*

Barcelona
P. Monts.Roca inv. 128–178 (4th c.), *21*
Berlin
Staatsbibliothek 10173 (14th c.), *3*

Cairo
Coptic Museum Lit. 15 (1634), *xvi, 12, 73, 83, 89, 97, 99*
Coptic Patriarchate Lit. 73 (1444), *44, 112*
Coptic Patriarchate Lit. 74 (1444), *44*
Coptic Patriarchate Lit. 117 (1910), *112*
Coptic Museum Lit. 253 (1364), *78, 113*
Dār al-Kutub Theol. 221 (1750), *xvi, 12*

London
British Library Or. 1239 (13th c.), *25*
British Library Or. 3580A (11) (10th/11th c.), *51*
British Library Or. 8778 (1726), *40*

Manchester
Rylands Copt. 426 (13th c.), *25, 132*

New Haven
Yale Beinecke Copt. MS. 20 (19th c.), *40*

Oxford
Bodleian Hunt. 360 (13th c.), *22, 25, 36, 98*
Bodleian Hunt. 572 (13th/14th c.), *58*

Paris
BnF Ar. 98 (17th c.), *xvi, 14, 16, 112, 116, 130, 135*
BnF Ar. 203 (1363–69), *xv, 4, 6, 39, 45, 47, 48, 52, 54, 57*
BnF Ar. 207 (14th c.), *xv, 12, 93, 97, 98, 99*
BnF Ar. 208 (1638), *xvi, 12, 72, 97, 99*
BnF Ar. 251 (1353), *39*
BnF Copt. 28 (13th/14th c.), *40*
BnF Copt. 129 (20) (9th/10th c.), *89*
BnF Eth. MS D'Abbadie 66–66bis (15th c.), *1*
BnF Gr. 325 (14th c.), *98, 132*

Red Sea
St. Antony Liturgy 446, 3

Scetis
Baramūs 6/278 (1514), *112*
Baramūs Canons 9 (1353), *15*
Monastery of the Syrians Lit. 383 (1255), *123*
Strasbourg
P. Strasbourg Gr. Inv. 254 (1523), *21*

Uppsala
Uppsala O. Vet. 12 (1547), *xv, 6, 38, 40, 41, 42, 43, 44, 45, 46, 47, 48, 49, 50, 52, 53, 54, 58, 59*

Vatican City
BAV Vatican Ar. 117 (1323), *15, 45, 58, 68*
BAV Vatican Copt. 17 (1288), *25, 95*
BAV Vatican Copt. 28 (1306), *98*
BAV Vatican Copt. 46 (1719), *16*

GENERAL INDEX

Aaron, 64, 66, 72, 76, 77, 108, 124, 143, 145, 146
'Abd al-Masīḥ Ṣalīb, Euchologion of, 75, 106, 134, 137
'Abdallah, Alfonso, 14, 16
ablution, 35, 56
Abraham (OT patriarch), 79, 114, 120
Abraham of Hermonthis, Bishop, 39
Absolution, 11, 96, 104, 156; of the Servants, 40, 41, 65, 72, 73, 104, 118; of women, 110; to the Father, 50, 118, 134, 149; to the Son, 50, 73, 118, 149
Abū al-Makārim, 45
Abū Sayfayn, church of, 139
Acts, 27, 42, 77, 80, 120, 122, 152, 156; *Incense Prayer of the*, 120, 122, 154
Advent, 36, 152
Afrahām ibn Zur'ah, Pope, 23
Ajbiyyah, 26, 37, 149
allegory, liturgical, 16
al-Āmir bi-Aḥkām-illāh, Caliph, 45
al-Ashraf, Sultan al-Malik, 2
altar, 14, 16, 40, 41, 55, 56, 57, 63, 66, 67, 68, 70, 72, 75, 83, 116, 117, 118, 125, 141; preparation of, 38, 66, 67, 112
ambo, 44, 84, 121, 150
anaphoral prayer, 26, 28, 59, 89–90, 95, 150, 151, 152
angels, 10, 11, 45, 47, 62, 71, 75, 80, 81, 82, 83, 90, 99, 113, 114, 117, 126, 139, 144
anointing of the sick, 5, 9, 14, 110
Antony, Monastery of Saint, x, 3, 4, 25
Arab conquest, 22, 23, 86
Arabic, scriptural readings in, 42, 78, 119, 120, 121, 153, 154
Arabization, 24, 77, 78
archdeacon, 8, 18, 33, 41, 44, 46, 51, 63, 77, 78, 79, 80, 82, 106, 107, 150
archons, 55
arkān al-islām, 9
asbasmus, 46, 150, 154. *See also* kiss of peace
'Awaḍ, Jirjis Fīlūthā'us, 3, 5, 31
awshīyah, 150. *See also* litany

Barcelona Papyrus, 20, 21
Basil the Great, liturgy of Saint, 14, 15, 23, 24, 25, 28, 36, 47, 50, 57, 59, 60, 89, 94, 95, 98, 108, 118, 127, 128, 129, 132, 134, 152
basilicas, 139,
bathhouse, 110
benedictus, 48, 156
Benjamin I, Pope, 46
bishop, 11, 18, 31, 32, 34, 38, 41, 44, 55, 56, 65, 70, 73, 75, 76, 78, 80, 96, 104, 105, 107, 130, 143, 149, 150, 151, 155
Books of the Kings, 34
Brakmann, Heinzgerd, 1
bread, eucharistic, 26, 32, 33, 52, 127, 151, 155. *See also* eucharistic gifts
Brightman, F.E., 25, 36
burial of Christ, 60, 81, 82, 88, 91
Burmester, O.H.E., 78, 134
Butler, Alfred J., 139
byzantine liturgy, 2, 6, 16, 19–20, 22, 28, 32, 40, 43, 45, 51, 67, 68, 89, 97, 104, 134
Byzantinization, 22

Cairo, 6, 8, 18, 24, 38, 43
candle, 32, 34, 76, 83, 96, 112, 115, 117, 121, 137, 138, 139

canons, church, 4, 31, 34, 36
catechumens, 27, 28, 32, 44, 86, 151
Catholic epistle, 27, 42, 77, 79, 80, 119, 120, 150, 153; *Incense Prayer of*, 42, 79, 119, 120, 153
censer, 16, 24, 31, 41, 42, 44, 46, 49, 55, 56, 57, 73–75, 76, 79, 90, 119, 120, 121, 125, 127; hymns of the, 41, 42, 119, 145, 147
Chalcedon, council of, 21
chalice, eucharistic, 14, 24, 25, 26, 29, 35, 39, 49, 51, 52, 53, 58, 59, 69, 70, 91, 96, 98, 99, 101, 104, 105, 106, 113, 116, 117, 128, 129, 133, 135, 137, 138, 140, 141, 152, 153; consecration of more than one, 52, 105
chanter, 6, 26, 29, 33, 42, 43, 44, 47, 53, 63, 72, 82, 98, 106, 110, 121, 122, 157
Christodoulus, Pope, 35, 36
Clement of Alexandria, 10
clergy, 4, 6, 8, 11, 17–18, 22, 27, 28, 32, 54, 64, 78, 105, 109, 110, 111, 118, 121, 137, 146, 152
cloth, communion/eucharistic (*lifāfah*), 38, 39, 106, 153
commemoration (of saints or faithful), 27, 28, 47, 49, 50, 94, 115, 123, 132, 156
commixture, 97, 135, 151
communion, 9, 14, 34, 35, 52–54, 104–106, 110, 137–139; call to, 29, 33, 96, 134; of infants, 137, 140
concelebration, 51
confession (sacrament), 55, 76, 122
confession (pre-communion), 51, 97, 98, 104, 135
consecration (eucharistic), 12, 20, 26, 28, 32, 38, 41, 46, 53, 58, 59, 60, 65, 70, 72, 87, 88, 91, 96, 101, 141, 152, 157
consignation, 132, 135
Copto-Arabic literature, 2, 4, 5, 10, 11, 12, 34, 69, 71, 94
Coquin, René Georges, 139
Covenant (Great) Thursday, 5, 46, 153
Creed, Nicene-Constantinopolitan, 9, 28, 46, 57, 72, 73, 88, 125, 126, 155
curtain, sanctuary, 32, 66
Cyril II, Pope, 36
Cyril III ibn Laqlaq, Pope, 15, 78
Cyril of Alexandria, 10, 21
Cyril of Jerusalem, 1
Cyril, liturgy of, 22, 24, 25, 36, 45, 47, 60, 118, 152

Damian, Pope, 23
David the prophet, 99, 100, 121, 143, 144, 146,
Davis, Stephen J., x, 10, 11, 17, 69
al-Dawādār, Baybars, 2, 3
deacon, position of the, 11, 45, 69–70, 72, 87, 112, 115, 117; service of the, 68–73, 84, 118
despotikon (pl. *despotika*), 50, 52, 53, 59, 105, 127, 133, 134, 135, 151

Diaconicon (book), 25, 151
dialogue before the anaphora, 89, 126, 150
Didascalia Apostolorum, 31, 32, 35
diptychs. *See* commemoration
disciples, fast of the, 48, 112
dismissal, 27, 29, 34, 35, 53, 106, 141, 151, 157

Engberding, Hieronymus, 89
epact calculation, 5
epiclesis prayer, 28, 40, 51, 59, 65, 91, 101, 123, 128, 129, 151–152
Ethiopian Church, 13
Eucharist, reservation of the, 35, 54; teaching on the, 9–10, 32, 35, 51, 59, 69, 92, 97, 99–103, 128, 130, 139–140; worthy reception of the, 9, 99–103, 125, 136, 139
eucharistic gifts, 57, 67, 101, 154; blessing of the, 39, 58, 115–116, 155; covering of the, 40, 117; selection of the, 26, 38, 58, 68, 113, 155
Euchologion, 13, 16, 19, 25, 61, 89, 95, 97, 152
excommunication, 34

farḍ (Islamic law), 62
feasts of Christ, 5, 9, 36, 37, 47, 54, 63, 66, 82, 83, 153
filling of the chalice, rite of the, 14, 25, 35
foot-washing, 65–66, 108, 109
Forty-Day Fast. *See* Great Lent
Fraction, Prayer of the, 23, 29, 50, 51, 95, 131, 133, 134, 152; rite of the, 51, 130–131, 133, 135

Gabriel II ibn Turaik, Pope, 24, 34
Gabriel V, Pope, 12–14, 139
Germanus, Patriarch of Constantinople, 1, 68
Gospel, book of the, 44, 83, 84, 121; *Mystery of the*, 44, 85, 121, 153; *Prayer of the*, 43, 57, 82, 120, 121, 154; proper conduct during the reading of the, 123–124; reading of the, 43–44, 83–84, 120–121; response of the (*maradd al-injīl*), 44, 124, 152
Great Ladder, The (*Scala Magna*), 4
Great Lent, 36, 37, 42, 43, 48, 53, 110, 112
Gregory the Theologian, Liturgy of, 24, 25, 36, 47, 48, 50, 51, 59, 60, 89, 98, 118, 127, 149, 152
Guide to the Beginners, The (*Dallāl al-mubtadi'īn*), 15, 45, 58, 68, 110
Gynaceum, 139

Hagia Sophia, 67
al-Ḥākim, Caliph, 109
Hammerschmidt, Ernst, 36, 48, 89
hand-washing, 28, 31, 46, 57, 104, 109, 125, 155
Hanging Church. *See* Al-Mu'allaqah, church of
head covering, 64, 96, 138
hegumen, 38, 55, 72, 78, 104, 152
Histories of the Monasteries and Churches, The, 45

History of the Patriarchs, 12, 13
homily, 9–10, 27, 99–103
Horologion. See *Ajbiyyah*

ibn al-'Assāl, Al-Ṣafī, 110
ibn Al-'Assāl, Al-Mu'taman, 5, 31, 71
ibn al-Muqaffa', Sāwīrus, 11, 69, 113
ibn Kabar, Abū al-Barakāt, 2–6, 17
ibn Sabbā', Yūḥannā (ibn Abī Zakariyyā), 7–11, 17–18
iklīrus. *See* clergy
incense, confession during the offering of, 55–56, 76, 120; *raising of* (liturgical rite), 37, 83
prayer of, 41, 42, 74, 79, 119, 120, 153, 154–155; offering of, 14, 27, 31, 41, 42, 44, 46, 54, 55, 56, 57, 74, 75–76, 77, 79, 80, 119, 120, 121, 122, 125, 145, 154; types of, 54–55
Inclination, Prayer of, 96, 134, 154
institution narrative, 58, 90, 127, 131, 150
Isaac (OT patriarch), 74, 114

Jacob (OT patriarch), 114, 144
Jacob Baradaeus, 54
Jacob of Edessa, 58
Jacobite, 54
Janeras, Sebastià, 81, 82
Jericho, 16, 121
jizyah, 13
John Chrysostom, 68, 93
John Fuller, 43
Joseph of Arimathea, 81, 82
Joshua, 16, 121
Joyous Saturday, 46
Judas Iscariot, 111, 125, 126, 138

Khalil, Samir, 2, 3, 7, 12
Khidmat al-shammās. *See* diaconicon
kiss of peace, 28, 32, 46–47, 48, 88, 123, 126, 145, 150, 154, 155; prayer of, 46, 150. See also *Prayer of Reconciliation* and *asbasmus*
Kitāb al-īḍāḥ (*The Book of Elucidation*), 11, 69, 71
Kiyahk, month of, 36, 43, 48, 53, 83, 152
kneeling, 34, 47, 48, 49, 61, 66

lamp, eastern, 34, 112
Lamp of Darkness, The (*miṣbāḥ al-ẓulmah*), 2–7, 31–59; contents of, 5; liturgical diversity in, 17; manuscripts of, xv; purpose of, 4–6, 17
Last Supper, The, 28, 46, 131, 150
lectern, 44, 121
lectionary, 5, 25, 27, 78, 121, 153
litany, 50, 74, 120, 125, 131
liturgical commentary, Byzantine 2, 16
liturgical year, 5, 36, 63, 106, 152
Lord's Prayer. *See* Our Father

Macarius the Monk, Nomocanon of, 34
Macarius, Monastery of Saint, 6, 23, 38, 44
Magi, 54
Majmū' uṣūl al-dīn, 5
al-Maqārī, Athanasius, 20
al-Maqrīzī, 3, 13, 109
Mark the Evangelist, liturgy of, 20, 21, 22, 24, 36, 51, 95, 98. *See also* Cyril, liturgy of; relics of, 13
Marqus ibn al-Qunbar, 55, 56
Mary Magdalene, 45, 140
Mateos, Juan, 19, 20
matins. *See* incense, *raising of* (liturgical rite)
Matthew I, Pope, 12
May you be saved, 40, 45, 116, 119, 124, 134
Melkite, church, 23, 43; liturgy, 22, 36, 51, 85–86, 98,
Mīkhā'īl of Damietta, 55, 56
Mikhail, Ramez, 14, 26, 35, 38, 39, 42, 64, 67, 109
Mistrīḥ, Vincentio (Manṣūr), 12
Moses bar Kepha, 2, 58, 68
Moses the prophet, 65, 66, 108, 121, 122, 123, 124, 130, 146
al-Mu'allaqah, church of, 3, 4, 5

Nativity, Feast of the, 5, 36, 47, 63, 152, 153
Nicaea, Council of, 34, 48
Nicodemus, 81, 82
Noah, 74
nocturnal emissions, 63
northern Egypt, 27, 43

oblation(s), prayer of the, 57
offering, prayer of. See *Prothesis Prayer*
Origen, 10
Our Father, 9, 29, 50, 51, 89, 95, 123, 134, 151, 152, 154
Our Father, Prayer after, 95, 134, 154

pastophorion (pl. *pastophoria*), 67, 154
paten, 16, 39, 49, 53, 58, 68, 69, 90, 96, 97, 98, 104, 105, 106, 113, 116, 117, 127, 130, 132, 133, 135, 136, 137, 138, 139, 140, 141
patriarch, consecration of the, 9, 88
Paul the apostle, 10, 55, 101, 146
Pauline Incense, Mystery of the, 42, 79, 119, 153; *Prayer of the*, 41, 119, 154
poll tax. See *jizyah*
Pontius Pilate, 51, 97, 102, 103
Praxis. *See* Acts
prayer, 9, 37, 61–62; posture during, 61–62, 72
pre-anaphoral rites, 28, 46, 88, 89, 125, 155
precommunion rites, 98, 131, 132–136, 151, 154

Precious Jewel, The (*Al-jawharah al-nafīsah*), 7–12; contents of, 8–9; interpretative method of, 10–11, 17–18; manuscripts of, xv–xvi
presbyter, 31, 32, 33, 38, 39, 40, 41, 42, 43, 44, 45, 46, 50, 51, 52, 53, 55, 57, 64, 69, 70, 75, 76, 77, 78, 80, 94, 104, 105, 107, 109, 110, 118, 146, 151, 152, 155, 156. *See also* priest
priest, assisting (*kāhin sharīk*), 44, 49, 52, 105, 118, 119, 121, 125, 137, 141; consecrating (celebrant), 29, 31, 32, 33, 38, 39, 40, 41, 44, 46, 49, 52, 56, 57, 65, 67, 72, 89, 95, 104, 105, 111, 118, 119, 120, 121, 125, 127, 131, 136, 137, 138, 140, 141, 151, 152, 154; proper posture of, 129–130
private devotion, 74, 92
procession of the offering, 26, 27, 39, 115, 116
prospherin veil, 40, 57, 72, 88, 117, 155
Prothesis Prayer, 40, 58, 117, 154, 155
prothesis rite, 26, 27, 31, 40, 41, 58, 67, 99, 115, 155
psalms, chanting of, 6, 29, 43, 44, 53, 82, 83, 106, 112, 120, 121, 136, 156
Pseudo-Athanasius, Canons of, 36
Pseudo-Basil, Canons of, 33, 39, 110
Pseudo-Dionysius, 10, 11, 17, 71, 81

qummus. See hegumen
Qur'ān, 122, 130

reader (liturgical rank), 26, 77, 78, 79, 80, 94, 105, 131, 149
Reconciliation, Prayer of, 46, 126, 154. See also *asbasmus*
Red Monastery, 113
reform, liturgical, 13, 15, 18, 19
Ritual Order, The (*Al-tartīb al-ṭaqsī*), 12–16; contents of, 14; interpretative method of, 15–16, 18–19; manuscripts of, xvi

sacristan, 36, 107
Samuel of Qalamūn, Monastery of, 13
Samuel, bishop of Shibīn al-Qanāṭir (Samuel al-Suryānī), 7, 112
sanctuary, 8, 11, 15, 27, 28, 32, 33, 34, 37, 38, 39, 40, 41, 42, 44, 45, 50, 51, 55, 56, 57, 64, 65, 66, 67, 68, 72, 73, 76, 77, 78, 79, 83, 85, 86, 87, 96, 102, 104, 105, 106, 107, 109, 111, 112, 117, 118, 119, 120, 121, 122
Sanctus, 28, 48, 90, 126, 156
Sarapion of Thmuis, prayers of, 20, 21
Sāwīrus of Ashmunein. *See* Sāwīrus ibn al-Muqaffaʿ
Scetis. *See* Wādī al-Naṭrūn
second coming, the, 60, 88, 91
sermon. *See* homily
Severus of Antioch, 49, 50, 93
Simeon the priest, 68
Simon I, Pope, 23
skeuophylakion, 67
southern Egypt, Liturgy of, 8, 23, 24, 43, 61
Strasbourg Papyrus, 20, 21
subdeacon, 64, 78, 79, 80, 84, 85, 105, 156
Sunni Islam, 8, 62
al-Suryānī, Samuel. *See* Samuel, bishop of Shibīn al-Qanāṭir
Swanson, Mark N., 8, 11, 12
Synaxarion, 4, 27, 156
Synodicon, West-Syrian, 58

Taft, Robert F., 2, 19, 86
taḥlīl. *See* Absolution
ṭawwāf chant, 83, 121, 156
Thanksgiving, Prayer of, 40, 55, 70, 71, 116, 118, 154
Theophany, Feast of the, 5, 47, 56, 63, 109, 153
Theotokia, 42, 43, 47, 53, 156
Trinity, The, 8, 10, 12, 33, 39, 40, 43, 58, 71, 73, 74, 76, 79, 80, 88, 90, 115, 116, 124, 139, 145, 149
Trisagion, 11, 27, 43, 80, 81, 82, 120, 122, 144, 156
troparion (pl. troparia), 37, 80

ūlūjiyyah, 29, 35, 53, 141, 157

veil (of the sanctuary), 28, 32, 42, 65, 86, 107, 121; *Prayer of the*, 23, 28, 45, 86, 121, 155
vessels, eucharistic, 5, 14, 29, 38, 46, 53, 67, 112, 113, 141, 154
vesting, 6, 26, 37, 64–65, 68, 105, 107, 109, 111, 141, 151; of bishops, 41, 72, 73, 105, 151
vestments, liturgical, 26, 38, 64–65, 66, 68, 72, 105, 107, 109, 111, 141, 151, 154
Villecourt, Louis, 7, 56
Virgin Mary, 11, 28, 36, 42, 47, 51, 69, 74, 80, 82, 83, 93, 97, 128, 135, 136, 146, 149, 156

Wādī al-Naṭrūn, 6, 23, 24
West-Syrian, 45
White Monastery, 23, 51, 61
wine, eucharistic, 10, 11, 24, 26, 28, 32, 39, 49, 58, 68, 69, 91, 101, 109, 113, 115, 116, 117, 155
Word, Liturgy of the, 6, 16, 27, 31, 41–45, 57, 74, 77–85, 119–124, 149, 150, 151, 152, 153, 154, 155, 156, 157

Youssef, Youhanna N., 113

Zacharias, Pope, 109
Zakhary, Milad S., 8, 9, 10, 11, 18, 71
Zanetti, Ugo, 43, 78, 95, 146

Arsenius Mikhail is Professor of Liturgical Studies at St. Athanasius and St. Cyril Theological School in Los Angeles. He is the author of *The Presentation of the Lamb: The Prothesis and Preparatory Rites of the Coptic Liturgy.*

CHRISTIAN ARABIC TEXTS IN TRANSLATION

Stephen J. Davis, T. C. Schmidt, and Shawqi Talia (eds.), *Revelation 1–3 in Christian Arabic Commentary: John's First Vision and the Letters to the Seven Churches*

Arsenius Mikhail, *Guides to the Eucharist in Medieval Egypt: Three Arabic Commentaries on the Coptic Liturgy*

www.ingramcontent.com/pod-product-compliance
Lightning Source LLC
Chambersburg PA
CBHW032037290426
44110CB00012B/838
* 9 7 8 0 8 2 3 2 9 8 3 2 7 *